FALMOUTH, JAMAICA

FALMOUTH

JAMAICA

Architecture as History

Edited by Louis P. Nelson and Edward A. Chappell
with Brian L. Cofrancesco and Emilie Johnson

The University of the West Indies Press
Jamaica • Barbados • Trinidad and Tobago

The University of the West Indies Press
7A Gibraltar Hall Road, Mona
Kingston 7, Jamaica
www.uwipress.com

A catalogue record of this book is available from the National Library of Jamaica.

ISBN 978-976-640-493-2

Cover and book design by Robert Harris
Set in Scala 10.5/15 x 27
Printed in Canada

Contents

Introduction

LOUIS P. NELSON

Jamaican architecture is complex, culturally dynamic and remarkably understudied. Occupied by indigenous peoples for millennia, Jamaica was settled by Europeans in the sixteenth century and heavily peopled by Africans through enslavement into the nineteenth century, and the earlier cultural landscapes of the island were marked by subjugation, creolization, accommodation and resistance. Under a regular battery of hurricanes and occasional earthquakes and volcanic activity, architecture in the Caribbean has also adapted to a challenging and often volatile climate. More recent architecture speaks to the challenges of economic survival after the collapse of the plantation regimes. The rich yet fragile historic landscapes of Jamaica reflect the complexities of cultures, the intensities of climate and the struggle for economic survival. As a place with much to offer and where much is at risk, the island is an ideal laboratory for the study of the many dimensions of historic preservation. For more than a decade, the University of Virginia's Falmouth Field School in Historic Preservation has been doing just that. For a month each summer, soon after graduation, we have travelled with fifteen or so advanced undergraduate and graduate students from the University of Virginia and other universities to live and work in the small town of Falmouth, located on the north coast of Jamaica between the major tourism centres of Montego Bay and Ocho Rios. This book is the result of that work.

One of the first priorities of the field school programme was to examine and record in close detail the surviving historic fabric of the town. On an island prone to rot, insect infestation and hurricanes, historic architecture in poor condition can disappear quickly. So it has been incredibly important to spend time producing carefully measured drawings of surviving buildings as a record of a fast eroding historic landscape. Through most of this work, I have worked in partnership with Edward Chappell, director of architectural and archaeological research at the Colonial Williamsburg Foundation. Chappell is a long-time advocate for Falmouth and a great support to the field school. In addition to assisting teams, he has helped to identify threatened buildings that are critically in need of recordation. Both Brian Cofrancesco and Emilie Johnson, this book's other two editors, began their careers as field school students. The student-produced field drawings have become a permanent record of the town's historic building stock and, simultaneously, they serve as the working drawings for active preservation of Falmouth's historic fabric. Special thanks to James Parrent and Matthew Webster for their years of advocacy in Falmouth and participation in the field school. And lastly, this project would not have been possible without generous support from Chris and Lilla Ohrstrom, who have long been advocates for the preservation of Falmouth.

Of course, the University of Virginia has not accomplished this work on its own – far from it, in fact. In establishing the Falmouth Field School, the University of Virginia partnered with Falmouth Heritage Renewal, a non-profit organization that has for nearly twenty years worked to stabilize the town's fragile historic fabric. Falmouth Heritage Renewal has been a partner from the beginning, providing safe, clean housing and regular, local cuisine at a reasonable cost. But, more significant than its practical assistance is the ideological and programmatic framework established by Falmouth Heritage Renewal and its articulated goals. These are (1) recording and restoring the built environment; (2) providing a lab for the training of local artisans in restoration technology; (3) improving the housing stock for local residents and (4) building a foundation for heritage tourism and eventual economic vitality. Very quickly, their goals became our goals.

In partnering with Falmouth Heritage Renewal, students have had the opportunity to participate in its active programme of crafts training and hands-on historic preservation programmes that take place year round. One of the primary intentions of Falmouth Heritage Renewal is the stabilization and preservation of the smaller historic buildings in town. In many cases, the restoration of these buildings depends on the working drawings generated by students of the previous summer. A large number of these smaller houses stand abandoned while many underprivileged (often elderly) Jamaicans struggle to find decent housing. By restoring these small historic houses and returning them to the housing stock at below-market rates, Falmouth Heritage Renewal simultaneously addresses economic, social and preservation challenges. Thus far, Falmouth Heritage Renewal has worked on twenty of these small houses. Many of these buildings stood open to the elements. Some had failing roofs and some were simply rotting in place. To realize this work, Falmouth Heritage Renewal has a team of full-time Jamaican carpenters and masons who have been trained by American preservation craftsmen who volunteer their time for the project. During the course of the field school, each student laboured under the tutelage of a Jamaican carpenter and a Jamaican mason, usually working on one of the town's small houses. In partnership with Jamaicans, these American students have worked to document and preserve the town's historic buildings. All of the profits from this book have been dedicated to the preservation of those same houses, creating, we hope, a sustained source of revenue for this important work.

This book was first produced as the field guide for the 2011 annual meeting of the Vernacular Architecture Forum, an American professional organization dedicated to the study of everyday buildings and landscapes. The reception of the field guide at that conference and the later peer-review process encouraged us to move forward with professional publication. As a review of the book's table of contents will make clear

FIGURE I.1. Three University of Virginia students measure a small house in Falmouth during the 2007 field season.

quite readily, this volume is dominated by histories of the most important heritage buildings in town. These entries are organized into five tours, each encompassing a portion of the city. Each entry includes a history of the building as derived from both the archival record and a close analysis of the buildings themselves. In this way, these histories remind us that the architecture is as much a historic record as the papers preserved in archives. But the volume also includes three essays. The first two help to synthesize the results of the decade of research on the town. The first, a history of the town, helps to reimagine the life of the community as it developed through the eighteenth and nineteenth centuries. The second essay is a more comprehensive assessment of the historic buildings as a collective; it works to help us understand that these individual sites tell a story about the community, a story impossible to understand from any single building. And finally, the book closes with an essay on the most substantial physical change to the community since its foundation in the late eighteenth century: the opening of the cruise ship terminal. This project, which unfolded through the course of our decade of work, fundamentally transformed this community. This final essay examines those changes – some good and some bad – as the most recent chapter in the community's history.

1

History of Falmouth

LOUIS P. NELSON

Falmouth, Jamaica, is a special place. Once the second port of Jamaica serving the richest expanse of sugar plantations in the British empire, Falmouth has an extraordinary collection of early nineteenth-century buildings ranging from churches and a courthouse to merchant storehouses to the small frame houses of the town's substantial free black population. A remarkable number of these buildings survive to the present and speak both to the town's dynamism in the decades after its founding and to the economic decline in the century that followed. It is this very condition – rich collections of historic buildings – that attracted the attention of Royal Caribbean Cruises Limited (hereafter Royal Caribbean) in 2007 when they committed to transforming this once central but long-marginalized community into a hub for heritage tourism. Falmouth's long and complex history is evident in the town's buildings. The careful preservation of those buildings is the careful preservation of the town's history for both local residents and their new guests. This is a story of Falmouth's extraordinary past.

The early history of Falmouth is inextricably linked with the vast acres of rich sugar plantations that rapidly spread across the north coast of Jamaica over the course of the eighteenth century. These plantations were a direct result of the spike in the demand for sugar in England in the first half of the eighteenth century. In 1660, England imported only 3,000 hogsheads of sugar, but by 1753 she imported 110,000 hogsheads of sugar, exporting only 6,000 to the continent.[1] As demand escalated through the eighteenth century, so did the investment in transforming the rich and fertile tropical soils of the north coast into sugar plantations. Through much of the eighteenth century, Montego Bay served as the small but only port town along the northwest coast of the island. But by the late 1760s, it became clear to some that the many plantations emerging along or near the twenty-mile-long Martha Brae River would require a new centre for export. As a result, the story of early Falmouth is the story of sugar and its exportation.

By mid-century a small community called "The Rock" emerged on the shores of the shallow-water lagoon just to the east of the mouth of the Martha Brae and served as the place of export for the sugar descending the river and intended ultimately for English and European ports.[2] But those shallow-water docks were soon to be supplanted by docks closer to the deep-water harbour just to the west. In 1769, a local planter and merchant, Thomas Reid, first subdivided his large parcel of land to the west of The Rock into what was the first development in Falmouth.[3] Reid's tract was situated along a straight stretch of shoreline near the mouth of the Marta Brae Harbour. This position accommodated larger ships than did the docks across the shallow lagoon at The Rock. Reid Town, as this section was soon called, was an early site for wharves extending out into the harbour. One year later, in 1770, another planter, Edward Barrett, followed Reid's example, and subdivided his property at Palmetto Point just to the west of Reid Town into his own Barrett Town. In that same year, Jamaica's House of Assembly passed an act that formally subdivided St James parish, centred on its port town of Montego Bay, by establishing a new parish to the west called Trelawny, named in honour of then-governor William Trelawny. In that same year, 1770, Thomas Reid sold

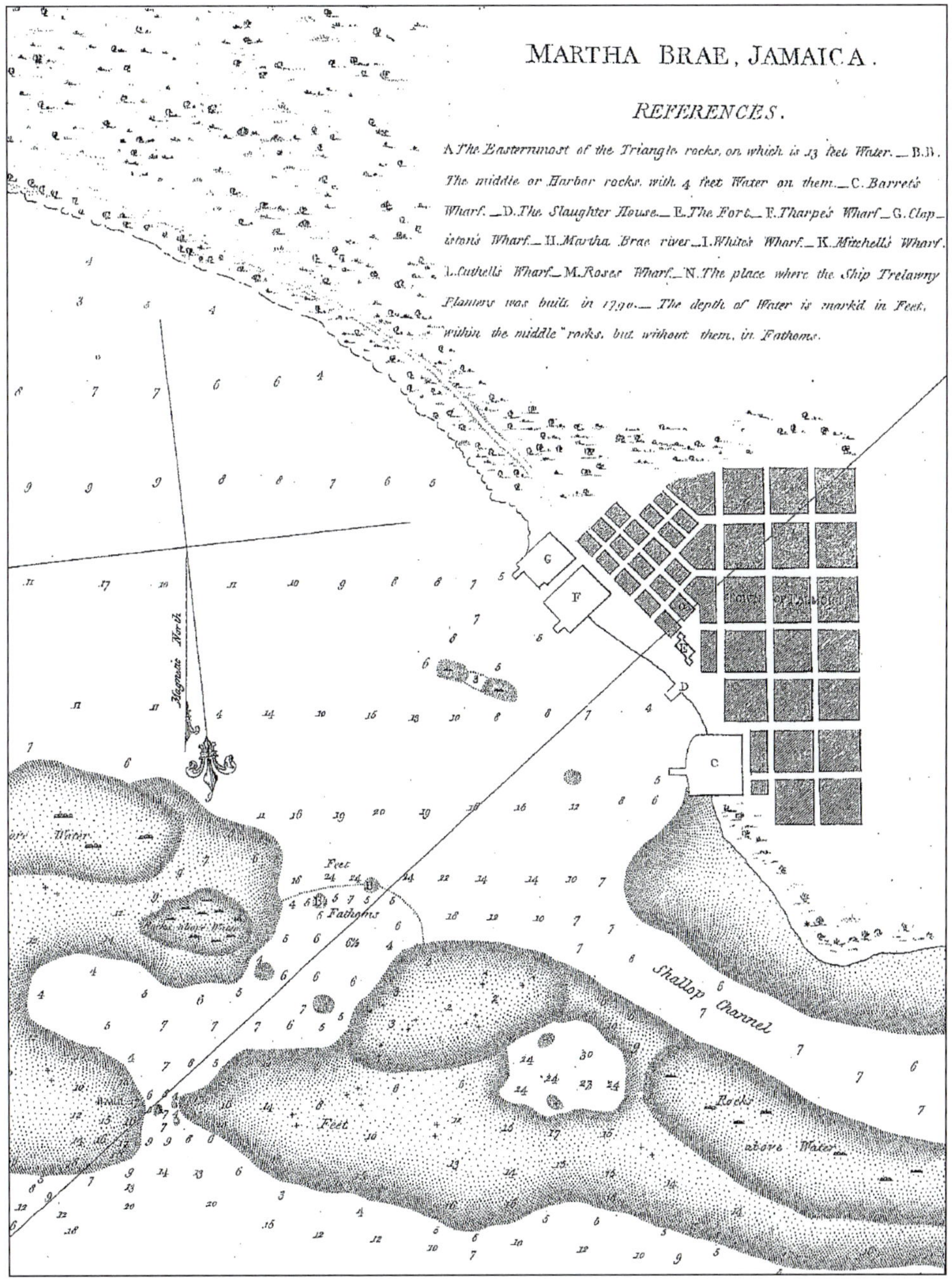

FIGURE 1.1. *Martha Brae, Jamaica*, by S.I. Neele (London: John Leard, 1793). © The British Library Board, Maps K.MAR.VII.53.b, Map 10.

"a lot of land at the place called Martha Brae Point otherwise known as Falmouth, Trelawny".[4] And with the sale of parcels by both Reid and Barrett, Falmouth was born.

A map of Martha Brae, Jamaica, published in April 1793 gives us an excellent window into the late eighteenth-century town of Falmouth. Far to the east, the settlement of The Rock still stands just to the east of the mouth of the Martha Brae River at the far end of the shallow lagoon. Farther to the west, the now-developing town of Falmouth stands closer to the mouth of the natural harbour, which was well protected by a shallow coral reef that jutted above the waterline in places and which required careful navigation. Even by the early 1790s, Reid's town had two major wharves, Tharp's Wharf and Clapiston's Wharf. Barrett's Wharf commanded the waterfront access from his larger, more easterly town development with larger square blocks positioned diagonally to the slightly earlier Reid lots. The intersection of these two grids created an awkward triangular space near the waterfront that by 1793 was dominated by a fortification. Just in front of the fort at the water's edge was the public slaughterhouse.

The opening decades of the town's history were marked by the emergence of a large free black population. Since the early eighteenth century, Jamaica had a significant population of free people of colour, both blacks and mulattos. Free people of colour typically lived in urban areas and, though the majority were poor, some individuals amassed considerable fortunes, becoming plantation and slave owners themselves. Free people of colour occupied an ambiguous position in Jamaica: unaccepted by white society, but wishing to distance themselves from enslaved blacks. In Falmouth, free people of colour lived in integrated neighbourhoods with white merchants and artisans. While no houses survive from this first generation, early descriptions suggest that the town had thirty houses by 1771 and more than two hundred by 1790.[5] Interspersed with these new houses were a few key institutions, such as the fort built almost immediately after its founding (and soon moved to the centre of town).

The expanding sugar plantations in the parish of Trelawny demanded a massive investment in the human capital of slaves. By the 1710s, blacks already outnumbered whites on the island by eight to one.[6] And the number of Africans on the island more than doubled between 1700 and 1705 and increased by a factor of five again by the end of the century.[7] Jamaica was by far the largest consumer of slaves in the British empire, and by the early nineteenth century, the planters of the parish of Trelawny owned more slaves than those in any other parish in the island. The parish census of 1811, which provides the most accurate early count of individuals in the parish, reports 27,550 enslaved Africans in Trelawny parish alone.[8] Simply put, British-African slavery was at its most extreme in the plantations that surrounded eighteenth- and early nineteenth-century Falmouth. Early advertisements in the newspapers for runaway slaves identify them as "Anthony, a Mandingo, RS on right shoulder" or "York, a Coromantee, to Mrs. Slack, at Falmouth, 5f. 3 I. the brand marks on his shoulders are illegible", or "Jack, a Congo, marked BL left shoulder". Such descriptions allude to the fact that the majority of Trelawny's early slaves was born in Africa, that their owners were familiar with the various tribal associations and that the practice of slave branding was common.[9]

The workhouse was intended as a house of correction for the troublesome among Trelawny's enslaved African majority. Newspaper accounts give us some sense for the range of offences that could result in imprisonment in the workhouse. Enslaved James Richards, found guilty of stealing crockery from a crate on the wharves, "was sentenced to hard labour in the Workhouse for 3 months. To receive 50 lashes in the Water-square before going in, and another 50 at the expiry of his imprisonment." "August" was found guilty of practising Obeah, traditional African religious practices, and was sentenced to "Confinement in the workhouse for life".[10] In the late eighteenth century, Falmouth had two critical institutions, the fort and the workhouse, the first to defend the emerging port city from potential naval attack from a European foe from without and from exploitation by crafty ship captains from within and the second to defend against the potential threat of the rapidly growing population of enslaved Africans which comprised the vast majority of the parish's population.

This rapidly expanding African majority had a profound effect on the

FIGURE 1.2. Falmouth Courthouse.

development of Falmouth in the early years of the nineteenth century. In July 1799, the parish declared martial law in an effort to suppress the many runaway slaves that were by that point terrorizing settlements and plantations. These runaways had escaped during the 1795 conflict between the British troops of Trelawny and the Maroons – descendants of Spanish-held slaves who had lived as a free people in the mountains since the late seventeenth century. The upper reaches of the parish were "infested by a body of the Armed Runaways on the frontiers, who have carried fire and devastation wherever they have appeared and have murdered several of the inhabitants", that "it appears to us that a great many of the old settlements have been deserted and inhabitants driven into the lowlands".[11]

The 1795 Maroon Wars and the continuing aftermath of assaults by runaway slaves engendered an atmosphere of fear across the parish.

Anxieties were surely exacerbated by the massive St Domingue slave revolt of 1791 which took the lives of more than one hundred thousand people and ultimately resulted in the establishment of the free black–governed state of Haiti. By 1803 the House of Assembly moved the fort from the centre of town back to its original location, on the grounds that "Falmouth is in danger of being set on fire whenever the guns of the said fort are fired", and out of concern for the defence of Falmouth from attack, a new site was selected.[12] One of the major advantages of the new fort was the construction of a substantially enlarged barracks, capable of housing seven hundred regular troops who could defend the city in times of attack. The construction of the new fort forced the relocation and expansion of the Falmouth workhouse. In 1803, the parish erected a small holding cell for disorderly sailors in the town square, not far removed from the city's wharves.[13] The parish also embarked on the construction of a much larger jail immediately adjacent to the workhouse. In this same season, Falmouth residents saw the rise of Falmouth's courthouse overlooking Falmouth Harbour, on the former site of Fort Balcarres.[14] The construction of the jail in 1814 and the courthouse begun the next year completed what had been a decade-long campaign to buttress the security of the town through the construction of a military fort, a courthouse, a new slave workhouse and a jail, the last two on adjacent parcels along the city's fringe at water's edge to the west end of town.

But even in the midst of such anxiety about defence and security, Falmouth thrived. In 1799, a coterie of Falmouth elite formed the Falmouth Water Company to implement a scheme to bring fresh water from the Martha Brae River directly into town. The scheme was financed by the sale of shares and a duty levied against every ship that entered Falmouth Harbour. The company bought property and built the infrastructure to feed fresh water into the heart of Falmouth from a still surviving and operational England-manufactured cast-iron Persian water wheel at a sluice off the Martha Brae through a series of aqueducts and mains to be stored in a round masonry reservoir in the middle of Water Square. The wheel was functional by 1805, giving Falmouth the claim to having had a municipal water source earlier than New York City.

FIGURE 1.3. Adolphe Duperly, *Water Square Market, Falmouth*, lithograph, *Daguerrian Excursions in Jamaica* (Kingston, 1846). Courtesy of the National Library of Jamaica.

By the early nineteenth century, Falmouth was also Jamaica's second-largest exporter of sugar after the capital city of Kingston, even though it was the third-largest urban centre in population, slightly smaller than Montego Bay and significantly smaller than Kingston.[15] And in 1809 Falmouth received free port status, allowing its merchants to export directly to England.[16]

This decade of remarkable productivity and profit together with two city fires in 1806 and 1809 resulted in a significant house-building boom between the 1790s and the 1820s, the season that saw the construction of many of Falmouth's earliest historic houses.[17] The most notable buildings are the mixed material merchant storehouse buildings that boast a masonry ground-floor shop that supports a timber-frame upper-storey residence that projects out over the sidewalk and is supported by a series of columns along the sidewalk. Primarily lining Market Street, but found originally on Duke Street as well, these buildings, when aligned cheek-by-jowl created a long stretch of sheltered access up and down the street.

One visitor described the houses of Falmouth as "neat in external appearance, but, as is the case in general on the north side of the island, exhibiting a very unfinished interior". The same writer also notes that the buildings seemed to respond directly to the climate: "For the admission of light and air, some are protected from the sun and rain, either wholly or in part, by jealousies, or by these and sash windows, with Venetian blinds." In addition to the jalousies, most houses and shops had "either a piazza enclosed by jealousies or an open colonnade. These being usually painted green and white, present a neat and interesting appearance."[18] Through the early nineteenth century, Falmouth developed a distinctive architectural signature. Market Street was Falmouth's social and economic heart; it boasted shops selling everything from essentials and grocery items to the finest imported wines and fabrics from shops and houses that clearly responded to their tropical condition.

Falmouth's elite were also vigorously social. A Scottish visitor described in 1802 a ball thrown for the governor that evening in a private house where "the saloons and ball-room were lighted up, and every preparation completed for the reception of the invited". Dancing com-

FIGURE 1.4. Adolphe Duperly, *Market Street, Falmouth*, lithograph, *Daguerrian Excursions in Jamaica* (Kingston, 1846). Private collection.

menced on the arrival of the governor: "The good old country dances, therefore, were the order of the evening, diversified occasionally by highland reels, danced *con amore* by the fair daughters and hardy sons of the Gael."[19]

Another great pastime in Falmouth was horse racing. In 1794, slaves from the workhouse were enlisted to transform the swampy lands to the west of town called Cave Island into a large and flat plain to be used as a horse track. This track was a major social centre for the north side of the island through much of the nineteenth century. One newspaper report in 1854 described "the studs of horses are unprecedented, both numerically and in the high mettle and general racing qualities. We are informed that there are no fewer than fifty horses now in Falmouth, to compete for the purses". The author went on to describe that the events attracted "all classes from the town and country" and complained that "the usual concomitants (vice and Sabbath desecration) have distinguished the conduct of the lower orders at the race course, where booths have been erected for many weeks past".[20] After the demise of the track in the late nineteenth century, this very large open space remained in public hands and was eventually transferred to lands in support of a regional hospital.

But the grandest public events were set in the 80-foot-long by 30-foot-wide great hall on the upper floor of the courthouse. One particularly spectacular affair was the annual Bachelors' Ball held in the ballroom on the upper floor of the courthouse, "the popularity of which was evinced by the numerous guests, which by nine o'clock crowded the great room nearly to excess". After dancing until about 12:30 in the morning, "the ladies and the rest of the company found easy access to the supper room, the tables of which were laid out with confections, fruits, and a variety of delicacies, accompanied with choice wines, which were sported with hospitable profusion". After supper, the "quadrilles and country dances", recommenced and lasted until 4:00 a.m.[21] In addition to balls, the courthouse great hall was also the stage for travelling theatre performances and concerts. Through the first quarter of the nineteenth century, Falmouth's elite staged spectacular soirees, but behind this frivolity lay a persistent if quiet anxiety.

Although Britain's slaves in the Caribbean received legal emancipation with the 1833 act to abolish slavery, the process was not one of immediate freedom. In 1834 began a season of "apprenticeship", in which former slaves continued to work for their former masters, except now for wages. Field slaves were to be apprenticed for six years while all others were to serve a four-year apprenticeship. The details of these arrange-

FIGURE 1.5. Unknown artist, West Indian scene, possibly Falmouth, Jamaica, *c.*1800. Courtesy of the National Gallery of Jamaica.

FIGURE 1.6. Unknown artist, *An Interior View of a Jamaica House of Correction*, c.1834–1838. © National Maritime Museum, Greenwich, London.

ments, however, were badly exploited by former masters, who now began to charge their "apprentices" for housing and food in the form of additional labour beyond the regulated forty-hour work week, even though such actions were not legal under the new law. Former masters also began to charge exorbitant rates for the early termination of an apprenticeship, far beyond the actual cost of the person's labour. The extremes of these conditions resulted in widespread unrest and ultimately resulted in the early termination of the apprenticeship period and the declaration of full emancipation for all former slaves in 1838.

Anxious times called for serious measures. In 1834, on the heels of abolition, the parish vestry authorized the construction of a new workhouse in the house of correction complex, and a fearsome treadmill was imported for use by the prisoners to grind cornmeal for their diet.[22] To some extent the officials were right to be afraid. Only a year later, in 1835, the *Cornwall Chronicle* reported "Riots in Jamaica". Jamaica's former slaves recognized that they were being exploited and they were not willing to submit to this new form of enforced labour. The former masters were deeply concerned about their own fate, and building the treadmill in the new workhouse was one step towards intimidating their former slaves into submission.

The immediate response to emancipation among the slaves was religious revival, the so-called Jamaican Awakening that lasted from 1838 to 1845. During this time, more than twenty thousand former slaves were baptized and nearly fifty Baptist chapels were built in the island. This revival cemented the authority of evangelical Christianity among the majority of religious Jamaicans and gave some sense of relief to Falmouth's white population.[23]

The history of Falmouth after full emancipation in 1838 is one of long slow change and general economic decline. By 1838, many of the lots in the former Reid and Barrett sections of town had been purchased and developed; in response, the Barretts converted space at the far western end of town into more parcels. Yet the fact that most of these new plots remained undeveloped until the early and mid-twentieth century is evidence of the town's general economic stagnation. Jamaica's plantations continued to produce sugar and rum, but their profits declined dramatically in the face of rising operating costs, the cheaper production of other non-British Caribbean islands where slavery persisted, and increased competition from the sugar beet, which could be grown more easily and in temperate climes. Another indication of Falmouth's slow decline was its shrinking population. The 1861 census reports Falmouth as having 303 white, 1,378 brown and 1,446 black, or 3,127 persons.[24]

The economic decline of the mid-nineteenth century was felt island-wide and resulted in increasing racial tensions. Although they had received legal emancipation in 1838, Jamaica's black population was largely denied the right to vote through a steep poll tax, and they had limited means to acquire land of their own to farm. As a result, racial tensions ran high. In October 1865, a group of black protesters freed an imprisoned black Jamaican who had been put on trial for trespassing on a plantation in the parish of St Thomas in the East. When he returned to the courthouse a few days later he and his supporters were met by a white militia. The resulting shots killed seven protesters. In response, the protesters rioted, killing eighteen whites and seizing control of the town. Widespread rioting broke out across Jamaica and the white governor's armed response under martial law resulted in the death of hundreds of black Jamaicans, some in firefights, others by execution. The Trelawny newspapers of those weeks make clear that the rioting and response resulted in a numerous lynchings in the plantations around Falmouth.[25] What eventually became named the Morant Bay Rebellion of 1865 was a critical turning point for race relations in Jamaica and stirred much debate in England about the authoritarian practices of the white controlled government. The limited response, however, meant that the status quo survived into the middle of the twentieth century. Only with independence from England in 1962 did black Jamaicans really begin to control their own futures.

If life for Falmouth's whites centred on the courthouse, life for Falmouth's black majority in these years centred on the residual space called Water Square. Well into the nineteenth century, Water Square remained simply an open area at the intersection of many streets and not a well-structured public space. The 1803 construction of the sailor's cage and the practice of public whippings in Water Square regularly reinforced the marginal social and economic condition of this awkward space. Nonetheless, the space was a major centre of gathering for Falmouth's black population. The 1844 Duperly view of Water Square shows the massive stone reservoir erected decades before by the Falmouth Water Company surrounded by a large number of black Jamaicans selling a variety of goods from baskets and fresh fish to fruits and vegetables, some from wheeled carts with awnings and shades and others from blankets laid out on the ground. The construction of a "shed for the Negro Market" in Water Square in 1800 suggests that this was a practice that reached back to at least that date, but likely back to the town's foundation.[26] Called the bend-down market by the mid-nineteenth century, market day in Falmouth was a critical event for the lives of newly emancipated slaves. The demolition of the cage in 1868 and the construction of the few buildings that now front the square in the same decades set the stage for the final act, the construction of a market building, the Albert George Market in 1894. Built as the first permanent market building in town, the market has a Georgian-inspired street façade that looks back to the architecture of the town's apogee in the early nineteenth century and a series of cast-iron sheds behind that emulate the architecture of train sheds, symbols of modernism in the late nineteenth century.

If local trade through the markets in Water Square sustained the local internal economy, the town's external economy was fuelled almost exclusively by the wharves. Into the twentieth century, Falmouth's docks remained a source of livelihood, and accommodating the harbour to the changes in shipping demanded occasional attention. In 1885, "Wealther Triangle Rock" in the Falmouth Harbour was finally removed. The rock was described as "54 feet long, 45 feet wide, and 14 feet below the surface". The newspaper account reports that it was a "long time coming to remove this dangerous rock".[27] In 1903, the national government finally agreed to blast out the rest of the rocks which had for so long guarded the mouth of the harbour and in 1938 the harbour channel was straightened and dredged to accommodate the increasing size of ocean-going vessels.[28] In 1905 the Jamaican government built a strong sea wall "to eliminate further destruction to the street and properties by the sea".[29] And these efforts sustained shipping in Falmouth into the mid-century. The construction of the many warehouses along the waterfront at the eastern end of town in the middle of the twentieth century is evidence that shipping remained a critical industry for the town into the 1950s. Writing in 1954, however, historian Dan Ogilvie reminisced about the days of his own childhood when "numerous schooners from Halifax with Fish stuff and lumber" were regular visitors to Falmouth. "Where are they today?" he opines. "Steamships have succeeded them and they all go to Kingston from where retailers of this and other parishes go to effect purchases. Kingston is thereby made richer and the other seaports poorer."

The harbour would be the only major source of income for Falmouth through the twentieth century. The Jamaican railroad, begun in 1845 from Kingston, reached Montego Bay in 1895, bypassing Falmouth, a move that would secure Montego Bay's economic supremacy over Falmouth through the twentieth century. Even for smaller transportation, Ogilvie saw Falmouth in decline: "Motor trucks have taken over this class of transport but instead of Falmouth they travel to Kingston with the belief and the hope of better prices and greater scope for their trading."[30] This sustained economic decline had a profound impact on the town and its population. The 1943 census reported the population of Falmouth as just over twenty-five hundred, a near 20 per cent loss of population since the 1861 census.[31] Falmouth's story through the twentieth century is one of slow economic decline.

This story of decline and neglect changed suddenly in 2007, however, when the Port Authority of Jamaica announced the Historic Falmouth Jamaica port development project. In partnership with Royal Caribbean, the Port Authority broke ground on the construction of a new eleven-acre wharf development in October 2009; by January 2011, the first cruise ships began to arrive. Royal Caribbean made clear that their interest in the town revolved around its capacity to introduce to visitors "historic" Jamaica. Such interest and investment were welcome in a town that had languished for more than a century. But it brings with it the complex questions of historic preservation: Whose houses and properties get preserved? Who pays for it? Who decides the prevailing preservation philosophy? It also brings questions of social and economic equity: What jobs are made available to local residents? Will Falmouth become a tourist town dominated by services for tourists? Will locals and their services be pushed to the margins? The many gated resorts that line Jamaica's beaches are in effect Jamaica's new colonialism: Will this port bring the exploitation of that new colonialism to Falmouth or will this be a different, more responsible, more integrative story? These are not easy questions to answer, yet these will be the questions that frame the next chapter in Falmouth's complex material and social history.

NOTES

1. Sidney Mintz, *Sweetness and Power: The Place of Sugar in Modern History* (Harmondsworth: Penguin, 1985), 39.
2. Daniel L. Ogilvie, "History of the Parish of Trelawny" (manuscript, 1954), ch. 2. Ogilvie is an essential source for the writing of the history of Falmouth, but it must be used with care. The level of specificity and his use of actual quotations implies that he had access to and used parish vestry records that no longer survive. Unfortunately, he did not footnote his sources. I have cited him only when it is clear he is citing a period source. Transcriptions of his manuscript are available on the web and those versions have been used here. The unpaginated format of this transcription means that I simply cite the chapter, rather than specific pages of his work (http://www.jamaicanfamilysearch.com/Samples/histre.htm). A second major source is Carey Robinson, *The Rise and Fall of Falmouth, Jamaica* (Kingston: LMH Publishing, 2007), which like Ogilvie, has no footnotes but is clearly depending on original source material. Robinson is cited here only when he is the sole evidence for a source that is now lost.
3. A valuable source for the early foundation of Falmouth is Ivor C. Connolley and James Parrent, "Land Deeds That Tell the Story of the Birth of Falmouth", *Jamaican Historical Society Bulletin* 11 (2005): 383–409.
4. Ibid., 387.
5. Ogilvie, "History", ch. 9.
6. Richard Dunn, *Sugar and Slaves: The Rise of the Planter Class in the English West Indies, 1624–1713* (Chapel Hill: University of North Carolina Press, 1972), 164–65.
7. Trevor Burnard and Kenneth Morgan, "The Dynamics of the Slave Market and Slave Purchasing Patterns in Jamaica, 1655–1788", *William and Mary Quarterly* 58 (January 2001): 205–6.
8. Ogilvie, "History", ch. 2.
9. *Cornwall Chronicle*, Trelawny, Gibralter, 5 November 1781; *Cornwall Chronicle*, 28 March 1810; *Cornwall Chronicle*, 21 March 1811.
10. *Cornwall Chronicle*, 13 September 1826, no. 30.
11. Ogilvie, "History", ch. 2.
12. *The Laws of Jamaica, 1799–1803* (A. Aikman, 1812), 293.
13. Vestry minutes from 1794, as reported in Robinson, *Rise and Fall*, 4.
14. Ogilvie, "History", ch. 5.
15. B.W. Higman, "Jamaican Port Towns in the Early Nineteenth Century", in *Atlantic Port Cities: Economy, Culture, and Society in the Atlantic World, 1650–1850*, ed. Franklin W. Knight and Peggy K. Liss (Knoxville: University of Tennessee Press, 1991), 121, 127.
16. Ibid., 125.
17. Ogilvie, "History", ch. 2; Robinson, *Rise and Fall*, 36.
18. James M. Phillippo, *Jamaica, Its Past and Present State* (London: John Snow, 1843), 64, 68–69.
19. Phillip Barrington Ainslie, i.e. "Philo scotus", published in 1802, reprinted in Georgian Society of Jamaica, *Falmouth, 1791–1970* (Kingston: Georgian Society of Jamaica, 1970), 28.
20. An 1854 newspaper report, cited in Robinson, *Rise and Fall*, 71.
21. *Cornwall Chronicle*, 26 July 1826, no. 23.
22. Ogilvie, "History", ch. 5.
23. Ibid., ch. 3.
24. Ibid., ch 2.
25. Robinson, *Rise and Fall*, 87.
26. Vestry minutes from 1800 as quoted in Ogilvie, "History" ch. 5.
27. *Falmouth Gazette*, Sept 25, 1885.
28. Ogilvie, "History", ch. 2, ch. 4.
29. Ibid., ch. 3.
30. Ibid., ch. 4.
31. Ibid., ch. 9.

2

Falmouth, Jamaica

Early Housing in a Caribbean Town

EDWARD A. CHAPPELL AND LOUIS P. NELSON

Jamaica was, quite literally, the plantation of Britain from the early eighteenth century until the 1830s. A population overwhelmingly composed of enslaved workers produced most of the sugar and rum consumed in the English-speaking world, and the wealth they generated fuelled the British economy. Sugar consumption in England expanded rapidly over the first half of the eighteenth century. If sugar was consumed only by the most elite in late seventeenth-century England, as Ralph Davis has argued, "by 1750 even the poorest English farm labourer's wife took sugar in her tea".[1] This massive rise in consumption was largely fed by Jamaica, Britain's biggest producer. In 1805, Jamaica's peak year for production, she produced 100,000 tons of sugar; the following year the island exported 6,760,000 gallons of rum, a product of sugar and a strong secondary export.[2] In both scholarship and the popular imagination, pre-emancipation Jamaica is primarily perceived today in terms of plantation agriculture: large teams of enslaved blacks harvesting and processing sugar under harsh conditions enforced by a small number of white planters and their overseers dominated the reality of life for most in Jamaica. And that understanding is not inaccurate. Yet all that sugar had to be exported by ship. The response to that necessity was the rise of Caribbean mercantilism and eighteenth-century port towns.

Coastal towns played a crucial role as centres of exportation but also as markets for goods consumed on the plantations. They also were principal points for the importation of enslaved workers until Parliament banned the slave trade in 1807, by which point Jamaica had imported over a million Africans as enslaved labourers.[3] While plantations commanded a huge role in the Jamaican economy, coastal port towns emerged as critical hubs for import and export. The character of dwellings and storehouses surviving in Falmouth and other West Indian port towns of this era is indicative of booming socio-economic development. Construction of relatively comfortable, well-finished and durable housing by a large number of people in trade (separate from a wealthy elite) is an important element of middling-class housing during and after the last decade or two of the eighteenth century. The architectural record is extremely clear. Economies as varied as those of coastal New England, the Chesapeake, Bermuda and Jamaica produced both an ability and a shared desire to occupy improved, better-finished housing, even when some of those economies are thought by historians to have been in decline.[4] The broad pattern of domestic architecture was a result of regional circumstances that commonly had some basis in labour produced by enslaved people. The visual record of this development in Jamaica grew, particularly towards the end of slavery and the decade following emancipation, when both Jamaicans and outsiders recognized that the absence of forced labour ensured that further change was underway.

In the early 1840s, daguerreotype photographer Adolphe Duperly produced a small group of images of Jamaican towns soon after emancipation, and he published lithographs based on those images. Duperly's engravings offer extraordinarily rich panoramas of the towns, notably Falmouth, where he crafted four views.[5] Duperly portrayed Falmouth as a well-ordered port and courthouse town of wide streets arranged in grids and lined with houses, their diverse size and elaboration precisely captured. These images offer remarkably detailed glimpses into life in the streets and at doorways. A ground-level view of Market Street shows the principal avenue linking the plantation interior with Falmouth's warehouses and docks (see figure 1.4). Most people visible on the street are black, all are fully clothed, not half-dressed like agricultural labourers. One or two whites also appear. A liveried black coachman drives a top-hatted merchant or planter towards the wharf. A black man carries a load of goods down the centre of the flat dirt street. Black women and men stand in the shadows cast by merchants' lofty residences partially carried on classical colonnades in front of ground-floor storehouses. Most proprietors of the storehouses and white residents of the elevated floors are little seen, although balconies and floor-length windows suggest they presented themselves upon occasion, elevated above the street.[6]

A second view shows a more modest avenue recognizable as Cornwall Street, which connects Market Street to Water Square, a block to the east (figure 2.1). Here black people share the street with horse-drawn vehicles

FIGURE 2.1. Adolphe Duperly, *Cornwall Street (Falmouth)*, lithograph, *Daguerrian Excursions in Jamaica* (Kingston, 1846). Private collection.

and walk on a raised sidewalk beside single-storey shops and two-storey houses. The shops open onto the street, with displays of house and kitchen wares in shuttered windows and a sales stand beside a shop door. A man whose colour is not evident leans against the doorway talking with a black woman shopkeeper. A sailor and local man negotiate the sale of a pig that slouches with them in the middle of the intersection. In the distance, one catches a glimpse of colonnaded buildings at the intersection with Market Street.

A third image shows Water Square, where fresh Martha Brae River water was delivered from an aqueduct to a central supply and carried by hand throughout the town (see figure 1.3). Duperly portrayed the square crowded with hundreds of black people conversing, collecting water, and buying and selling market goods from baskets and fabric-covered stalls. In the background are storehouses located below residences of varied sizes.

Most panoramic is a fourth view, looking from the Anglican church tower down Duke Street towards the harbour where merchant ships stand at anchor (figure 2.2). This is a more diverse and verdant scene, showing houses and their fenced yards filled with tall royal palm trees and dense foliage. People walk in the middle of the wide street, without sidewalks or many porches. From his perch, Duperly portrays at least three distinct forms of houses. Expressing typological interest in modest as well as large buildings, he focuses the foreground on a small two-bay house. Three ladder steps rise from a neat but unfenced yard to a side door. Unlike the Cornwall Street shops, it has no visible doorway to the street. Rather, a sizeable window looks through the short end towards Duke Street. Across the intersection are two small gable-entry shops. Further east are conventional-looking Georgian buildings that housed successful merchant families in rooms stacked two deep on two well-lighted floors. Also, at the corner with Princess Street, is a storehouse with partial colonnade supporting a residential second floor. The image illustrates a socially mixed pre-industrial community, one in which people of widely varied wealth occupy the same street or block.

In spite of this diversity, a few general observations can be made about Falmouth's architecture. The buildings in the Duperly views are almost universally covered by either a single hipped roof or two to three such roofs running parallel to one another, with open valleys. The double and treble roofs are based on older English roof construction, modified in the western hemisphere and usually employed without the parapets that, when complete, required that all rainfall be carried away by gutters. Such open-ended multiple roofs became more common in Jamaica and other island colonies in the eighteenth and nineteenth centuries than they were in contemporary Britain. The Falmouth roofs are covered with shingles, much like those on most British North American roofs of the same era, not clay tiles or slate. Some are given an exotic Jamaican flourish with wood caps and small prow-like projections, now called a "cap and comb", at the ridge. Wall material, too, varies somewhat from British practice. Duperly shows weatherboards and exposed brick or stuccoed walls, sometimes the former used on a storey raised above the latter. The views

FIGURE 2.2. Adolphe Duperly, *Falmouth (Taken from the Church Tower)*, lithograph, *Daguerrian Excursions in Jamaica* (Kingston, 1846). © The British Library Board, Maps 19.b.12, pl. 19.

exhibit very few chimneys. Heating was unnecessary for comfort in the Caribbean, and fireplaces in Jamaican households were usually confined to kitchens and other work buildings, inevitably removed from the core of affluent households. Even Duperly's smallest Duke Street house lacks a chimney, and elsewhere they are glimpsed only on ancillary buildings. The fenestration is familiar to observers accustomed to European and North American building tradition: windows and doors seem placed evenly along the walls, balanced in respect to exterior massing or interior partitions. The chief point of difference is the appearance of louvres arranged in vertical rows flanking conventional windows or filling small openings in secondary locations, like small rear wings.

In short, the four views portray a community with buildings, streets and activities somewhat resembling those of other British-American towns, but with an exotic quality reflecting the tropical climate, a predominantly black population and an economy distinctive to Jamaica. Yet, as extraordinarily detailed and seemingly reliable as Duperly's views are, they pierce no walls. They offer snapshots of life on the public streets in the bright light of day, but the images say little about the spaces and lives they moulded and contained. The delineations tell us little about arrangements and activities in the chambers and in the yards where many people spent much of their waking time.

The greatest means for understanding the nature of most life in Caribbean towns in the three or four decades before emancipation is the careful study of standing buildings and archaeology. This paper addresses the former. Countless such buildings survive, many of them now in deteriorating condition and scattered thinly in coastal communities. A rich range of surviving houses and outbuildings in Falmouth expresses the town's prosperity from about 1790 to 1835. They and nearby plantation housing exemplify much of the superior or durable construction that Jamaica supported in the last half-century of British slavery. A recent survey of Falmouth identified nearly one hundred buildings that predate 1850, but imbedded beneath later layers and obscured from street view there are surely many more.[7] Graphics from the 1830s and 1840s illustrate how much of the town's early fabric has disappeared, but far more survives here than in most Jamaican towns and especially in Kingston, which has suffered greater large-scale destruction. The north coastal town is a worthy object of preservation action and research, which have proceeded in tandem since the late 1990s. Construction of a vast cruise ship terminal that has now remade the shape of Falmouth Harbour newly threatens the survival of delicate historic buildings as well as the residents and small businesses who occupy them, just as it offers potential for somewhat better-funded preservation of selected landmarks.

Falmouth provides a portal into the character of houses for planters, merchants, tradesmen and domestic workers, and it is broadly representative of affluent early nineteenth-century towns in Jamaica. There are surprising unities in planning and construction within the range of distinctive regional practice. That practice is related to the vernacular architecture of other Caribbean nations and of British North America, but it is endemic – recognizably different from construction of buildings anywhere else. This paper will characterize and interpret that practice, to begin filling a void in the region-by-region study of North America's first generations of extensive refined and durable housing. Most historical scholarship on the pre-emancipation Caribbean has focused on plantations as the dominant institution in the region's role as sugar producer in the Atlantic economy. Jamaican town buildings and landscapes in particular now call for more inquisitive study.

Popular perceptions and colonial policy in eighteenth- and early nineteenth-century Britain sought an uneven relationship in which colonies provided raw materials that were finished or manufactured in Britain to support a refined lifestyle that was absent or incomplete beyond the metropole. Colonial elites might grow rich from production and trade, but they remained relatively uncultivated in the metropolitan view.[8] The sugar islands, source of the greatest commercial wealth, were seen as especially savage and sensual due to a punishing climate, tropical diseases, majority population of black slaves, and a major gender imbalance with a higher percentage of males among whites, as well as perceived absence of many major plantation owners. In visual representations as well as writing, British critics portrayed white in addition to black

Jamaicans as wild and uncultivated. See, for example, an 1802 London engraving *Segar Smoking Society in Jamaica*, lampooning the behaviour of Jamaican elites, including cigar-smoking, hard-drinking and publicly sprawling white women (figure 2.3).[9] The image represents a collection of white men and women ungracefully reclining in their chairs with their feet resting high on the walls or on the top of the table. The size of the glasses and the large volumes of wine on the table are the artists' critique of excessive consumption. In these same years, this kind of lounging was referred to as "creolizing", probably used by British observers to identify the position of Caribbean-born whites.[10] Popular British perception that the whites' dissolution further resulted from their thoughtless domination of enslaved workers grew with the rise of abolitionist publicity.[11] The lone shoeless and shirtless male slave standing at attention and ready to serve white "creoles" in the image is a poignant commentary on this issue as well. Slaveholding Jamaicans were increasingly alienated from public opinion in Britain between the 1790s efforts to ban the trade and Parliament's ending of slavery in the colonies in 1834. Yet well-off Jamaican society materially developed in the same decades.

FIGURE 2.3. Abraham James, *Segar Smoking Society in Jamaica*, etching, 1802. Courtesy of the Lewis Walpole Library, Yale University.

It was in the era of Falmouth's ascendency, from about 1790 to 1835, that a broad creole culture flourished in Jamaica and other British sugar islands, with well-built houses as a clear marker of individuals' refinement – and their removal from slavery. White planters and merchants and commercially successful free people of colour created a manner of permanent building that they perceived as refined, on their own terms. It drew upon certain British elements but recast them in a regional vernacular that was different from standards of the homeland. An important characteristic of 1790–1835 Falmouth houses and contemporary houses surviving elsewhere in the island is the continuity of essential forms among different sizes and qualities of building. In finish as well as form, the smallest two-room urban houses bore certain similarities to the largest mansions of the era, to a degree not paralleled farther north.

Initially looking past the fine houses of wealthy residents, one sees a middle ground: housing far more modest than the best-known great houses and markedly superior to the earthfast and thatched abodes of most agricultural workers until the last century. The line between houses that could be used for entertainment and those that could not is far less evident than on the mainland. Planters, merchants and their attorneys economically dominated towns like Falmouth, Montego Bay and St Ann, but architecturally the clearest barriers were between enslaved and free rather than along strict lines of colour. The absence of strict racial lines in housing is most evident in surviving plantation houses like the well-appointed two-storey stone house with six refined rooms that the wealthy Trelawny planter and Falmouth trader John Tharp (1744–1806) is said to have built for his mixed-race son John Harewood (d. 1812) and overseer at Good Hope plantation.[12] The point is also expressed in the well-built and expandable small houses free people of colour built in the towns. Residents continued using the established manner of arranging, framing and finishing building after emancipation and the subsequent decline of the export economy. Yet durable house construction dramatically slowed in mid-century Falmouth and Jamaica in general until near 1900.

A number of factors led to the development of a self-confident creole culture supporting a market for new, improved housing. By 1790, a much more varied racial landscape had developed. Race in Jamaica was more a matter of distinct skin colour difference in 1690 than it was a century later. Over the course of the eighteenth century there developed increasingly complex strata constituting a broad grey scale. Far more than in the Carolinas and Chesapeake, not to mention New England, Jamaican free people of colour owned and occupied properties in town, and they plied skilled trades from their premises. Others owned estates in the hinterland. As early as 1754, one census of Spanish Town on Jamaica's south coast reported a total free population of twelve hundred, and a full one-third of these were "Negroes and Mulattoes".[13] Frank Pons has estimated that just prior to full emancipation in 1838, Jamaica had a free black population of forty-two thousand, most of whom lived in towns.[14] As Jamaica's third-largest town, it seems safe to assume that free blacks comprised a substantial minority of Falmouth's population as well. Examination of Falmouth's earliest land deeds indicate that by the turn of the nineteenth century a number of free blacks already owned lots. These included carpenters Samuel Reeves and John Sylvester, the brick mason Thomas Love, the tavern-keeper Thomas Neale, and the spinster Rebecca Lake, among others. Free blacks in Falmouth and elsewhere were artisans, small planters, tavern-keepers and professionals who were born free or had made enough money to purchase their own freedom.[15] As freedmen and women, landowners, and skilled tradesmen, McGhie, Reeves, Sylvester and Love were well positioned to erect the small timber-frame buildings that survive in Falmouth from the nineteenth century. Slightly later, prominent free black families owned houses and substantial buildings in town on Duke Street, Trelawny Street and other principal streets. Surviving substantial houses include the two-storey tavern erected by Thomas Neale on Duke Street and the substantial galleried house adjacent to Fort Balcarres built or remodelled by Thomas Davidson in 1838. Free people of colour were, in Falmouth as elsewhere, substantial property owners.

Both surviving buildings and the early views of Falmouth illustrate a large number of small but well-built houses: handsome houses that are relatively spacious, well-finished and well-lighted. The most distinctive are single-storey wooden houses with a small number of rooms. These must be the houses of successful free black tradesmen as well as their white counterparts, given the large numbers of free people of colour who worked at trades in pre-emancipation towns and who owned property in early Falmouth. Indeed, successful African Jamaican tradespeople as well as enslaved workers who rebelled, most effectively in 1831–32, form a background for Jamaicans' transformative efforts towards liberation in the following century.

Among the most distinctive survivals in Falmouth are small houses from the early nineteenth century that contain two rooms of comparable size.[16] This pair of spaces forms the core of early Falmouth's well-built houses. Builders set two-room houses either parallel with or at right angle to the streets, favouring corner lots, and placing the slightly larger room at the front when a short end faced the street. In spite of this, the houses generally open into a side yard rather than the thoroughfares, unlike nineteenth-century Barbadian urban houses of similar scale, with their doors and small porches commonly facing the street. Builders of a highly representative 17-foot by 10-foot house at 31 Duke Street balanced windows on the end wall facing the main avenue and a long side wall facing the secondary street, for example, and placed doors on the two walls looking towards the yard (figures 2.4 and 2.5). Working at 36A Cornwall, another builder set a 20-foot by 12-foot two-room house parallel to the street, placing windows in the front and ends, and both its two doors in the rear wall. A contemporary 24-foot 3-inch by 14-foot 3-inch house at 28 Trelawny has two rooms, the larger one 14 feet square and with no street-facing doors.

Although most two-room houses are set at a right angle to the street, there are relatively few early buildings of this size with doorways aligned on short front and inner walls, and in virtually all cases the front doors are late additions. Evidence in the framing shows, for example, that the 20-foot by 12-foot house with two rooms of identical size probably built by a woman of colour named Elizabeth Somerville soon after 1836 at

FIGURE 2.4. 31 Duke Street.

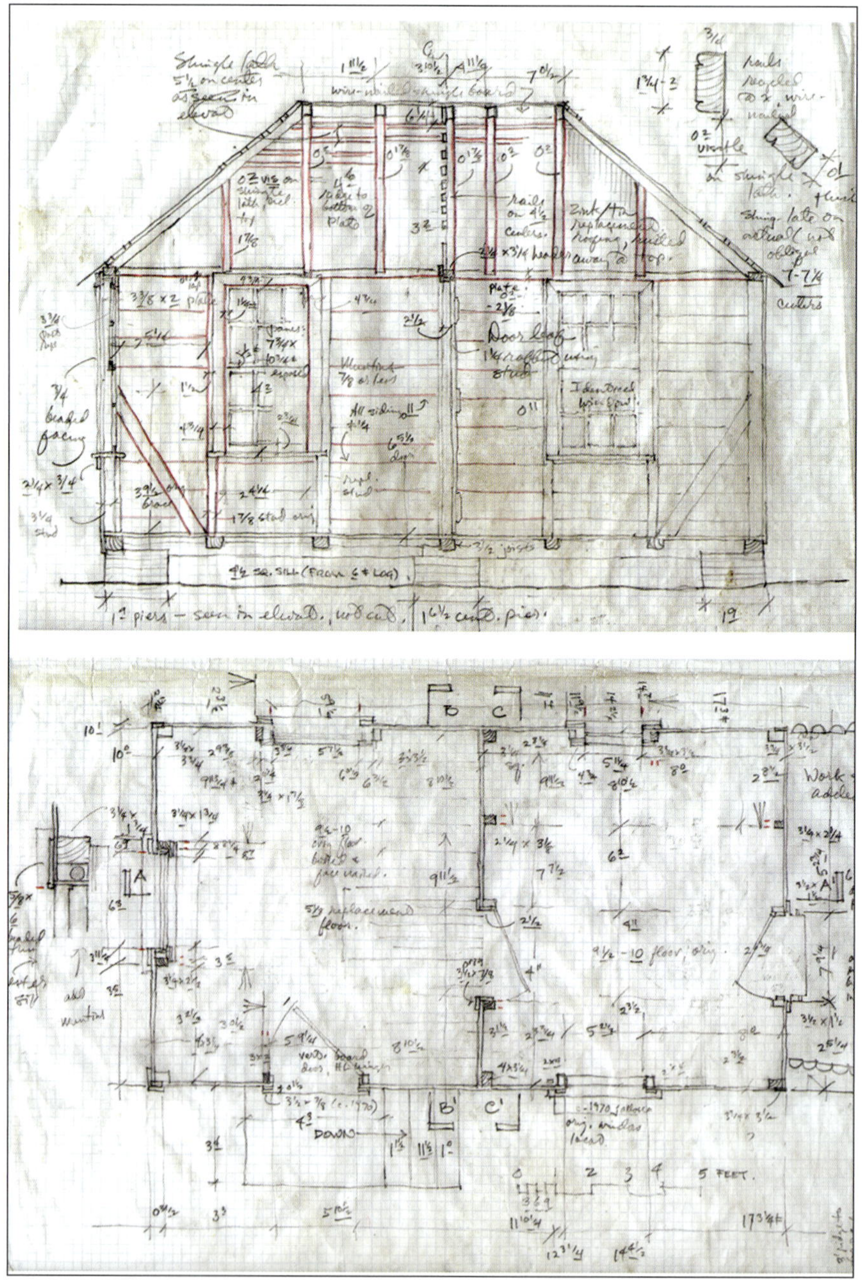

FIGURE 2.5. 31 Duke Street, Falmouth, plan and section. Red lines represent beads on framing and finish. Field notes, Chappell.

8 Trelawny Street, began with a three-part front window that was not replaced by a doorway until about 1900.[17] Indeed, it was common to use a tripartite window to ornament the narrow front and light the better room in two-room houses, while placing doors on the long side walls. A few blocks away, the house at 32 Duke Street is similarly disposed to 8 Trelawny. The patterns in Falmouth and elsewhere along the north coast are for small front-entry houses to date after the late nineteenth century. Often when front doors were added to the narrow ends of houses like 8 Trelawny Street (figure 2.6), it was part of a larger remodelling that extended the rear of the house or added lateral wings, and included an ornamental porch. As a result, the building form architectural historians often characterize as shotgun houses – two-room houses with street-end doors – are nowhere in evidence in the early period.[18] Unlike windows, commonly centred within rooms, interior doors in small Falmouth houses were usually located at one end of their partitions, preserving as much unbroken wall space as possible. Two rooms could both contain

FIGURE 2.6. 8 Trelawny Street.

beds as well as provide space for visiting and eating, which also took place outside. The common lack of a street-side entrance meant that most inside gathering could happen in the rear room, as it often does today for the sake of privacy, or in the front room, which was marginally larger and virtually always superior in quality. The smaller size of the building and the tropical climate also suggest that occupants spent much of their life out of doors under the protection of shade trees, enlisting spaces in the rest of the lot as "rooms" in the house, a practice that persists to the present. In short, the builders of the smallest surviving houses generally buffered them from the street by manipulating door placement.

This core two-room arrangement could be expanded in a variety of ways for diverse purposes. The two rooms could be raised above a commercial ground floor, as at 36 Cornwall Street (figure 2.7). There the two rooms are generous in size, originally reached by exterior stairs from the rear yard. Both were given conventional windows facing Cornwall, so the long frontage was of three uneven bays, but the larger room was also given a three-part end window overlooking the side street. The result was a substantial edifice, but one containing only two domestic rooms without internal communication with the ground-floor commercial spaces and with an exterior appearance that would have been considered peculiar in contemporary Britain or North America. Similarly, two-bay 6 King Street began with a pair of rooms on both of two floors with no connection between the floors, so they could be employed as separate apartments. There the larger of the two upper rooms was reached by exterior stairs to an end doorway. Another King Street house with a pair of rooms on two non-communicating floors has rear exterior steps leading to the larger upper room. The upper rooms were provided with louvre-flanking

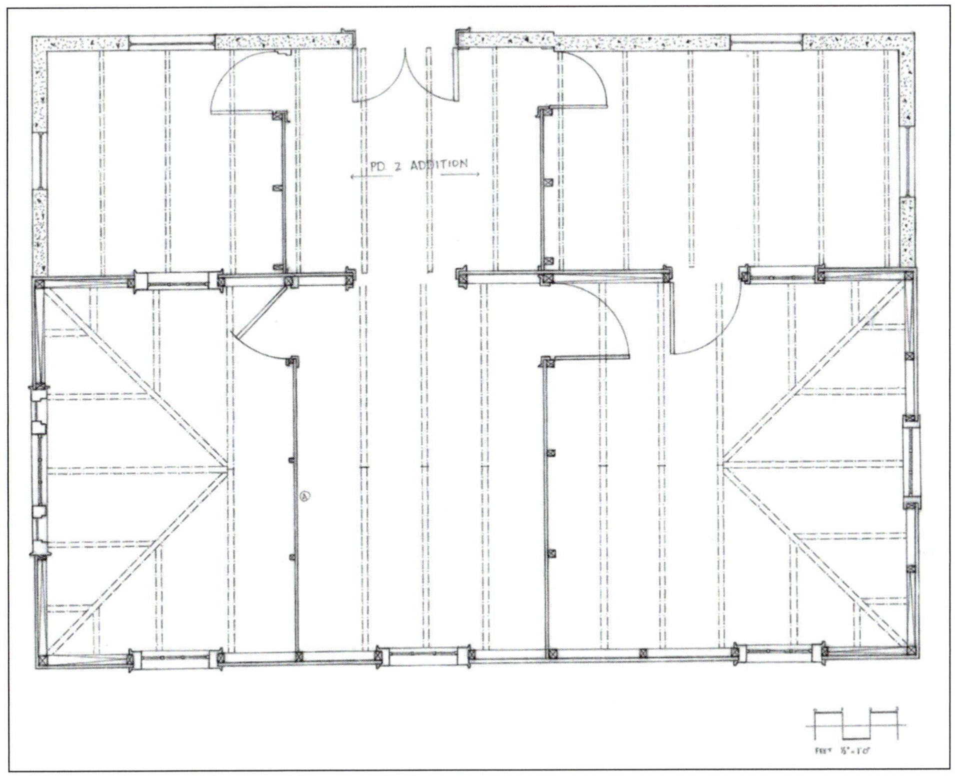

FIGURE 2.7. 36 Cornwall Street plan, drawn by Kelsey Reynolds, 2010. The north (upper) space and the southwest partition are late additions.

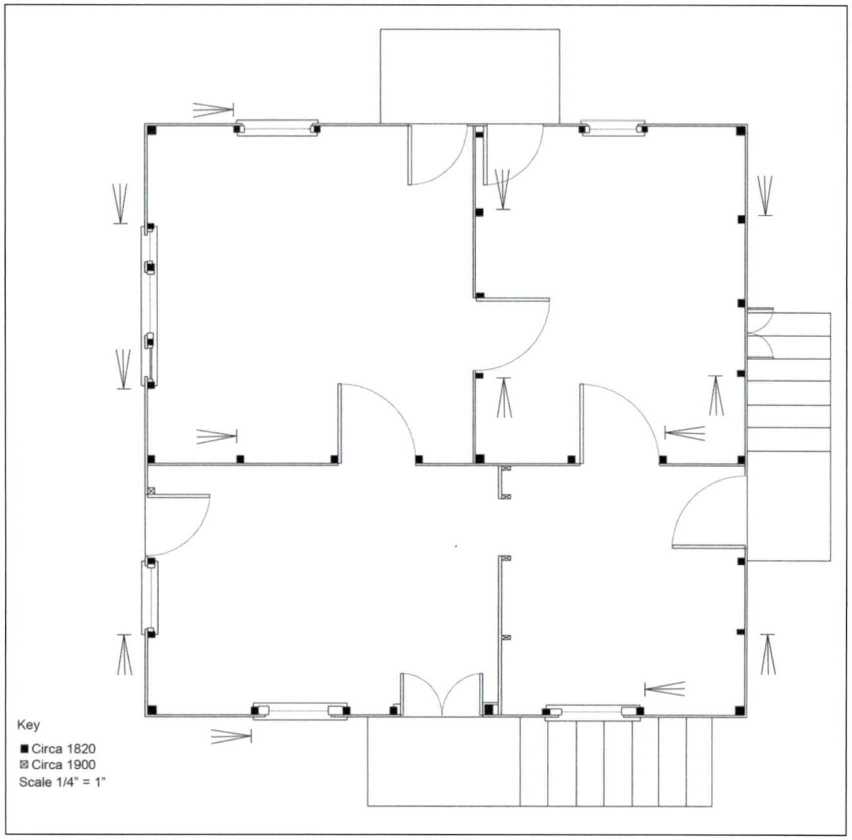

FIGURE 2.8. 18 Pitt Street plan, drawn by Kristin Hennings, 2007. Front partition added c.1900.

windows, and the smaller chamber was always partitioned to have a large closet. In a pattern often seen in two-storey Jamaican buildings of the era, the lower apartment was given only conventional windows, without louvres.

Small-frame Jamaican houses of the early nineteenth century were conceptually modular, so that a builder could double the depth as well as the height of the building, as part of original construction or as an addition. Soon after construction of 6 King Street, the owner added a pair of smaller chambers at the rear of both floors. Expansion towards creating larger social space was also no challenge for the house grammar; it could be achieved by simply adding a larger room running the length of the house. Double-pile houses (to use the British term) at 18 Pitt Street and 3 Lower Harbour Street both have a single long room facing the street and two small contemporary ones at the rear, as though a reception room were placed in front of the basic two rooms, which then could become solely bedchambers (figures 2.8 and 2.9). A sizeable and more public front room encouraged use of a front door.

But doubling the house did not inevitably shift its access to the street, following the normal pattern for free-standing double-pile English and North American townhouses. A circa 1820–30 house on Lower Harbour Street has always been entered from two doorways, both facing the yard, with only windows facing the two streets intersecting there. Neither street nor yard orientation was universal for larger houses. The Pitt Street house is more pretentious, raised on a high base with a continuous stone

FIGURE 2.9. 18 Pitt Street, Falmouth: house and ancillary building, 2009.

foundation confined to the front and slender brick piers at the sides and rear. There the street-side elevation is symmetrical, with windows flanking a door. While the residents of small Falmouth houses generally favoured side- or rear-yard access, in part to create a separation from the street, they as well as higher-placed inhabitants favoured street-side placement of the best room. An institutional example is that provided by the Falmouth District Prison, for which builder John Robey was paid £2,349 in May 1814 (figure 2.10).[19] Above ground-floor incarceration cells, Robey constructed two three-room keepers' apartments. An enclosed porch reached by high exterior steps gave access to the long front room of each apartment with a pair of rear chambers for both. A pair of hipped roofs, one behind the other, covered the two banks of rooms, following a common arrangement for double-pile Jamaican houses. Even a relatively grand Falmouth residence could have as few as three rooms: a sizeable reception room in front of two chambers. The commercial lower storey of 9 Seaboard Street has a yellow-brick façade laid in carefully trimmed Flemish bond and the remnants of a brick-fronted side porch that originally gave access to the well-finished apartment upstairs. The frame upper floor contained only three big rooms: a 30-foot by 15-foot front reception room lighted by three tripartite windows in the façade and opening directly into two long rear chambers, each with its own tripartite window in the back wall, and no passage. Each of the rooms was covered by its own hipped roof. In sum, Falmouth offers a wide array of smaller and middling, well-built houses that all seem to derive from a critical two-room core.

Several construction characteristics make these buildings regionally distinctive. The first is the common practice of multiple roofs. As Duperly's views suggest, pre-industrial Jamaicans generally favoured multiple roofs rather than a

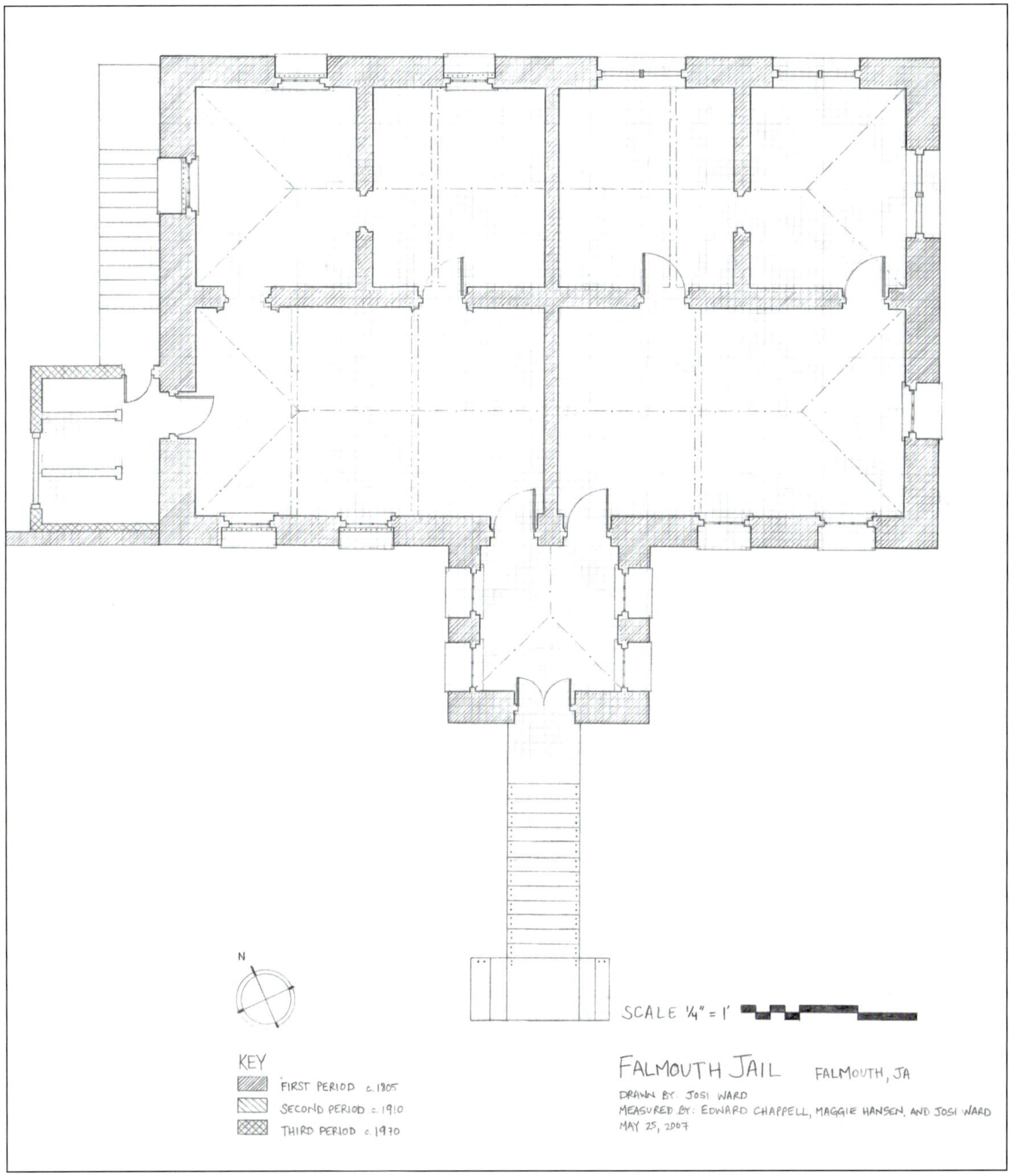

FIGURE 2.10. Trelawny Gaol, plan of the upper floor, drawn by Josi Ward, 2007.

single cover for buildings two or more rooms deep. The spans were kept relatively short, and the roofs in town were usually plainly framed with common rafters, simply birdmouthed onto light plates, often even omitting collars. Two such parallel hipped roofs cover the front and rear rooms at the Pitt Street house. Broad rear additions to 36 Cornwall and 6 King Street and a long side elevation at 27 Newton Street were all covered with independent hipped roofs, and the same roof arrangement is used for similar houses of a single period. All-encompassing roofs offered an occasional alternative, illustrated by an original single hipped roof with a central truss on the 3 Lower Harbour Street house.

Another regional distinction is quality. To close observers of eighteenth- and early nineteenth-century architecture with a North American or British perspective, they are surprisingly well-built little houses, indicating pride in accommodation and sufficient funds to afford non-functional niceties provided by professional builders and imported materials. Their frames are fully joined with carefully cut mortises and tenons, without any of the rougher lapped joinery or earthfast posts that characterized most small housing in the Chesapeake or the rustic roof frames exposed in larger landowners' houses in Bermuda through much of the eighteenth century. Furthermore, the materials did not come cheap. Jamaica is a forested island, but it is richer in hardwoods than in species like yellow and white pine that are favoured for most framing and non-luxury finish. As a result, most of the wood for framing, wall finish and shingles was imported, much of it from the coastal United States or Canada.

Well-built Jamaican houses of about 1790 to 1835 combine an economy of framing (small size of timbers and straightforward joinery), which contemporary mainland frames share, with planed and lightly ornamented surfaces on virtually all exposed pieces. Posts, braces, studs, plates, joists, tie beams, rafters and roof collars are all normally planed and beaded, dramatically unlike most mainland construction of the same era. All surviving original exposed timbers in even the smallest professionally built houses, like the one-room dwelling behind 16 Duke Street and two-room ones at 31 Duke and 36A Cornwall, are treated in this manner. Only in the later nineteenth century do such houses cease to have such consistently beaded frames, and exposed surfaces of framing continued to be planed into the twentieth century.

FIGURE 2.11. Beaded wallplate, stud and rafter foot, Falmouth, Jamaica.

The early houses are also well-finished beyond the frames. Even the plainest siding on surviving early Falmouth houses is executed with relative care: commonly 1-inch-thick boards bevelled or rebated at the top to slide into a groove at the bottom of the board above it, creating the appearance of flush boards inside. Siding is often milled and planed to a decorative shape, precociously resembling what was later called novelty siding in the United States. The lower exterior edge is occasionally moulded, resulting in a striated pattern outside and neat, flush board facing inside, superior to cladding used in New England and Chesapeake for houses of comparable size. Sometimes the interior face is beaded, as at 31 Duke and 8 Trelawny, and often it is only planed smooth, as at the costly 7 Market Street. Such work was tightly fitted for reasons of appearance, not comfort in the Caribbean climate.

Openings are usually finished with beaded frames or classical architraves outside and inside. On the smallest houses, planed boards with a beaded inner edge and no backband frame the windows, provided with thin sills. Builders used boards ornamented with cyma or cavetto shapes at the ends to shield the joint between weatherboards and window sills, in favour of beefy moulded sills. Inside, beaded door trim was offset on the wall frame to create rebates for door leaves hung on HL or butt hinges. Roman architraves played the same role for slightly larger houses. At 3 Lower Harbour, joiners fitted doors from the big room to the chambers with double architraves on the front and single ones on the rear.

Joinery nevertheless was expensive in the pre-industrial Caribbean, and builders sought ways to create refined appearance at reduced labour cost. One common choice for Jamaican builders from the 1790s into the twentieth century was to apply planed and moulded stiles and rails, or "sticking" to the outer face of board doors. This created the appearance of panelled doors without the cost of carefully joining stiles and rails together and grooving them to receive the precisely bevelled edges of independent panels. Board doors with faux panels were selectively used in other regions, but they became a standard choice for well-finished but non-elite Jamaican houses, to a degree unknown in the mainland colonies and states. Such leaves were used as the best doors in small houses and in lower status locations in fine houses. At two-room 31 Duke Street, for example, exterior board doors were finished with cyma-moulded stiles and rails outside, and the sole interior door was left plain, with battens nailed to the back side of beaded boards. Larger 36 Cornwall has similar sticking attached to the outer face of both its exterior and interior doors, with beaded battens facing the smaller room. At three-room 3 Lower Harbour Street, stiles and rails planed with thin neoclassical mouldings were applied to create the appearance of six panels on the front-room face of board doors, leaving the plain boards fully visible in the rear chambers. The upper apartment at 6 King Street began with a true panelled exterior door with glazing and a partition door with faux panels.

FIGURE 2.12. 3 Lower Harbour Street, 2008.

Such respectable little houses were well-lighted, and builders used relatively expensive windows. Stylish windows were those with large panes of glass and narrow muntins – as transparent as possible. With panes as large as 10 inches by 1 foot 3 inches and delicate muntins of ¾-inch thickness, stylish sash were used earlier and in smaller houses in towns like Falmouth than among houses of comparable size in North America, from Georgia to Maine.[20] Most of the smallest refined Jamaican houses also employed counterweights and metal pulley wheels to ease use of the windows, and the sash slide in grooves separated by parting beads – a refinement confined to expensive houses further north. The appearance of properly glazed windows in these smaller early houses was a marked improvement over the closing decades of the previous century when glazed windows in Falmouth were described by a contemporary as "a very unusual comfort at that time in Jamaica except in Kingston".[21] Such a comment reinforces the quality of construction, especially in the smallest of houses in Falmouth.

Conventional windows with six-over-six panes in sash were often

FIGURE 2.13. 7 Lower Harbour Street elevations, drawn by Elizabeth Milnarik, 2004.

paired with narrower louvred openings to create tripartite openings, a West Indian variation on tripartite windows in Regency Britain. Wooden louvres were made adjustable by pegging them loosely to stiles with wave-shaped edges allowing free movement and a tight fit when closed. A 12-foot 4-inch wide by 21-foot 5-inch deep two-room house at 27 Newton had a 5-foot 11-inch by 4-foot 2-inch such window centred on the front wall, lighting the marginally larger front room. Similar windows were given the same street-front role in comparable houses at 32 Duke, 7 Lower Harbour and Elizabeth Somerville's 8 Trelawny Street. Such windows raised the quality of front rooms, just as they embellished the narrow façades of the small houses.

A certain West Indian informality and response to climate played a role in building finish in well-constructed houses, beyond the common use of wall louvres. Year-round heat and humidity led the builders of wooden houses and masonry houses with wooden partitions to expose wall and roof frames inside rather than to sandwich walls with two layers of wood or plaster and to seal off ceilings. Heat, ravenous wood-consuming insects and a willingness to eschew some formality led builders to expose most building frames. This, in turn, provided reason to plane and bead all visible pieces of the wall and roof frame in well-built houses. Builders sawed, planed and beaded posts, braces, studs, plates and rafters in all the circa 1790 to 1835 two- to four-room Falmouth houses. The absence of attics and ceilings below most roofs allowed builders to omit joists at eaves level, replaced by a single thin tie beam joined to longitudinal wall plates and used to frame the top of partition studs. Partitions seldom were carried up solidly more than 1 foot above the eaves. Especially in small houses, builders applied beaded horizontal battens to studs or braces above the partitions, creating a visual sense of separation between rooms while allowing air and sounds to pass unobstructed from one to the other. Shingle lath as well as rafters were planed and beaded, so only the underside of the narrow shingles were visibly unfinished overhead in the rooms.

If the smallest surviving wooden houses in Falmouth demonstrate a quality of construction, they also offered a clear sense of spatial hierarchy, expressed in arrangement of wall and door finish. Sheathing was confined to only one side of each wall in the small houses. Such boards were favoured over exposed framing, even if most of the frame was exposed, and *consistency* of finish was a concern only in the best spaces of the more expensive houses. In two-room houses like those at 27 Newton, 31 Duke, 36A Cornwall, and 8 Trelawny, partition sheathing is consistently placed on the side of the largest room. At three-room 18 Pitt and 3 Lower Harbour Street, builders attached the sheathing to the front of the longitudinal partition and one side of the shorter transverse one, so the front room and largest rear room both had a single board-faced wall, and the smallest room had none. The larger the house and more public the space, the more consistent the finish. For example, a double-pile house at 30 Duke Street has stone outer walls and frame partitions, with boards facing the larger of two front rooms and a rear passage, leaving studs exposed in the small front and both rear rooms.

The Jamaican system of favouring boarded surfaces while accepting exposed frames is fully expressed in Falmouth houses that are three or more spaces deep. Usually this includes a single large reception room in front of an axial passage extending between bedchambers and leading to one or more rear spaces. In these more complex houses, the sheathing faced superior rooms and circulation spaces even when this required redundant finish. Fully framed houses with a third tier of rooms make the system more emphatic. A single-storey wooden house with this form stands near the sea at 9 King Street, covered by three parallel hipped roofs. The front reception room, 21 feet by 11 feet, is quite open, with three exterior doorways and two windows. This room is fully sheathed: even exterior walls are boarded inside. A central passage opening into the back of the reception room through an arched doorway is also fully sheathed, as is the sizeable rear room into which the passage leads through a second arched doorway, without the separation of door leaves. So the builders completely hid the frame from public view in the three linked public spaces, while leaving it exposed in the principal pair of bedchambers and a smaller rear chamber, in a house of about 1820–35.

A similar approach to plans and finish was used in more substantial house-storehouse combinations, where a fine residential floor was raised above a commercial ground level opening onto the street. Such buildings are related to urban merchant residences located over relatively unfinished commercial space in much of the Caribbean and Iberian South America. In Falmouth, they have a particular range of forms that distinguishes them from non-regional relatives and connects them to the smaller houses in Jamaican towns. One might, without much seriousness, call these elevated bachelor houses.

The grandest surviving array of such buildings line Market Street, some of them pictured in Duperly's view midway along the principal commercial route. Most are free-standing. In a simple version, at 39 Market Street, a 23-foot 5-inch by 34-foot 4-inch deep rectangular block encloses a front room running the width of the upper floor, lighted by two front windows and side windows flanked by louvres. Smaller rooms set two deep flanked an axial rear passage, with access to a stair. As at 9 King Street, front room and passage connect through an oversized and arched doorway, without leaves to close it. The Jamaican planter and historian Edward Long referred to such doorways in 1774: "the greatest expence is bestowed upon the arch of the principal hall, which is generally of mahogany, and some houses well-executed".[22] Long was describing grand early houses like the Hibbert House in Kingston and Seville in St Ann parish, and the pattern became more widespread in later decades.

At the largest, most visually dramatic buildings in Falmouth, much of the long front reception space was carried on classical columns or piers set evenly along the edge of the street. Shaded central doors and secure windows opened into the storehouses, which consisted of sizeable undivided spaces with little specialized treatment beyond sheathed walls and

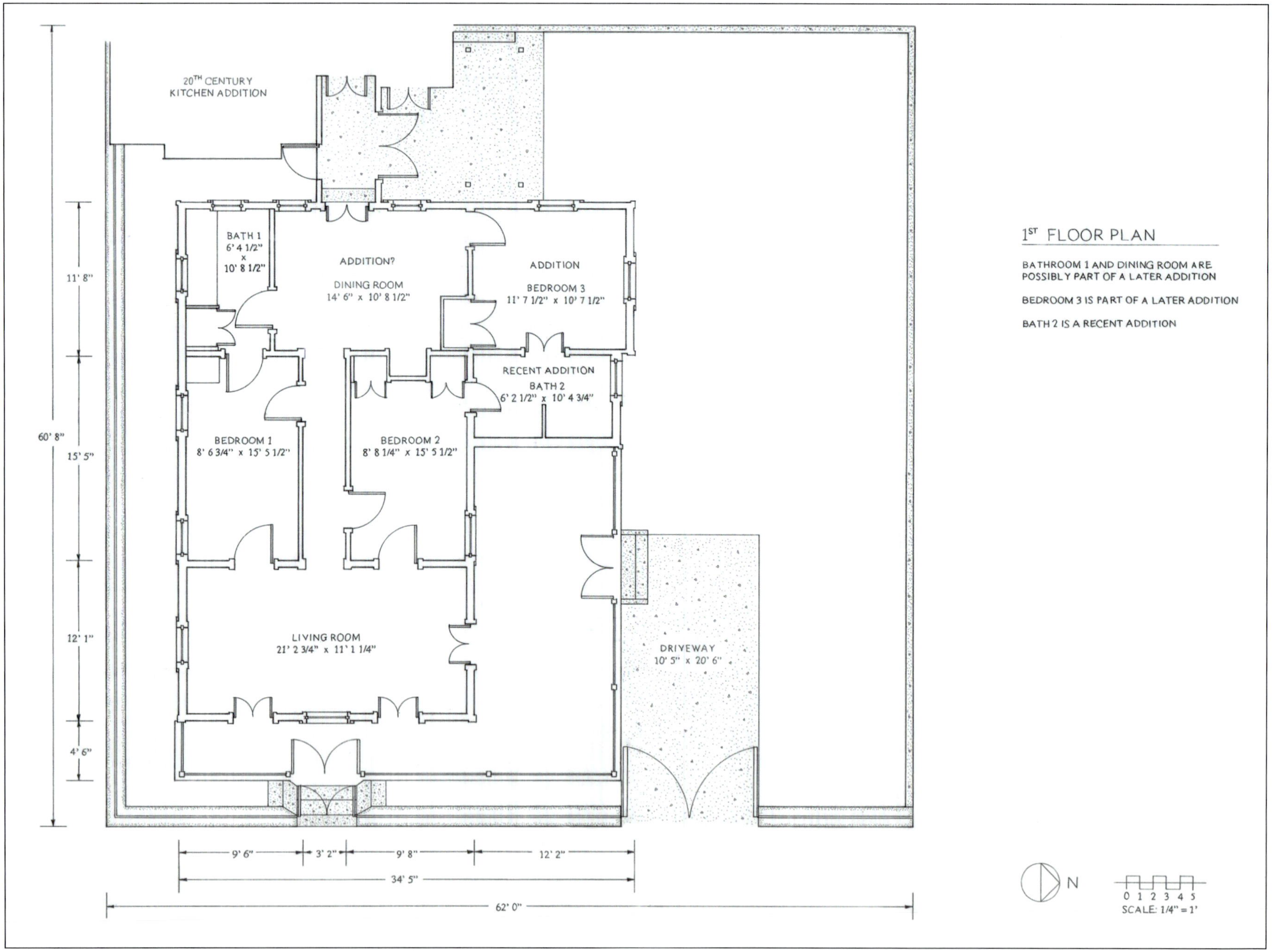

FIGURE 2.14. 9 King Street plan, drawn by Elizabeth Moore, 2006. Plan measured after alteration to finish.

well-finished framing overhead. Phillip Barrington Ainslie described such storehouses in Falmouth:

> There appeared to be several large shops, or, in Jamaica parlance, "stores", all open in front, and apparently filled with an omnium gatherum, consisting of silk mercery, woollen and linen drapery, hardware, saddler, groceries, &c. I observed in some of the larger of the stores several gentlemen, who I opined were leading men in the country, carrying on a lively conversation, which, doubtless, was increased by potations of sangaree, which was free circulating amongst them.[23]

The residential form was long-lasting. The Moulton Barrett House at 7 Market has a cornerstone dated 1795 (although stylistically a later date is plausible), and the present post office at 17 Market was built around 1833, probably by the Englishman Robert Vermont, living in Jamaica. In these and similar buildings, the front reception room dominates in size, visibility and finish. The grand room at 17 Market is 34 feet 8 inches by 15 feet. The front rooms set lofty heights, such as 12 feet below a tray ceiling and topped by a quasi-classical cornice at 17 Market Street. The space overhead was most often so finished only in the front room. The reception room was substantially glazed to capture breezes and display fashionable parties to people along the street, as they were in Kingston, Spanish Town and other Jamaican towns. No less than nine windows open up the outer walls of the room at 21 Market, filling the space with light and air. At both 7 and 17 Market, tripartite windows with glazed side openings are centred on the front and at both ends of the room, alternating with conventional windows.

Special fittings further opened the best rooms to overlook the street. Wrought-iron balconies equal to what one

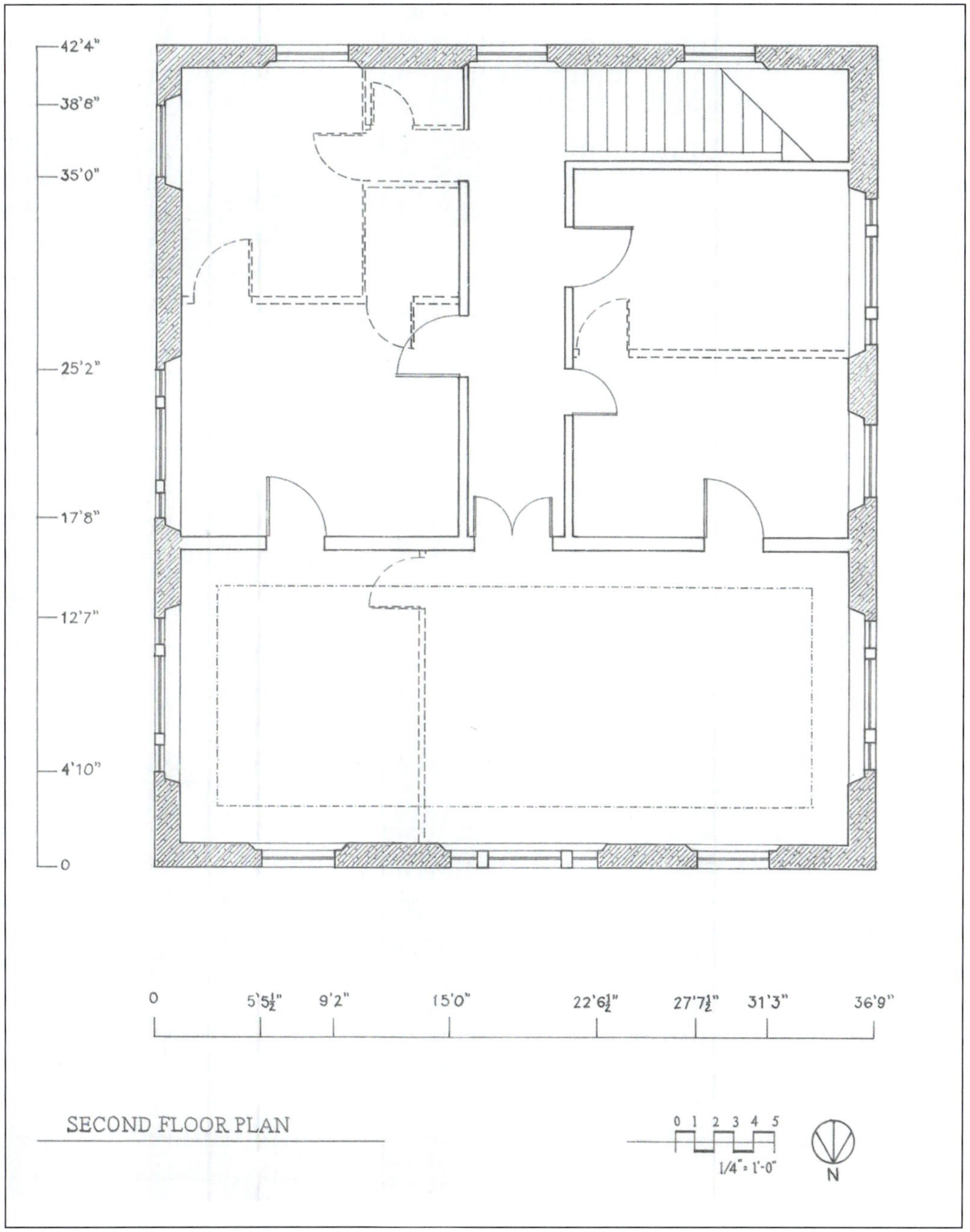

FIGURE 2.15. 17 Market Street, second-floor plan, drawn by Kevin Riddle and Elizabeth Milnarik, 2004.

FIGURE 2.16. 17 Market Street, post office, Falmouth, 2009.

can find on a fashionable Bath crescent fronted what may have been two reception rooms behind the 60-foot-long façade at the 1799 Edward Barrett House at 1 Market Street. Here the half-round balconies were fronted by crisscrossed wrought-iron bands with cast-lead rosettes at the intersections. Others with neoclassical guilloches between cast-iron balusters ornamented a raised room farther south on the street, allowing guests to step out above the crowds, as did Portuguese revellers over Brazilian commercial streets in the nineteenth century.[24] In other raised Falmouth party rooms, triple-sash windows descended to the floor without the addition of balconies. In all these, the front reception room was originally reached by way of a circulation space, usually an axial rear passage leading to a stair, bedchambers and occasionally a second reception space. Often 5 feet to 6 feet wide, they resembled the passage in smaller 9 King Street. At the expansive Barrett House the circulation space was broadened to be a sizeable square room ornamented with neoclassical doorframes and accessible to an interior rear stair.

Variation in finish marked status in comparable ways and now offers clues about functions. At 7 and 21 Market Street, the front room, passage and a rear lobby were fully sheathed, while most spaces were enclosed by a single layer of boarding located on the superior side of each wall. Only at the Moulton Barrett House was there an additional reception room, probably a separate dining room, fully sheathed, beside the passage. Bedchambers were generally bounded by exposed frame walls, often with one or none sheathed on their face, depending on the room's position in the pecking order. Partitions

FIGURE 2.17. 7 Market Street elevation, drawn by Emilie Johnson, 2007.

Trelawny Street, with its frame exposed inside. It contrasts with the rare second reception room across the passage: longer, fully sheathed and lighted by two side windows spaced so that a sideboard or serving table could be centred on axis with the passage door.

Predictable though the system initially seems, there is much variation, in the choice of construction technology and its employment towards functional purpose, marked by finish. Stone walls extend two stories high at the 17 Market Street house-storehouse, circa 1820–40, for example. There, the outer three walls of the reception room are plastered while the inner wall and passage are boarded. At the Moulton Barrett House, the rear of the passage is extended to create an elevated projecting space carried on a pair of turned columns and providing a panoramic view of the rear yard. One envisions family members seated here, keeping a controlling watch on workers in the walled yard. This small observation space was marked as superior by the use of wall sheathing, a tray ceiling moulded at the edges, and an ornamented archway opening into the passage. The space is flanked by two small shed-roofed extensions, seemingly closets, chamber-pot toilets and sleeping space for personal servants. The small rooms were lighted and louvred for ventilation, and one of them opens into the best chamber, through a louvred door providing more ventilation for residents of the big room. A smaller house-storehouse at 15 Falmouth Street has a less finished elevated rear room connecting exterior steps with another axial passage leading past two chambers to the front reception room. Its present resident characterizes the front room as "where the big men ate".[25]

between bedchambers would be sheathed on the side facing the best room, giving front chambers one finished face and the rear chambers none. Chambers usually remained open to the roof, without cornices, essentially like those in houses a third their size. Such plainly finished rooms were nonetheless lofty – their heights set by the front room – and relatively well lighted. Tripartite windows with side glazing or louvres enhanced comfort in the rooms while ornamenting and helping visually balance the side elevations, particularly when visible from a side street.

The best chamber at the Moulton Barrett House stands behind the reception room, and is served by a tripartite window in a wall facing

FIGURE 2.18. Rear view of 7 Market Street, Moulton Barrett House, Falmouth, 2009.

Entrance to the large upper-floor residences was generally at the rear of the building, as at smaller ones such as 36 Cornwall. Separating access to the residence from the storehouse below it permitted a more decorous approach and allowed the levels to be let to different tenants. Unlike Brazilian merchant families and their guests who entered raised quarters through ornamented street-side doorways often grandly positioned at the centre of tiled house-storehouse façades, Jamaicans made their way through rear doorways to enclosed interior stairs connected to the upper passage, or up exterior steps leading into small porches or interior circulation spaces. This pattern of back-door arrival is not regionally limited. It can also be seen in contemporary refined residences constructed above retail shops from Boston to Savannah, although some in the early republic were built with entrances through the façade. Clearly arrival and departure from the elite quarters were visually celebrated once one reached the upper floor ornamented with arches and pilastered doorways, often at both ends of the axial passage. But for reasons that became less persua-

FIGURE 2.19. 15 Duke Street, Falmouth, 2010.

sive after emancipation, access to and from the rear, a side street, or through an enclosed yard, was conventional.[26] At 27 King Street, exterior stone steps with ornamented ironwork are reached by a gate in the property wall along the side street (Cornwall). At 9 Seaboard Street, a street-side doorway through an extension to the lower brick façade led to a side porch housing a stair up to the residential floor, somewhat reminiscent of Charleston single house access via an end doorway to a side porch opening into the main storey. A similar two-storey porch contained a stair climbing to the upper level, opening into a side passage at 15 Duke Street, above a storehouse without colonnade.[27]

FIGURE 2.20. 21 Duke Street, Falmouth, 2010.

Elite houses recessed from the street and offering refined living quarters on two floors, without a commercial ground floor, resemble Georgian houses elsewhere in varying degrees. Outwardly, post-1790 houses such as three-bay brick 21 Duke Street seem inspired by small English Georgian houses in all but their multiple roofs and occasional window louvres. One finds great freedom in how spaces were handled in these houses, however, and sometimes their spatial arrangements are reflected in non-canonical façades. Some features common in Britain and North America are absent here, and other plan elements are more common in their presence than in the specific manner in which they were assembled. Most Jamaican house builders avoided central passages extending to the front, for example, and allowed direct access into principal ground-floor rooms. Using yards, property walls, and fences to separate the principal entry from the street encouraged direct entry into a large and usable space, reminiscent of directly accessible front rooms at smaller houses like 18 Pitt and 9 King Street. In the larger houses, however, this was seldom the best and never the sole oversized room.

Among Georgian boxes on the island, a substantial entrance hall and a superior reception room on the floor above were a normal combination. A front door in the pretty yellow- and red-brick Georgian façade of 21 Duke Street opens directly into a room running half the depth and seemingly all the length of the house. This (later subdivided) in turn opens into a generous corner rear passage, in which a mahogany stair rises to a shallower passage above it. The upper passage sacrificed depth for the sake of a large and fine reception room occupying two-thirds of the three-bay front. This arrangement left space for two bedchambers on the upper floor and one below it. Probably dating circa 1820–30, the house has a somewhat more refined finish than the single-floor quarters, but it remains eclectic in choice of wall surface, even within spaces. The interior face of exterior walls is plastered, while all studded partitions are

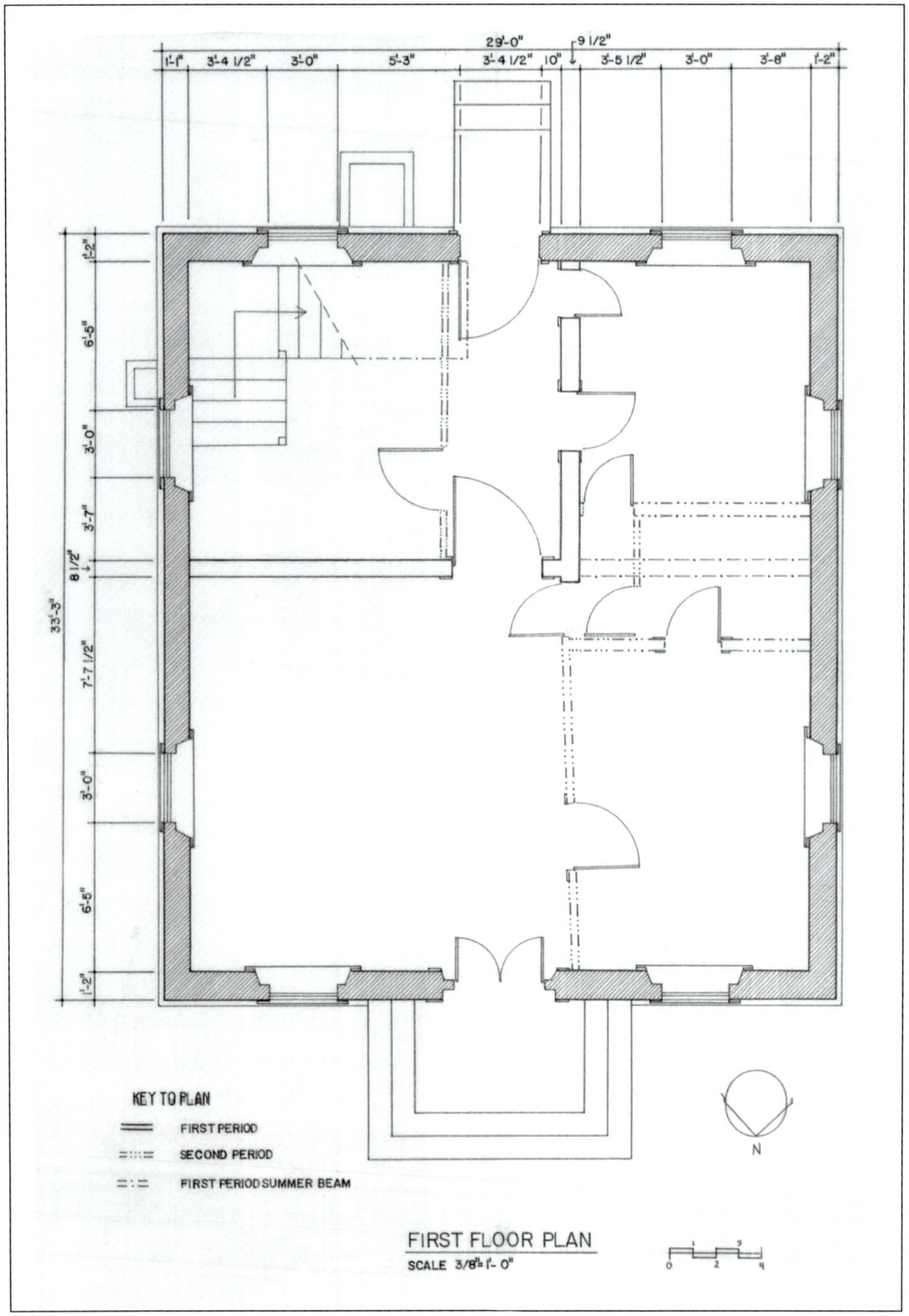

FIGURE 2.21. 21 Duke Street, first-floor plan, drawn by Patricia Slovinac (n.d.).

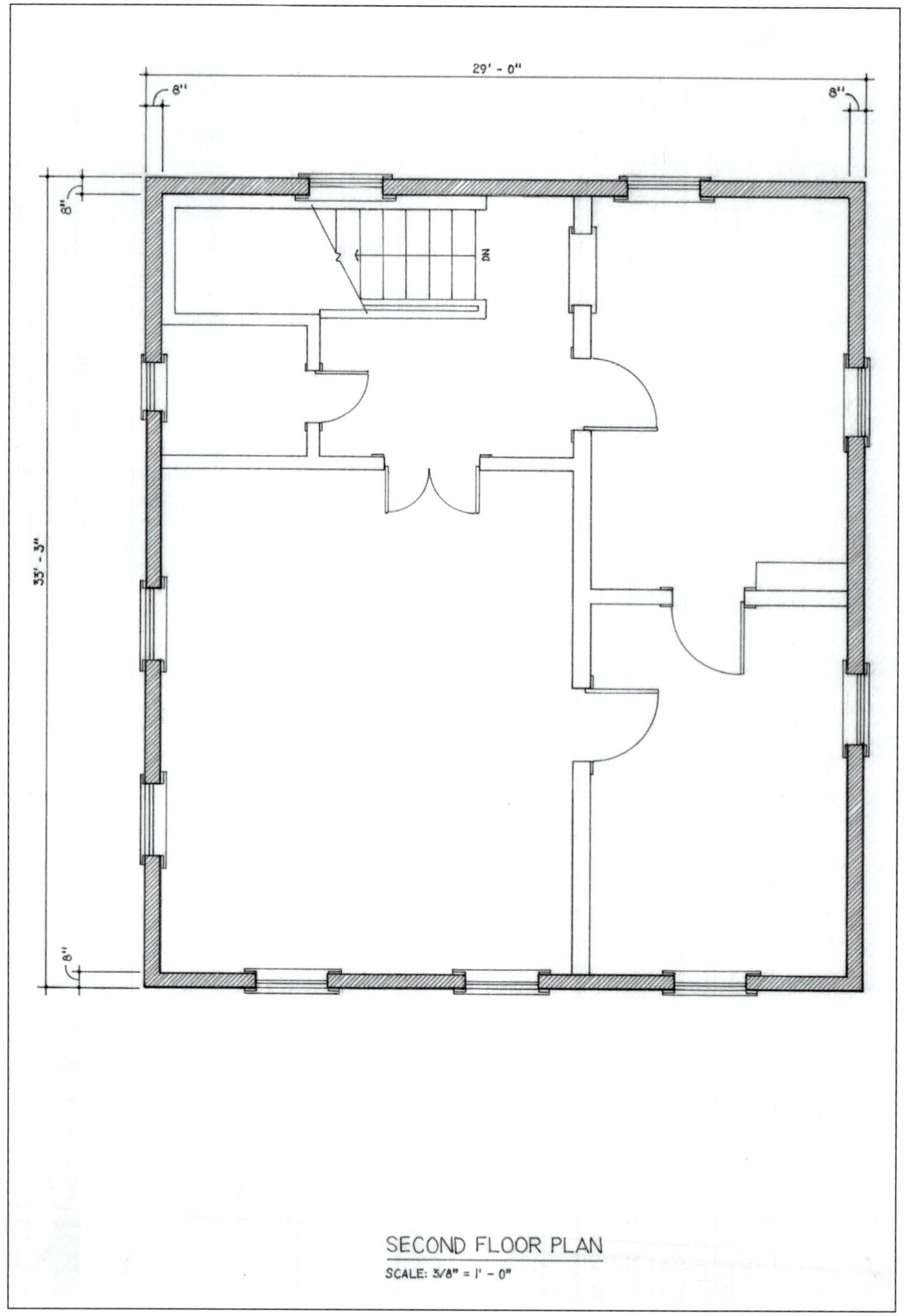

FIGURE 2.22. 21 Duke Street, second-floor plan, drawn by Michael Yengling (n.d.).

sheathed on both sides, except in an original closet, where vertical framing remains exposed. Planed and beaded horizontal framing on the main floor carries flooring that likewise was planed and beaded to be seen from below. Superiority of the best room upstairs was announced by sunken-panel surrounds and Greek-inflected corner blocks, used to trim its door in the passage and on all its own openings. Ordinary architraves and beaded frames were used everywhere else in the house.

Such conventional Georgian exteriors give few clues to the interior arrangement. A larger two-storey and three-bay house on a pair of lots at 43 Cornwall provides similar accommodation – direct entry into large space, big upper reception room, and three or four chambers – in a form that resembles the raised plans over storehouses. Here the front door opens into a long front room with a leafless arched opening to a rear passage between chambers ventilated by louvres in their walls and a straight shot to the back door. At the outer end of the front room, a second arched opening provides an entrance to the stair, also accessible from a private exterior doorway. Climbing the stair carries one directly into a fine upper reception room, 31 feet by 16 feet, stretching the length of the façade. Midway along its back wall is a more richly decorated arched opening, giving access to two more chambers and an enclosed miniature rear porch reached by exterior stone steps. Varying wall and ceiling finish as well as the relative elaboration of the arched openings marks the upper front room as best. The entry space has boarded as well as plastered walls, and exposed joists overhead carry planed and beaded flooring. Upstairs, the front room has all plastered walls and a tray ceiling above a frieze and cornice. The rear chambers have plaster on outer walls and sheathing on their transverse partition, and exposed roof frames.

An inflated version is found behind a boisterous brick and stone façade at 16 Church Street in Montego Bay. The Georgian house is raised over cellars and set behind a low property wall with a gate and fence between brick pillars. Here the front door originally opened into a room running the full width and more than half the depth of the house. This broad space is spanned by impressively large transverse and longitudinal summer beams carrying joists, all planed and beaded. An arched door-

FIGURE 2.23. 16 Church Street, Montego Bay, 2010.

way opens into a relatively broad (15 feet wide) central rear stair hall, with a fine curved and cantilevered stair, made of tropical hardwood. The stair sweeps up to a narrower second-floor passage, well lighted by a tripartite window that nearly fills the outer wall. As one now expects, the rear circulation space on both levels opens into side chambers, and the upper one leads through another ornamental doorway into a superior, full-length front room overlooking the street. A three-part middle bay opens onto a balcony.

In terms of general arrangement, this expansive sort of Georgian house looks back to some of the grandest colonial houses of an earlier era, such as Drayton Hall in South Carolina and Thomas Hibbert's house (now called Headquarters House) in Kingston. Hibbert was prominent among a group of wealthy merchants who built large brick mansions set behind brick walls and iron gates in the southern port town in about 1755. Both it and Drayton Hall have grand entrance halls leading on axis to centred rear circulation spaces with dramatic stairs expensively built with tropical hardwoods, which deliver guests and family to upper chambers and to the finest reception space at the upper front. In both those cases, guests could move easily from the upper room onto a front portico, looking down on the approach. With chambers or small withdrawing rooms flanking the entrance and rear halls, the lower floor at Hibbert House and the now single-storey Seville plantation house somewhat resemble the one-storey English house Edward Long describes in 1774 as common in Jamaica: "the centre room is a hall, communicating at each end with a bed-chamber; the back part, usually a shed, is divided in the same manner, and communicates with the front, or principal hall".[28]

Rich Jamaicans of the later generation like the Trelawny planter John Tharp could also favour houses with a single refined floor containing two reception rooms in addition to a broad entrance space, all raised over storage space for their com-

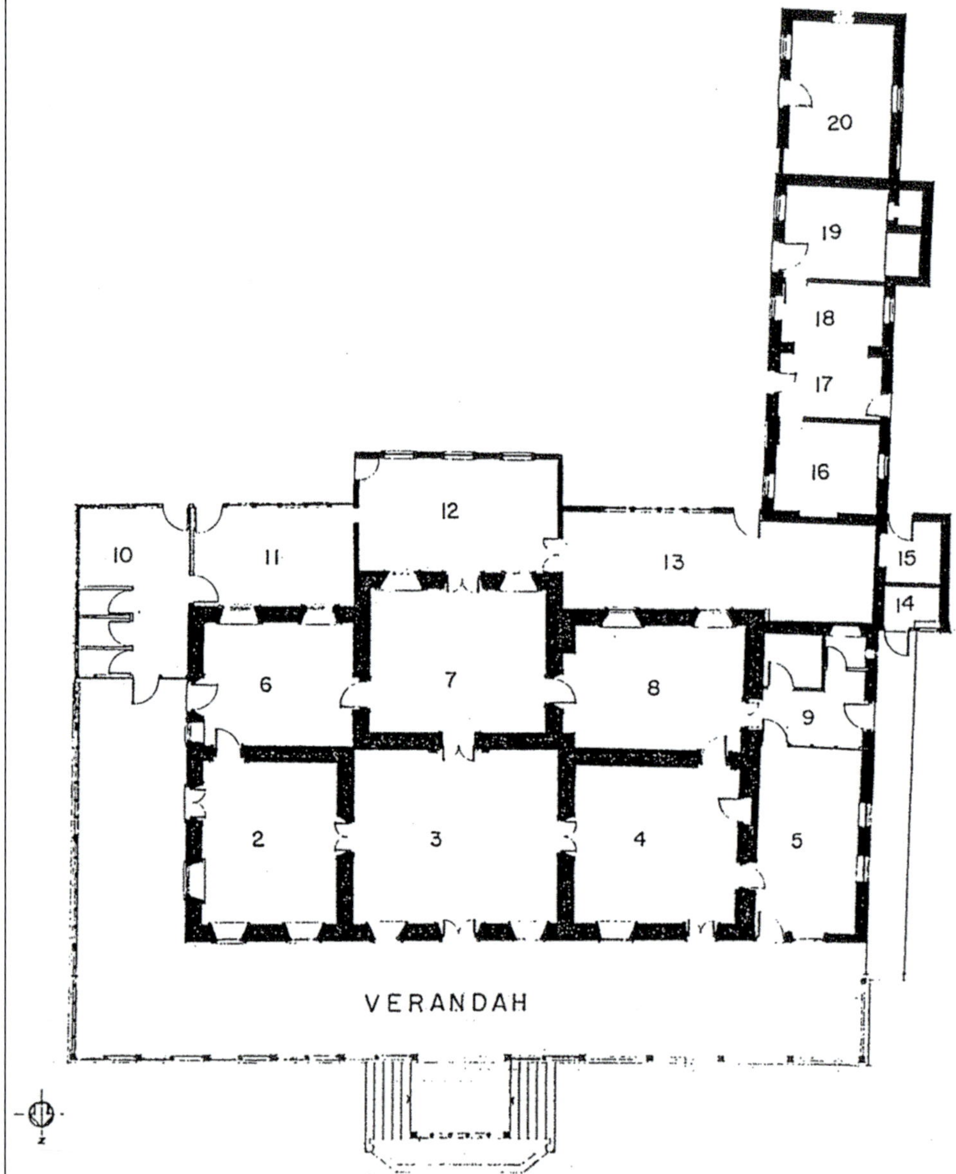

FIGURE 2.24. Seville Great House plan. Courtesy of the Jamaica National Heritage Trust.

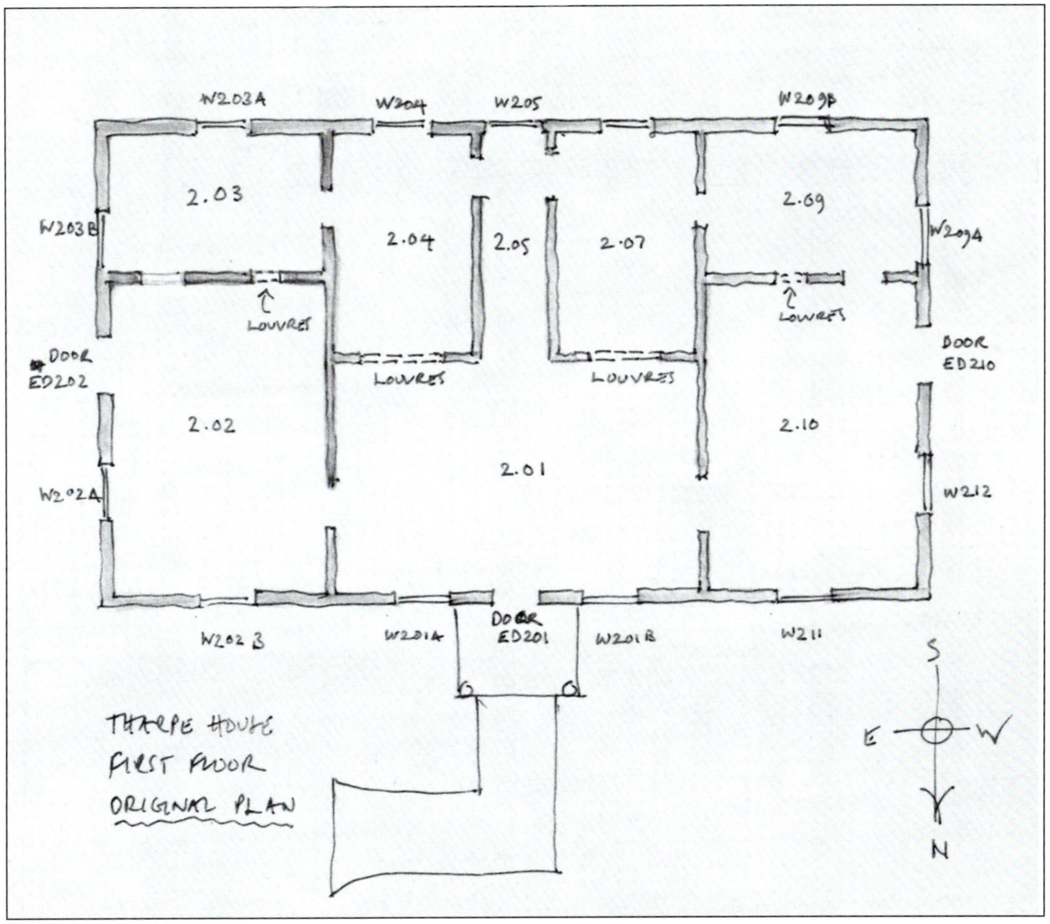

FIGURE 2.25. Tharp House, main-floor plan, restored, drawn by Peregrine Bryant (n.d.).

mercial loot. Tharp built such a house on his Falmouth wharf and another where he lived at nearby Good Hope plantation.[29] Both Tharp's houses are articulated with varied fenestration and multiple roofs suggesting certain features of the plan. Front steps rise to long transverse entrance halls leading on right and left to entertainment rooms and straight ahead to narrow passages.

Tharp's townhouse is the more controlled of the two, with a symmetrical plan inside a rectangular box built of nogged frame above stone cellar walls. Here the large entry room opens into a pair of matched reception spaces ornamented with small lions'-head friezes. Outside, these reception rooms were distinguished by triple-sash windows flanked by louvres, descending to the floor, contrasting with windows of the same height but lacking louvres in the entry.[30] The outer rooms in the suite and a narrow passage in the familiar axial location led to four rear chambers. Each of the chambers had openings with moveable louvres providing ventilation between them and the reception spaces. At frame-walled Good Hope, the entry space is proportioned more like a longitudinal passage, leading to outer front reception rooms that project forward and are marked by tall round-headed windows flanked by louvres, a Caribbean variety of Venetian window. Here the left wing contains two large rooms, both heavily ventilated with exterior louvres. The largest and plainest is a rear dining room, near a long stone-walled kitchen in a common position, facing the rear yard from one side. The fourth and most ornamented reception space is in the right wing, its less provision for ventilation perhaps indicating a more limited use than the breezy opposite pair. An arched and ornamented central doorway opposite the front entry leads to four chambers in the manner now familiar from Falmouth houses. Roof frames are visible and finished above all the reception spaces, with early ceilings over the axial passages, as seen in similar Falmouth passages. In short, the two houses of Trelawny's richest planter can be read as variations on the arrangement of Falmouth houses, built atop storehouses or free-standing. Conceptually they expand the usual front hall with an axial rear passage leading to bed chambers by simply adding more reception rooms and chambers to both ends.

The extensive use of louvres for ventilation marks a significant development among houses of the richest resident Jamaicans away from mid-eighteenth-century Hibbert's house and Seville, which lacked them, to

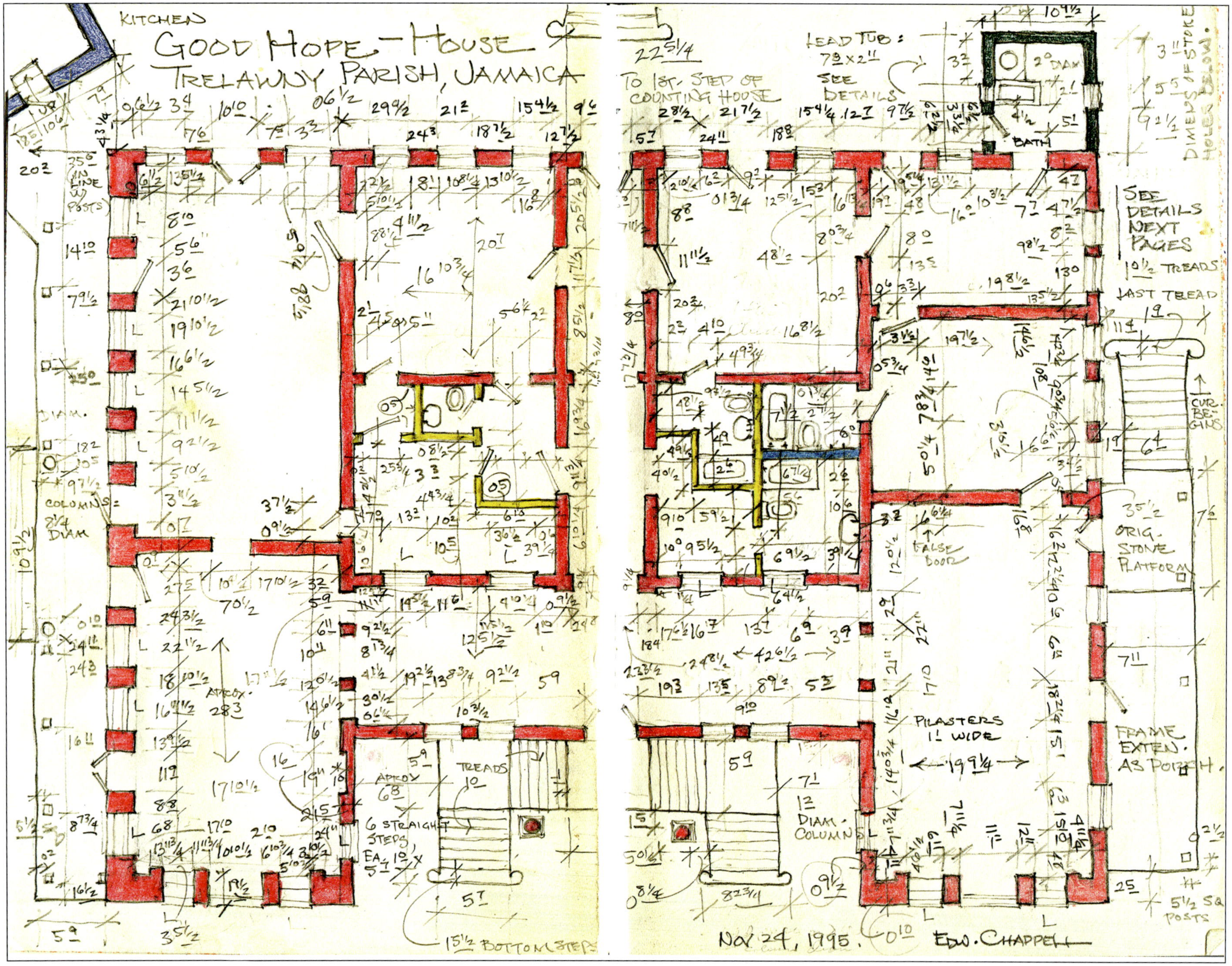

FIGURE 2.26. Main-floor plan, Good Hope, Trelawny. Field notes, Edward A. Chappell, 1995.

Tharp's very late eighteenth-century houses, which included them in both interior and exterior walls. The latter reveal a growing concern for physical comfort and willingness after about 1790 to move further from British practice.[31] This provides some context for the extensive use of louvres in smaller houses of the same era and thereafter. Nineteenth-century houses in Kingston and Spanish Town made even further use of louvres, often fully enclosing full-length upper verandahs with them.

The varied roof forms and windows within a single elevation like that of Tharp's townhouse also give the large Jamaican houses a freewheeling quality that is rare among their counterparts in Britain and North America. Within a disciplined "Georgian" aesthetic, the front fenestration at 16 Church Street in Montego Bay gives the three-bay house a very unruly appearance. Two conventional upper windows flank the wide balcony doorway with multiple sidelights above a main doorway flanked by tripartite windows, with the variation emphasized by exaggerated rustication draped around each opening. Exterior walls shift in materials with equal freedom. Most Market Street house-storehouses have masonry lower walls and wooden upper ones, in contrast to the older Hibbert House. Those on Duke Street favour stone lower walls and brick upper ones. The two-storey house at 43 Cornwall Street, similarly, has ashlar stone below and refined brick above. By the 1790s, Jamaican elites enjoyed their freedom from homeland convention, architecturally as well as in their social behaviour.

The overall shapes as well as fenestration and materials of sizeable houses broke British design rules. A pair of large reception spaces with the superior one upstairs could also be housed in unconventional wrappers at houses like frame-walled 29 Cornwall Street, located directly on the edge of the street. This has a distinctive elevation, with two front upper windows flanked by louvres and a not-quite-symmetrical three bays below without louvres: a Georgian façade on tropical holiday. The slightly off-centre doorway originally opened into the largest ground-floor space, at front left. Walking through this to a rear room, one would have found a stair rising directly into the superior reception room, running the full depth of the left side rather than across the front. One of the louvred and glazed façade windows served the best room and the other offered light and air to a front bedchamber.

FIGURE 2.27. 29 Cornwall Street, Falmouth, 2009.

A yellow-brick-walled variation on this arrangement is the more altered house at 2 Trelawny. There, the front fenestration is the same – two triple windows above two single windows and a door – while the overall fenestration offers stronger clues for the location of the best rooms. A front door flanked by conventional windows now leads through rearranged space giving access to a back corner hall containing a fine

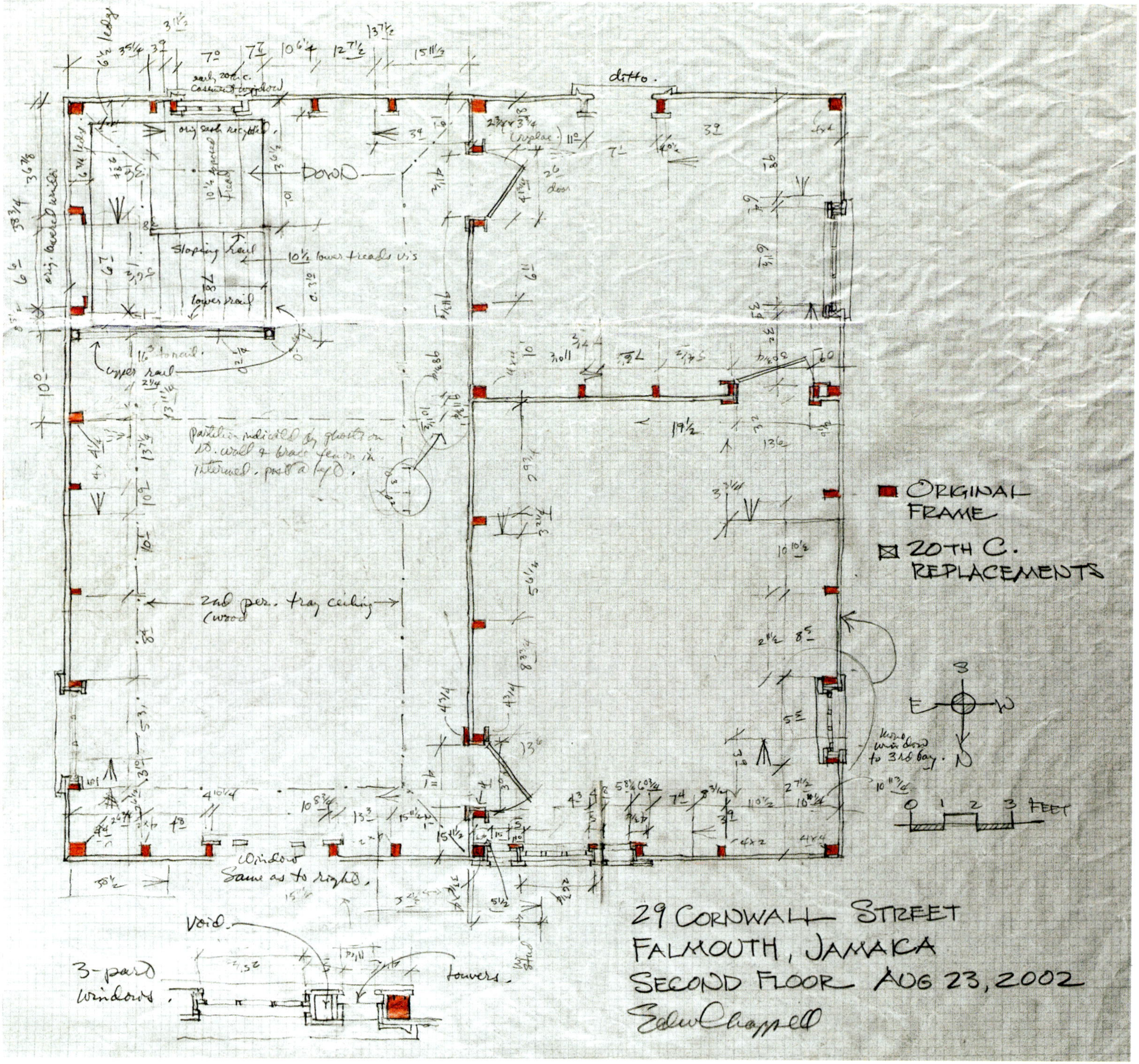

FIGURE 2.28. 29 Cornwall Street, second-floor plan. Field notes, Edward A. Chappell, 2002.

mahogany stair. The stair rises to a mahogany-floored passage that originally led to a 26-foot 2-inch by 16-foot 5-inch reception room lighted by three tripartite windows and two adjoining smaller spaces, probably a withdrawing room and chamber, both with a single three-part window. The two best rooms together running the depth of the house, were given tropical hardwood floors, contrasting with North American pine floors in the lesser ones. They also received superior finish, although wall framing is exposed and beaded on the back of their shared partition, just as it is in the rear room of two-room houses.

A number of familiar characteristics employed in the arrangement of two-storey, two-bay houses with pairs of oversized reception rooms is best exemplified in 20 Duke Street, an expensive yellow-brick house at the front of two large walled yards of service buildings, occupying much of the half block between Queen and King streets. The 28-foot narrow façade is set close to Duke Street, behind a low wall and fence but was originally separated from it by placing only two tripartite windows on both levels of the front and confining access to a rear doorway. As at upper-floor quarters over storehouses, family and guests entered the property from a gate and made their way through the yard to a doorway well removed from street life. This opened into the lower of two L-shaped passages, connected by a stylish mahogany stair with cantilevered steps rising through an apsidal well. The lavish means of circulation provided dramatic access to a pair of deep reception rooms, stacked one above the other. The lower passage opened through two double doors into the first reception room, extending two-thirds the 46-foot 6-inch length of one side. The drawing room upstairs is superior, with a more elaborate frieze and cornice than those in the dining room below, and both are better finished than all other spaces. Two hipped roofs run front to back and parallel, with their valley over the frame spine wall. The left roof exposes its planed and beaded rafters and purlins to chambers and passage, while its partner has unfinished framing hidden by a tray ceiling in the drawing room and flat boarded ceiling in the adjoining front room. The circulation is freer downstairs, with all rooms opening into all adjoining spaces, and fewer doors upstairs limiting guests' access to the two best rooms.

Circulation is relatively free and flexible in most of the houses studied, when compared to mainland arrangements of the same era. In small houses, of three rooms for example, all adjoining spaces connect: chambers connect with each other and with the larger principal space. The substantial three-room residence over a storehouse at 15 Duke Street has each room opening into its adjoining room as well as all opening into a side passage with doorway from a side porch. Chambers located behind front reception spaces over Market Street storehouses commonly open directly into the front room as well as the passage. The second reception room at 7 Market Street connects to both the front room and passage. Reception rooms on both floors at 20 Duke Street connect with their adjoining smaller room, as though a chamber could serve as a withdrawing room when needed in a fashionable house where not all rooms connect. The chamber as well as withdrawing room on the upper floor of 2 Trelawny Street connects to the main reception rooms, so that all three could form a circuit with the passage for large gatherings, and air would circulate reasonably well. Certain control is evident in large houses of two floors, because the expanded number of rooms allowed more specialization and less need for flexibility. At 43 Cornwall, for example, both rear chambers open into the front reception room, but neither rear room connects with the entrance hall and second front room on the lower floor. At 16 Church Street in Montego Bay, too, all first-floor spaces connect only by way of the rear passage. The non-connecting spaces underscore that ventilation was not the sole motivation for openness.

The porosity in Jamaican houses indicates desire for relative freedom of movement and function. Especially in the raised quarters, bedchambers became public spaces for parties, and reception rooms served along with bedchambers as private sitting spaces when visitors were absent. Locks on virtually all doors offered control when residents desired it, and doors within passages were often staggered rather than aligned as a subtle means of aiding privacy, so the presence of many doors did not mean access was always free and easy. On the other hand, long front reception rooms virtually always opened into axial passages through large doorways that generally lacked leaves, at least after about 1790. When the front

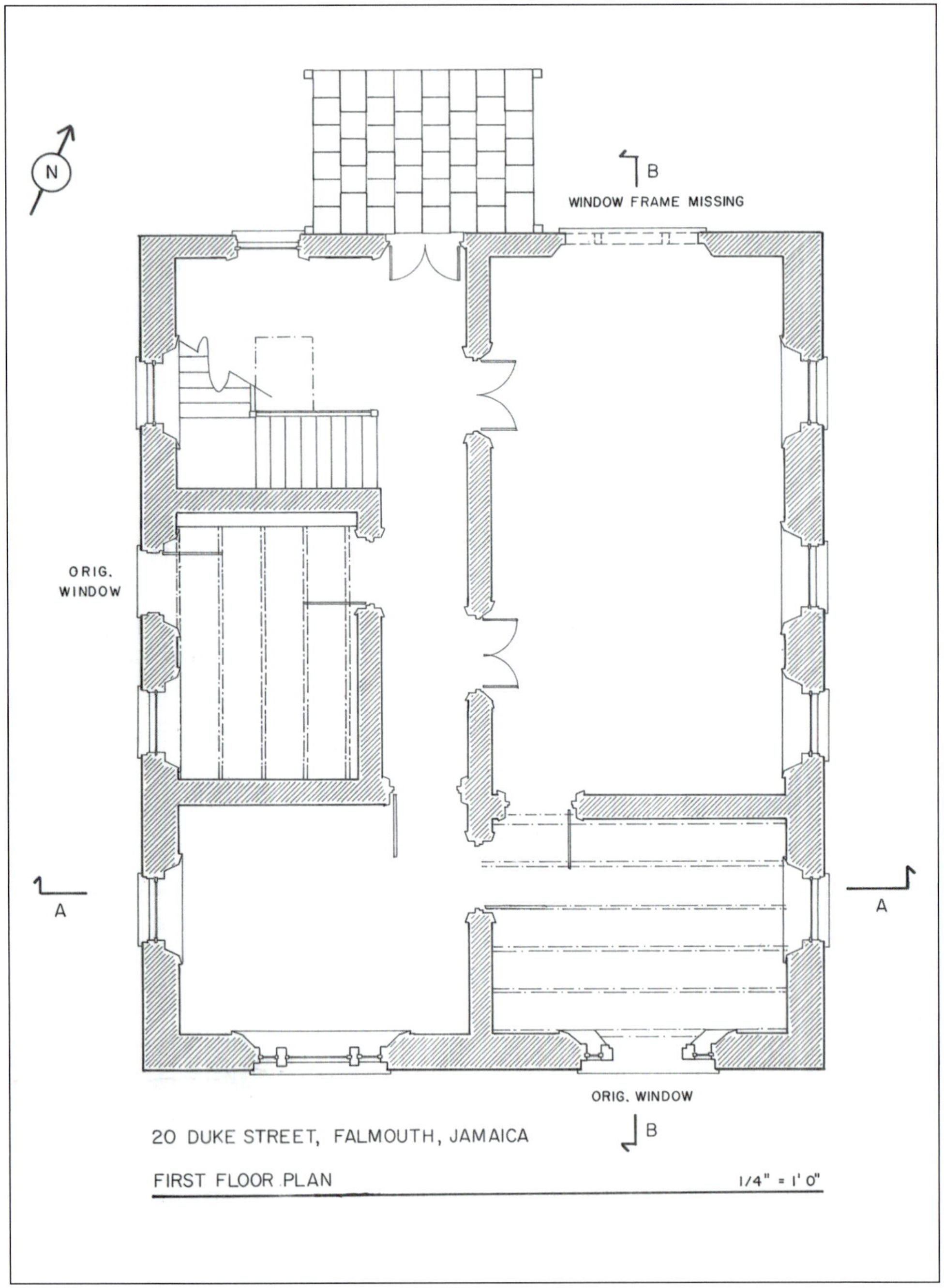

FIGURE 2.29. 20 Duke Street, first-floor plan, University of Virginia Falmouth Field School, 2004.

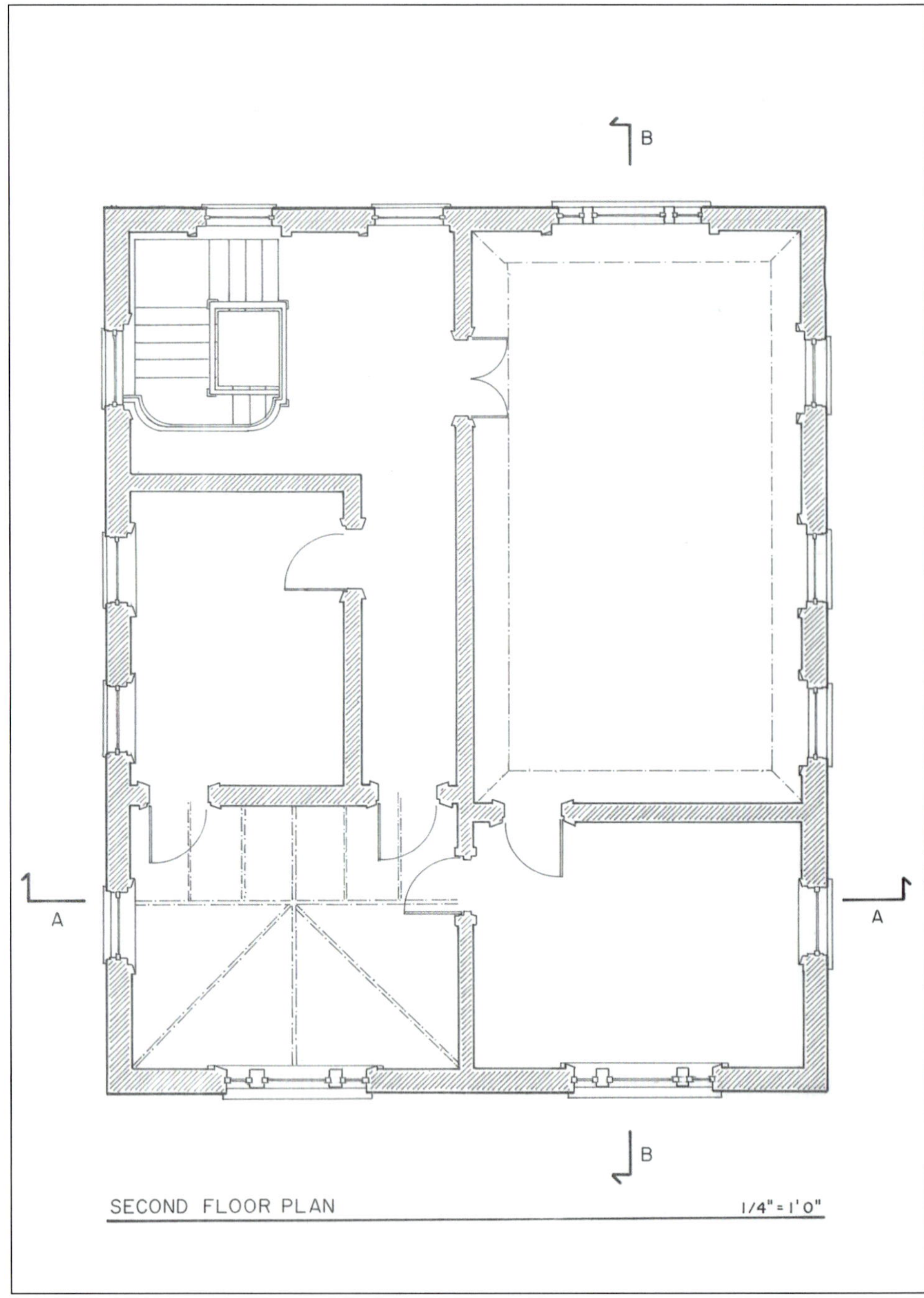

FIGURE 2.30. 20 Duke Street, second-floor plan, University of Virginia Falmouth Field School, 2004.

door opened directly into sizeable halls, the superior room was well-buffered from the street in all but the smallest three-room houses. As we have seen, even in houses as small as 3 Lower Harbour, there was a preference for entering from a side or rear yard. Larger residences had multiple points of control. Reaching the reception room over storehouses usually involved entering the property and then a door at some distance from the street, climbing a stair and traversing a relatively dark passage before arriving in the room full of light and guests. The route to reception at two-storey Jamaican Georgian houses could be less circuitous, but the ultimate position of achievement could be similarly attenuated: through the front gate and front door, into the entrance hall, and eventually up a stair to an elevated room for parties.

An essential functional characteristic of households in all the examples discussed here, from two rooms to eight or more, is the absence of cooking from the main residence. Even the smallest surviving street-side houses lack fireplaces, and evidence for detached kitchens is present at a number of them. Elsewhere, self-consciousness among slave owners about their domestic chattel grew in the decades after the American Revolution. Revolutionary rhetoric and the rise of abolitionism caused concern for how visible the delivery of food and service was to property owners and guests in the United States and certain slaveholding British colonies. Elites increasingly felt that reduction in visibility of black servants contributed to refinement in cultivated social settings. Indeed, English prints lampooning the unrefined behaviour of Anglo-Jamaican elites included shoeless and often shirtless black servants and onlookers as an additional hilarity in the ribald scenes. The degree to which this affected Jamaican slave owners themselves and their houses is an interesting question.

Large free-standing residences, especially two-storey Georgian houses, generally offered secondary access for service to the first floor, via a back door. However, houses such as 43 Cornwall were rare in providing extensive alternate service routes to the superior room or upstairs in general. In that case, servants could apparently reach the best room by way of rear steps to the upper axial passage as well as through a side doorway to the interior steps. Residences above storehouses were more limited in their choices. In most cases, food was delivered along the same route that guests and residents used – up the same stairs and down the same passage, with the limited exception of perhaps serving through rooms otherwise used as chambers. Judging from arrangement of circulation, domestic slaves were simply an accepted fact of life, although the same reading might be made of fashionable residences above shops in early US cities.

Most of the known Falmouth kitchen-service buildings are located at a property line, behind and/or beside the house, often set against one side of the rear yard. Windows and doors usually face the yard. Outer walls can have windows if they face the street but are normally unpierced where they face an adjoining property. In form, the buildings resemble substantial kitchen-quarters at the largest contemporary and earlier houses in Spanish Town and Charleston. Even some of the grandest plantation houses such as Good Hope and Seville placed kitchens and domestic slave lodging in linear buildings at one side of the rear yard rather than in one of two large balanced flankers as at Rose Hall in about 1770.[32] Sizeable work buildings used for laundering as well as cooking usually locate the oversized fireplaces on the outer side wall, turning their backs to their neighbours' property, as also seen at the Miles Brewton House in Charleston. Now-altered examples remain behind 21 Duke Street and the Masonic Hall, believed to have been converted to a Baptist manse, on Market Street. Unlike Carolina and Chesapeake urban examples, quarters for workers were usually placed farther back along the side property line or against the rear of the property rather than above the work rooms.

An alternative seen at the Tharp House was to house domestic workers in rooms running back from near the house along the most public property line and place kitchen and laundry elsewhere. Workers and work appear to have been accommodated in small cells with their brick walls built into side and rear property walls at the 20 Duke Street complex. A multi-room brick kitchen and quarters perhaps built just after emancipation extend along the rear property line of a two-storey edifice thought

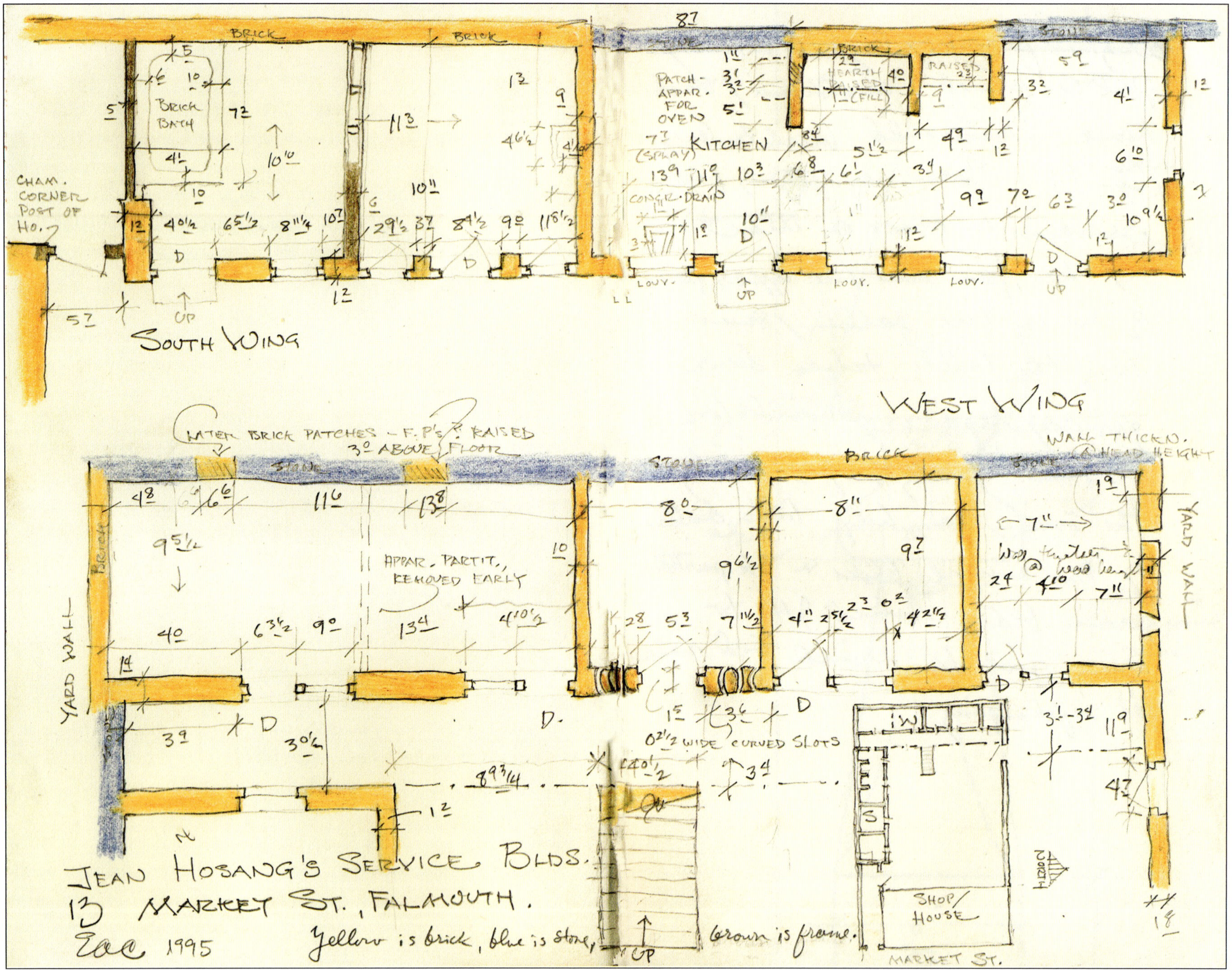

FIGURE 2.31. Kitchens, quarters and other ancillary spaces arranged along the left and rear property lines of the house-storehouse at 13 Market Street. Field notes, Edward A. Chappell, 1995.

to have been unmarried officers' quarters, dated 1838, opposite Fort Ballcarres. Among the houses discussed here, only the Hibbert mansion in Kingston shows any evidence for specialized cooking in the cellar, and Hibbert's property contained a large and detached multi-storey building for service and workers.

Distance from kitchen to house varied according to lot size as well as to degree of wealth. The kitchen-laundry closely adjoins the Georgian house at 21 Duke Street, and the remains of a bake oven indicate the kitchen at 16 Church Street in Montego Bay was immediately behind the big house. Remarkably, the yellow-brick cooking fireplace with oven at two-room 36A Cornwall Street is located 39 feet behind the house. By contrast, the foundations of a kitchen with only 3-foot 10-inch-deep floor space in front of the cooking fireplace are a mere 3 feet 7 inches from the rear of the shop and about 5 feet from the three-room house at 3 Lower Harbour Street, built on a substantially divided lot.

Placed near or far, the implication of detached kitchens is that free people's disdain for domestic labour in a land dominated by slavery, as well as the punishing climate, removed cooking from the centre of households with few or no servants. This contrasts, for example, with Pierre-Joseph Leborie's conception of how a hearth for cooking should be included in the front room of every 10-foot by 20-foot apartment assigned to two slaves in barracks for British West Indian coffee plantations.[33] Edward Long wrote that "almost every dwelling-house throughout the island is detached from the kitchen and other offices; which, though different from practice in England, is a very judicious arrangement for this climate, where the fumes and smoak of the kitchen, and the stench of other necessary offices, would be intolerable in too near a neighbourhood".[34] Long was referring, of course, to white-led households. Such separation of portable domestic work from the main house follows the pattern of other substantial slaveholding regions in the Caribbean and British North America. What is most interesting is that in Jamaica it extends to properties with such small houses. When residents of the smallest surviving Falmouth houses like those at 36A Cornwall and 31 Duke Street lacked a cook, a family member had to cook outside or in a separate building, increasing inequitable gender relations within the family. While it is conceivable that some residents of small well-finished houses cooked in the open air, as do some present residents, especially unattached males, the physical evidence suggests most of the present houses had free-standing kitchens, however roughly constructed.

Kitchens and quarters extend the range of construction quality, even if we rely only on surviving structures for evidence. Certain expensive houses in Falmouth and Spanish Town from around 1790–1835 had well-built brick or frame ancillary buildings, primarily ones incorporating masonry property walls. However, masonry was often confined to the kitchen chimney and sometimes its adjoining wall, as evident at the substantially rebuilt kitchen behind 43 Cornwall Street. Even elite houses such as 29 Cornwall show evidence for relatively mean workers' accommodation, buildings with small windows in low and roughly constructed walls. A spindly frame building 13 feet behind 8 Trelawny Street also appears to have been a kitchen. A small service building behind the comparable three-room 18 Pitt Street house probably also contained cooking space.

A cheaper quality of construction in the smaller work buildings helps define the superior manner in which the surviving houses were built. Most common among the smallest Falmouth kitchens are flimsy frame walls filled with rough masonry: usually brick or small pieces of limestone in mortar or slurry. Nogging or filling frames was not an innately inferior construction method. Carefully crafted hardwood frames with filling of brickwork were used for the upper walls at the Tharp House and for the principal floor at substantial plantation houses like Hampstead. If the exterior was stuccoed and the interior plastered, nogged walls were a secure and genteel choice. But the technique also offered a means towards economy when building, by adding bulk and strength to lightly framed walls. The Masonic Hall kitchen employed a relatively slender frame with nogging, for example, beyond a masonry property wall incorporating the chimney.

Filling a light frame with low-quality brick or stone masonry was better than but akin to use of wattle and daub: forcing bent lath, often woven around sticks, between framing members of the wall. This also required

FIGURE 2.32. Service building (*at left*), Thomas Davidson House, 1 King Street.

FIGURE 2.33. 29 Cornwall Street, service building: wall frame and brick nogging, 2009.

some variety of exterior rendering to survive very long. Edward Long reported in 1774 that planters had generally built their houses in what they called "a make-shift" way, so that it was not unusual to see a plantation with expensively built masonry sugar works and "the owner residing in a miserable thatched hovel, hastely put together with wattles and plaster, damp, unwholesome, and infected with every species of vermin". Long suggested that Anglo-Jamaicans had much improved on the quality of their houses in the previous two decades, in both the countryside and towns.[35]

Less durable construction methods descended the social scale and by the later eighteenth century were increasingly associated with buildings for poorer Jamaicans, particularly African Jamaicans. Matthew Gregory Lewis wished to be progressive in treatment of his slaves in the last decade of slavery, and he wrote positively about their houses, "composed of wattles on the outside, with rafters of sweet-wood, and well plastered within and whitewashed; they consist of two chambers, one for cooking and the other for sleeping".[36] Phillip Gosse described the Westmoreland houses of recently emancipated slaves as "small huts, generally made of wattle, or hurdle-work, and thatched with the fronds of some of the Palms".[37] Their use continued through the nineteenth century. Turn-of-the-century photographs of rural Jamaica show numerous houses and other small buildings with round posts on 2-foot to 3-foot centres set into the ground and extending up to a plate and round end joists, or in some cases, up to gable rafters.[38] Jamaican historian B.W. Higman observes that plantation maps show small slave houses shaped like tents as well as those with walls and roofs, citing James Kelly's 1831 observation that groups of houses for enslaved workers resembled "so many villages of bee-hives thatched almost to the ground".[39] Spaces between framing members filled with what seem to be riven strips of wood sprung around slender round studs. Some such walls were daubed with clay, but many were left entirely exposed. Woven fibre mats appear to have been a less substantial alternative. The roofs were commonly covered with palm or straw thatch, overhanging the eaves and gables, the latter executed by extending the round plates. Others were shingled, so these represented available technologies rather than a predictable system. Most photographed wattle-and-frame houses appear to have contained one or two rooms, and some were larger than their well-finished small houses in town.

Detailed images of modest earthfast and thatched Jamaican buildings are rarer from about 1790 to 1830, but some exist, notably the sketches of an English artist named William Berryman (d. 1816), who lived on the south coast of the island from 1808 to 1815. His drawings show small houses and work shelters and their carefully observed enslaved residents. Berryman's buildings are thatch-covered over light frame walls, some earthfast and at least one set on a low stone foundation. The buildings range from small open-sided huts and shelters with poles lashed together, to fully enclosed houses with walls rendered outside, apparently with clay.[40] The smallest seem akin to the large number of residence huts regularly shown on Jamaican plantation plats and found archaeologically at Stewart's Castle and Seville, but his "View of Negro Village" labelled "Near Rodon Hall" shows larger houses that may have sheltered extended groups of workers under hipped and thatched roofs.

There was, then, a vast distance between the ephemeral dwellings of most rural slaves and the durable houses for skilled free blacks and poorer whites as well as the showy edifices planters like Tharp built for processing sugar, stabling their best horses, housing relatively high-status employees and – in cases like Good Hope and Orange Grove – treating large numbers of sick slaves.

It is difficult without archaeology to know if such impermanent buildings were a familiar sight in Jamaican port towns, although R. Cartwright and R.A. Leighton include two buildings with lofty thatched hipped roofs in the picturesque setting of their portrait of King Street Chapel in Falmouth, published in 1840.[41] Present in town or confined to the countryside, the ephemeral frame buildings provide a vivid contrast with surviving urban houses. Raising buildings with relatively unworked frames having little or no joinery, without masonry foundations or glazed windows could be done quickly with little investment in materials and skilled labour, by the residents or their owners. Even the smallest known Falmouth houses required both available funds and sufficient personal confidence to invest in fully worked material, most of it imported, and skilled tradespeople for construction. Concentrated in the port towns, there developed in and after the 1790s a sizeable middling population with sufficient funds and confidence in their future to build houses that offered a certain refinement in living. Architecturally, that refinement shared some character with elite townhouses of the same date. In the era when anti-slavery campaigns most assailed Jamaican elites and their system of labour, those planters and urban elites more lavishly cultivated the same building arts to create a lifestyle that was as comfortable as possible and self-assured in its variation from British standards of refinement. The freedom with which they styled their houses reflected their general approach to life in the tropics, while keeping a sharp eye on London.

By means of conclusion, it is useful to return to the illustration *Segar Smoking Society in Jamaica*. As a lampoon image, it works to communicate a certain message about the poor physical and moral comportment of Caribbean colonials and the jarring distinction between white privilege and black enslavement. But a careful examination of the surviving built environment expands dramatically on this limited representation of early nineteenth-century Caribbean culture. First, the architectural historical record of Falmouth suggests historians of Caribbean urban populations are right to highlight the broad racial, social and economic scale of indi-

FIGURE 2.34. Isaac Mendes Belisario, *Highgate, Jamaica*, c.1836–1842. Courtesy of the National Gallery of Jamaica.

working individuals, some white, yet most people of colour.

Second, this full range of scales from Elizabeth Somerville's two-room house to John Tharp's very large townhouse is remarkably undifferentiated except in scale. Given a comparable context like Charleston, South Carolina, the quality of workmanship, materials and architectural ornament in the largest house in Falmouth is just not that dramatically different from that in the smallest. This physical evidence suggests that given the large population of free mulattos, architecture drew stronger distinctions between free or enslaved status than it did between whites and people of colour. Even more striking, the surviving body of architecture points to a remarkable degree of openness and fluidity: plans where movement from room to room is largely uninhibited, at least when doors were unbolted. The casual physical comportment of white sitters represented by the British cartoonist in *Segar Smoking* seems to correlate to the largely unregulated openness of spaces. The architectural evidence supports the general historical assertion that the tight social controls expected in contemporary British society were not at play among Jamaican creoles.

Finally, this attention to the built environment suggests that it is a very useful body of evidence in the historical discussions about cultural processes of creolization. Kamau Brathwaite's seminal work *The Development of Creole Society in Jamaica, 1770–1820* offered a cultural model for creolization that ignited a flurry of investigations into the processes of formation and reformation of cultures in the Caribbean and beyond. Studies of foodways, religion, music and most especially linguistics have

viduals in British Caribbean towns and cities. Yes, there was a clear distinction at each end of the spectrum between enslaved Africans and elite whites, as suggested in the image. But the wide range of architectural scales surviving in Falmouth points to a large population of free people who fell in between these extremes. Small two-room houses were built by free women of colour like Elizabeth Somerville or Sarah McGhie. Those rooms could be elevated over a commercial ground floor for those who could afford to do so. And there was a range of other options all the way up to the substantial dock-front townhouse of John Tharp. The architectural record reinforces the historical evidence for a wide range of free profited richly from this model. But the evidence of historic architecture has played precious little role in this discussion.[42] This examination of the architecture of Falmouth provides some of the strongest non-linguistic evidence yet that affirms Brathwaite's understanding of creole culture as a historically affected socio-cultural continuum within which there are four interrelated and sometimes overlapping orientations, European, Euro-creole, Afro-creole and West Indian. In light of Trevor Burnard's strong argument that plantation Jamaica was clearly differentiated between whites and all others, the architectural evidence of Jamaican towns suggests far greater social complexity.[43] The social complexity of urban life played a critical role in the formation of a broadly shared creole culture.

Falmouth's architecture supports this argument in two ways. First, the fact of a clear family of plan types, and the use of discrete options among materials, building units, and ornamentation reinforce Brathwaite's notion of a "common colonial creole experience". Such a discrete – even shared – architectural vocabulary is not found, by contrast, in contemporary Charleston, South Carolina, or Bristol, England. Second, the scale of planning options within the range, from the two-room house to the large townhouse, validates the "infinite possibilities within these [racial] distinctions". For those of us who look carefully at surviving eighteenth- and early nineteenth-century buildings, Falmouth's jarring lack of sharp distinction among classes reinforces the claim that all these builders understood themselves in some way to participate first and foremost in something vaguely understood to be "creole" society. In this way the sharp racial distinction between the slave and the creolizers in *Segar Smoking* is a visual and political polemic that does not fully reflect the complexity of everyday life in Jamaica's towns. While the sitters might be creolizing, they are not an accurate reflection of creole society. Creolization in Jamaica, and elsewhere in the Caribbean, produced a huge range of artificial categories between African "black" and European "white" that belied racial binaries. Falmouth's historic architecture is astonishingly rich evidence of the complex social, economic and racial reality of life in "creole" Jamaica.

NOTES

1. Ralph Davis, *The Rise of the Atlantic Economies* (Ithaca: Cornell University Press, 1973), 251.
2. B.W. Higman, "Jamaican Port Towns in the Early Nineteenth Century", in *Atlantic Port Cities: Economy, Culture, and Society in the Atlantic World, 1650–1850*, ed. Franklin Knight and Peggy Liss (Knoxville: University of Tennessee Press, 1991), 120.
3. David Eltis et al., *The Transatlantic Slave Trade: A Database on CD-ROM* (Cambridge: Cambridge University Press, 1999).
4. Edward A. Chappell, "Housing a Nation: The Transformation of Living Standards in Early America", in *Of Consuming Interests: The Style of Life in the Eighteenth Century*, ed. Cary Carson, Ronald Hoffman, and Peter J. Albert (Charlottesville: University of Virginia Press, 1994); Edward A. Chappell, "The Bermuda House", *Post-Medieval Archaeology* 45, no. 1 (2011): 93–143.
5. For information on Adolphe Duperly, see Tim Barringer, Gillian Forrester and Barbaro Martinez-Ruiz, eds., *Art and Emancipation in Jamaica: Isaac Mendes Belisario and His Worlds* (New Haven: Yale University Press, 2007), 420. See also Allister Macmillan, *The West Indies Illustrated: Historical and Descriptive, Commercial and Industrial, Facts, Figures, and Resources* (London: W.H. and L. Collingridge, 1909).
6. We assume certain of the people and animals in Duperly's lithographs are the artist's additions because their movement would have constituted problems for daguerreotypes, and some of the figures are out of scale with their settings. The scenes nevertheless appear realistic.
7. Survey of University of Virginia and Falmouth Heritage Renewal carried out by students and staff, summer, 2009.
8. Virginian William Byrd II experienced this inequality. Byrd claimed a dominant political and social role in his colony but met with limited acceptance in England in spite of his erudition and English education. Kenneth A. Lockridge, *The Diary, and Life, of William Byrd II of Virginia* (Chapel Hill: University of North Carolina Press, 1987); Mark R. Wenger, ed., *The English Travels of Sir John Percival and William Byrd II* (Columbia: University of Missouri Press, 1989).
9. Also see "The Torrid Zone: Or, Blessings of Jamaica", in Barringer, Forrester and Martinez-Ruiz, *Art and Emancipation*, 335–37.
10. John McLeod, *Narrative of a voyage in his majesty's late ship Alceste, to the Yel-*

low Sea (1817): "Creolizing is an easy and elegant mode of lounging in a warm climate; so called, because much in fashion among the ladies of the West Indies; that is reclining back in one arm chair, with their feet upon another, and sometimes upon the table."

11. For example, "A West Indian Sportsman. Make haste with the Sangaree, Quashie, and tell Quaco to drive the birds up to me – I'm ready", by James Sayers, published by William Holland, London, 1807, in Douglas Hamilton and Robert J. Blyth, ed., *Representing Slavery: Art, Artefacts and Archives in the Collections of the National Maritime Museum* (Aldershot: Lund Humphries, 2007), 286–87.
12. Harewood's refined upper rooms include a 22-foot-long entrance hall and 39-foot-wide reception room.
13. James Robertson, *Gone Is the Ancient Glory: Spanish Town, Jamaica, 1534–2000* (Kingston: Ian Randle, 2005), 91.
14. Frank Moya Pons, *History of the Caribbean: Plantations, Trade, and War in the Atlantic World* (Princeton: Markus Weiner, 2007), 205, 317.
15. For published work on free blacks in Falmouth, see Ivor C. Connolley and James Parrent, "Land Deeds That Tell the Story of the Birth of Falmouth", *Jamaican Historical Society Bulletin* 11 (2005): 383–409.
16. Few houses built with a single room survive. One, a 14-foot 4-inch by 9-foot 6-inch building now behind the two-storey brick house at 16 Duke Street, was a two-bay house with off-centre front and rear doors.
17. Elizabeth Somerville bought this lot from Samuel Barrett Moulton Barrett in 1836 for £60, an amount that suggests the lot was then vacant. Samuel Barrett Moulton Barrett to Elizabeth Somerville. Deeds, Island Record Office, volume 806, folio 172.
18. The canonical work, of course, is John Michael Vlach, "The Shotgun House: An African American Legacy", *Pioneer America: Journal of Historic American Material Culture* 8 (January 1976): 47–70. For more recent work, see Jay Edwards, "Shotgun: The Most Contested House in America", *Buildings and Landscapes* 16 (Spring 2009): 62–96.
19. Daniel L. Ogilvie, "History of the Parish of Trelawny" (manuscript, 1954), ch. 11. Available at http://www.jamaicanfamilysearch.com/Samples/histre.htm.
20. Panes are 9 inches by 1 foot 2 inches at 9 King Street; 10 inches by 1 foot 3 inches at 32 Duke Street; 10 inches by 1 foot 1 inches in the jail. These are the full size of the panes, including puttied edges.
21. Phillip Barrington Ainslie, that is, "Philo scotus", published originally in 1802. Reprinted in Georgian Society of Jamaica, *Falmouth, 1791–1970* (Jamaica: Georgian Society of Jamaica, 1970), 28.
22. Edward Long, *The History of Jamaica* (1774, Danvers, MA: General Books, 2009), 16.
23. Georgian Society, *Falmouth, 1791–1970*, 28.
24. Five front windows with triple sash were provided with half-oval iron balconies with cast ornaments at the Barrett House. Duperly shows balconies on the opposite side of Market Street near Duke, and a neoclassical iron balcony from one of the Market Street residences was moved to the Pinto House on Trelawny Street around the 1970s. The upper floor of the Barrett House is now lost, but it was recorded in measured drawings and photographs in the 1970s, and some of the balconies survive.
25. Keith Whitehead to Chappell, 8 June 2012.
26. The stair at the Moulton Barrett House was moved to a front space accessible from a façade door in the late nineteenth century, and an exterior front stair was added to the Barrett House, an arrangement commonly seen in St John's, Antigua.
27. A second doorway, from the porch to the reception room, is an addition.
28. Long, *History of Jamaica*, 16. Both the Hibbert House and Seville are more complex in development than what Long describes as normal, including the fact that both began with T-shaped plans that added well-lighted space to the front of the entrance hall at Hibbert House and to the rear hall at Seville.
29. Tharp was born in Jamaica to an affluent family and well represents his generation of the plantocracy's desire to partake of English gentry culture. He was educated at Eton and Trinity College, Cambridge, and in 1792 he paid £40,000 for a Cambridgeshire estate, Chippenham, with a house said to contain thirty rooms. In 1796–97, he spent £3,000 to renovate his London house. Tharp and his younger second wife, Ann Gallimore, moved to Chippenham in 1795, intending to remain in Britain, but he returned permanently to Trelawny in 1802 after Ann engaged in an affair with Tharp's son-in-law, an Anglican minister. In short, Tharp must have built the two surviving Trelawny houses between about 1785 and 1795 or 1802–6. The family's social ambition is illustrated by his oldest son's marriage to Lady Susan Murray, daughter of the fourth Earl of Dunmore. At John Tharp's death, he owned several thousand acres in Trelawny and more than twenty-five hundred slaves. See Sarah M.S. Pearsall, " 'The Late Flagrant Instance of Depravity in My Family': The Story of an Anglo-Jamaican Cuckold", *William and Mary Quarterly*, 3rd ser., 60, no. 3 (July 2003): 549–82.

30. The front openings were changed to conventional two-sash windows, probably late in the nineteenth century. The original openings were discovered in 2011.
31. For more on the increasing importance of physical comfort in Anglo-American culture, see John Crowley, *The Invention of Comfort* (Baltimore: Johns Hopkins University Press, 2001).
32. James Hakewill reported that in 1820 one of the Rose Hall flankers housed "servants' apartments and offices" and the other, elegant apartments for a member of the owner's family. Hakewill, *A Picturesque Tour of Jamaica* (1825), quoted in B.W. Higman, *Jamaica Surveyed: Plantation Maps and Plans of the Eighteenth and Nineteenth Century* (Kingston: Institute of Jamaica, 1988), 234–35.
33. P.J. Laborie, *The Coffee Planter of Saint Domingo* (London: T. Cadwell and W. Davies, 1798), 95–96.
34. Long, *History of Jamaica*, 16.
35. Ibid., 16–17.
36. Matthew Gregory Lewis, *Journal of a West India Proprietor* (London: John Murray, 1834).
37. D.B. Stewart, ed., *Gosse's Jamaica 1844–45* (Kingston: Institute of Jamaica, 1982), 35.
38. See, for example, James Johnston, *Jamaica: The New Riviera: A Pictorial Description of the Island and Its Attractions* (London: Cassell and Company, 1903), 37, 73, 102–3.
39. Higman, *Jamaica Surveyed*, 245.
40. The graphite and watercolour sketches are now in the Library of Congress. Barringer, Forrester and Martinez-Ruiz, *Art and Emancipation*, 326–31.
41. From *Five Views of Baptist Chapels in Jamaica*, reproduced in Barringer, Forrester and Martinez-Ruiz, *Art and Emancipation*, 517.
42. Edward (Kamau) Brathwaite, *The Development of Creole Society in Jamaica, 1770–1820* (Oxford: Clarendon, 1971), 310.
43. Trevor Burnard, *Mastery, Tyranny and Desire: The Anglo-Jamaican World of Thomas Thistlewood and His Slaves, 1750–1786* (Kingston: University of the West Indies Press, 2004).

FIGURE T1.1. Map of Water Square and Market Street.

TOUR 1

Water Square and Market Street

EMILIE JOHNSON

Thomas Reid, a wealthy planter and merchant, first subdivided land that would become Falmouth in 1769. Reid Town, as this eastern gridded section was called, was an early site for wharves extending out into the harbour. In 1770, Edward Barrett followed Reid's example and subdivided his property at Palmetto Point into Barrett Town. The two plans did not align; the space between them became known as Water Square and has always been Falmouth's centre for gathering, marketing and socializing.

Water Square was already developed before the Falmouth Water Company purchased buildings and lots there in 1799, in preparation for the construction of the water system that brought potable water from the Martha Brae River into a massive circular stone reservoir at the centre of the square. Its proximity to the wharves made Water Square a logical place to build a stone retaining cell for disorderly sailors in 1803, which was dismantled in 1894 to make way for the Albert George Market. Water Square was also the site for public corporal punishment. The 1844 lithograph of Water Square shows Water Square as a vibrant public space, full of people. Built in 1894, the Albert George Market formalized a long tradition of weekly marketing among Jamaicans, a tradition continued today at the bend-down market.

Even in the twenty-first century, Water Square is a location for street parties and large-scale civic gatherings, although the recent transformation of the square threatens to resign the square over to commercial operations geared to cruise ship tourists rather than residents. Such a change threatens to end Water Square's history as the town's heart and soul. The bend-down market still happens weekly just outside downtown Falmouth and attracts vendors and purchasers from as far away as Kingston.

Market Street was the primary commercial artery of the Barrett Town development in Falmouth, stretching southwards from Barrett's Wharf. Market Street had the highest concentration of merchant storehouses in Falmouth, the distinctive two-storey building type that featured a masonry ground level for storing and selling commodities, and a framed upper level that housed the merchant family. The upper storey projected over the ground level, often supported by masonry or wooden piers, creating a sheltered walkway for browsing customers. The density of this building type on Market Street created a protected loggia that extended almost the entire length of the street. Scholars of consumerism have discussed how architectural changes that improve physical comfort indicate changing consumption habits and patterns. In the harsh sunlight, intense heat and torrential downpours, it is easy to understand how a covered passageway could revolutionize people's activities.

Falmouth Courthouse

(1815, 1926–29)

CALLIE WILLIAMS AND EMILIE JOHNSON

When the parish of Trelawny was subdivided from the parish of St James in 1770, the town of Martha Brae was chosen as the parish seat, and a courthouse was built there. In January 1794, however, residents of Falmouth began to agitate to have the courthouse moved from Martha Brae to Falmouth.[1] During the late eighteenth century, Falmouth eclipsed the upriver town of Martha Brae as the important port city serving the parish's vigorous sugar trade. With its deep-water harbour and extensive wharves, Falmouth became the seat of Trelawny and the courthouse was moved to the growing port town. Court activities were first held in a tavern located at the corner of Market and Duke Streets, but by 1815 construction began on this building overlooking Falmouth Harbour, on the former site of Fort Balcarres, which was moved to its current site (the Falmouth All-Age School) in 1802.[2] The courthouse does not face the houses, shops and markets of central Falmouth, but rather the sea to the northeast, emphasizing the importance of the harbour and making it a symbol of the town's civic pride, genteel taste and status to those arriving in the port. The courthouse is a striking example of Jamaican Georgian architecture, constructed in the Palladian style, with a central block and a ground-floor arcade fronted by a large central portico. Early records tell us that John Robey was paid £16 for his drawings of the courthouse.[3] At the centre of the portico's pediment is a round covered opening which once housed an eight-day clock, donated in 1844 by Samuel Magnus, a member of the justices and vestry.[4]

The courthouse served numerous functions for residents of nineteenth-century Falmouth. Not only were legal and legislative procedures carried out here, the large rooms on the upper floors also hosted social functions for the town's elite. One of these events, the Trelawny Bachelors' Ball, was held on 21 July 1826. The *Falmouth Gossip*, a local weekly newspaper, reported that the guests crowded the great room almost to capacity. A supper room provided refreshments to the party-goers, who spent the rest of the evening dancing quadrilles and country dances. The party lasted from about 8:30 p.m until 4:00 a.m.[5]

In 1926, a fire that began in a store nearby ravaged the courthouse and destroyed much of the original fabric. According to local histories, the Falmouth Courthouse was reconstructed quickly after the fire within the original masonry shell. An iron gate within the main arcade supports a decorative element bearing the date "1929". The courthouse reconstruction preserved the basic design and overall aesthetic of the original building, except for the window frames and the roof structure. The most significant change to the overall look and design of the Falmouth Courthouse was the reconstruction of the roof. The roof was reoriented at a ninety-degree angle, significantly changing the building's appearance.

FIGURE T1.2. Falmouth Courthouse elevation, drawn by Todd Mattocks, 2008.

Rather than seeing a large, unbroken mass above the cornice of the façade, three hipped gables of the roof structure are now visible. Metal frame windows also replaced the original wooden windows lost in the fire. In May 2007, Falmouth Heritage Renewal removed the metal frame windows and replaced them with wood-frame windows based on a 1798 mould pattern, with funds provided by the Tourism Enhancement Fund and the Tourism Product Development Company.

NOTES

1. Daniel L. Ogilvie, "History of the Parish of Trelawny" (manuscript, 1954), ch. 5. Available at http://www.jamaicanfamilysearch.com/Samples/histre.htm.
2. Ibid.
3. Ibid.
4. Ibid., ch. 3.
5. *Falmouth Gossip*, 26 July 1826, no. 23, National Library of Jamaica.

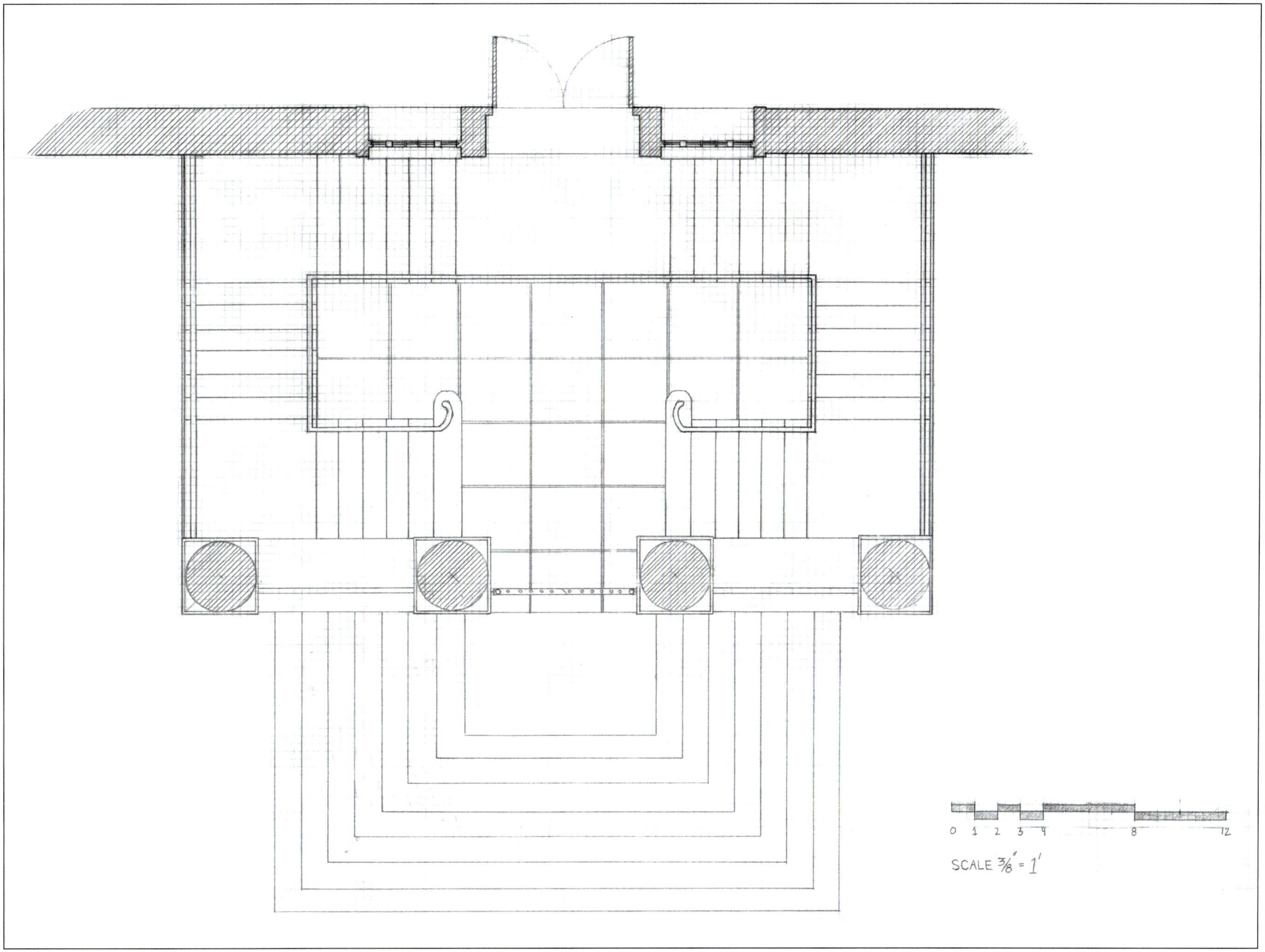

FIGURE T1.3. Falmouth Courthouse stairs plan, drawn by Todd Mattocks, 2008.

Barrett House

1 Market Street (*c.* 1799)

GREY GRAHAM AND EMILIE JOHNSON

At the corner of Lower Harbour and Market Streets, the Barrett House was one of the largest and finest houses in Falmouth. The building footprint was approximately 50 feet wide by 60 feet deep, more than twice the width of houses nearby. The keystone above the main entrance bears the date of 1799, a clue to the date of construction. The house has long been associated with Edward Barrett, who owned much of the land that became Falmouth and who laid out the lots in the grid that extends south and west from this house. Edward Barrett died in 1799, and he may have initiated the construction of this house, but records show that his primary residence was at Cinnamon Hill plantation in the parish of St James. If not built by Barrett, the house may have been built by his son-in-law Charles Moulton, who leased the wharf across the street from Barrett in 1786.[1] Charles Moulton was missing from Edward Barrett's will, which bequeathed his Falmouth lots and wharf to his grandson Samuel Barrett Moulton (Charles's son), under the condition that Samuel change his last name to Barrett. Samuel conceded; in later documents, his name appears as Samuel Barrett Moulton Barrett.[2] Regardless of its builder, the structure was closely associated with the important Barrett family and was one of the most spectacular examples of the distinctive Falmouth merchant-house type.

During the early nineteenth century, the two-storey merchant storehouse with covered, colonnaded porches developed as a popular building type in Falmouth. This type was deeply connected to changes in consumer culture in the Atlantic world in the late eighteenth and early nineteenth centuries. Architectural evidence suggests that the wood-framed upper level housed the merchant family and the masonry lower level was the location of commercial activities. Overhanging upper stories, which extended along building fronts, sheltered potential customers and collectively created a shaded sidewalk down the entire street. The living space on the second storey extended over the porch, supported by columns or piers. The porch was a transitional space, providing a sheltered walkway connecting neighbouring buildings and inviting passersby to linger in comfort around the doors and windows of the ground-floor shop.

The seven-bay lower level originally had three doors spaced between four windows, although later changes to the façade left the ruin with two doors and five windows. The six columns that supported the upper storey were turned from the whole trunks of a Caribbean hardwood tree, likely bullet wood, a dense indigenous material able to withstand rot. Inside,

---

This entry depends on an extensive on-site field report and analysis of surviving historic fabric written by Edward A. Chappell in the summer of 1997, 2003 and 2009.

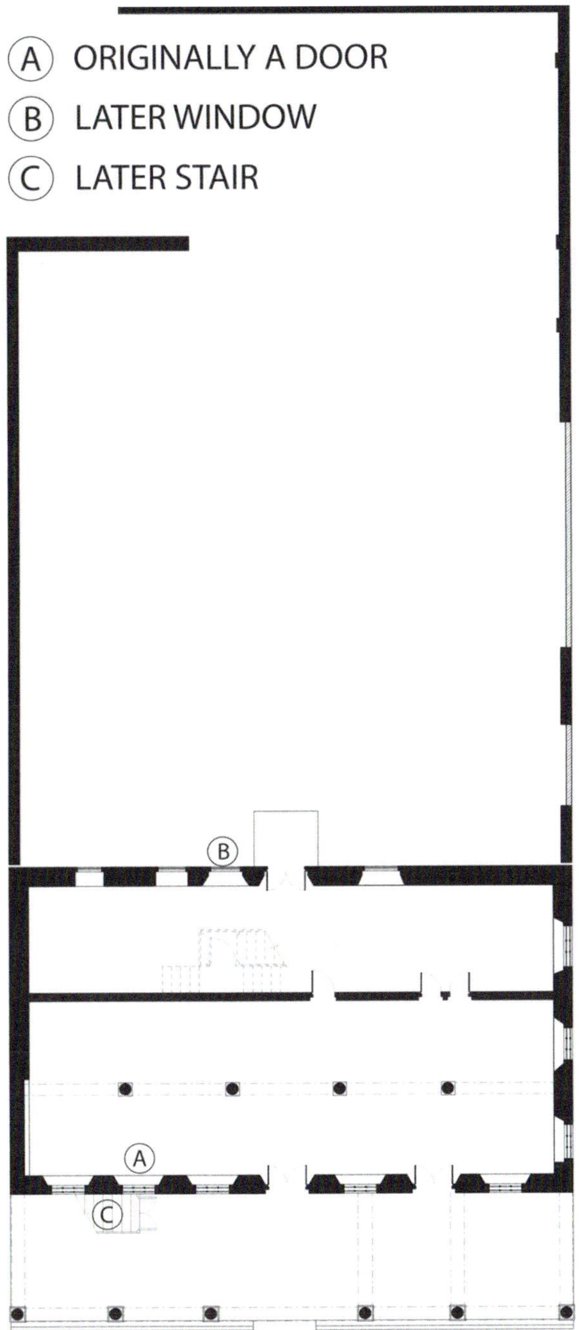

FIGURE T1.4. Plan of 1 Market Street (n.d.).

the ground floor was entirely open with only a longitudinal row of interior columns to support the structure above. This colonnade divided the room into zones for merchandise display and sales in the front, and storage in the rear. A small staircase at the southern end of the porch, probably added in the nineteenth century, may have led to a store office above. Double doors in the central bay welcomed the public and likely permitted the convenient delivery of goods. The walls of the first floor were limestone, with stones carefully laid in jack-arches over the street-side doors and windows. Practicality dictated the use of masonry on the ground level: the stone was flood-proof and windproof in a hurricane-prone area; it kept the goods inside cooler than a frame structure; masonry construction protected the valuable merchandise in the store from theft; and stone was rot-resistant, serving as an extended foundation.

The merchant and his family lived on the upper level, accessible from another interior stair in the rear of the ground floor that led directly into the primary circulation space above. Much of the interior architecture was lost during a storm in the 1990s and by exposure to the elements in the years that followed. Historic photographs show that five tall, triple-sashed windows with intricate iron balconies adorned the front façade. Evidence in the ruins suggests these windows lit the formal reception rooms at the eastern end of the house, allowing guests and passersby below to observe each other. The upper-storey woodwork was well crafted with apparent bead and bevel moulding on the exterior siding. Most of the original studs were pit-sawn, a common method of the era.

At various times since its construction, the Barrett House has been painted with pigments of ochre and limewash, or covered with stucco and scored to suggest ashlar masonry. Most of the surface treatments on the ruinous masonry walls have fallen away, allowing glimpses of the rough stone. This sturdy underpinning is why the house has survived so long in its abandoned state.

The Barrett House is no longer functional as a living space, but nonetheless holds the distinction of being the grandest of its kind on a street filled with similar structures. It is worthy of preservation as an example of a nineteenth-century Falmouth merchant-house.

NOTES

1. Edward Barrett to Charles Moulton, 1 January 1786. Deeds, Island Record Office, volume 348, folio 65.
2. Edward Barrett will, 12 March 1799. Wills, Island Record Office, volume 65, folio 169.

FIGURE T1.5. Barrett's Wharf from a plan of the town of Falmouth in the parish of Trelawny. Courtesy of the National Library of Jamaica.

FIGURE T1.6. 1 Market Street, 2010.

Moulton Barrett House

7 Market Street (*c.* 1795, 1825–1850, 1875–1900)

BRIAN L. COFRANCESCO

The stately building at the corner of Market and Trelawny Streets is known locally as the Moulton Barrett House. The plot on which the house stands was purchased from Edward Barrett in 1775 by Rebecca Lake, a free woman of colour, along with another lot on Market Street for £130.[1] Lake was a substantial landowner in Falmouth; in addition to the two lots from Edward Barrett, Lake also bought a lot from Thomas Reid in 1771 and owned at least one hundred acres of land in Trelawny.[2] Lake presumably sold the corner lot back to a member of the Barrett family. A cornerstone, at the northwest corner of the house, reads "MB 1795", which traditionally has been interpreted to mean "Moulton Barrett" and the year of construction, although interior finishes suggest the building dates to the second quarter of the nineteenth century.

An important example of the merchant storehouse typology in Falmouth is 7 Market Street, with commercial space on the first floor and a residence above (see figure 2.17). The original block of the house is three bays wide and three bays deep, with the ground-floor exterior walls now covered in twentieth-century stucco, disguising a lightly framed wall with masonry nogging. The upper storey of the house is of timber-frame construction with exterior horizontal clapboard siding clad in shingles. The grand, second-storey reception room, which occupies the full front of the building, projects over the ground floor, creating a sheltered porch and walkway below, supported by four original turned wood neoclassical columns. This second-storey façade has three six-over-six sash windows, the centre window flanked by two-over-two sidelights, and the spacing determined by the intercolumniation below. The lower façade also features three openings, though not all original nor so evenly spaced: to the far left is a six-over-six sash window like those above, at the centre is a wide double door into the original commercial space, and the door to the right is a later addition opening into the interior staircase.

The plan of the ground floor has changed substantially over time, and is currently subdivided for office space. Originally, a narrow central passage aligned with the rear door and divided the space into two halves, with the left half entirely open for commercial functions and storage. An original partition on the right side suggests a possible subdivision of spaces, and a neoclassical door in this wall once led to the original stairway in the rear right corner of the house.

At the front of the house is a late nineteenth-century stairway that replaced the original stair at the rear of the house, and provides access to the reception room on the second storey. The reception room is one of the best rooms in the house with sheathed walls, bases and surbases, and the possibility of once having a tray ceiling. The focal point of the room is an arched opening with scrolled keystones and panelled

---

This entry depends on an extensive on-site field report and analysis of surviving historic fabric written by Edward A. Chappell in the summer of 2004.

FIGURE T1.7. 7 Market Street, 2005.

FIGURE T1.8. 7 Market Street side elevation, drawn by Noel Makubwa, 2007.

columns, which frames an off-centre passage and a similar archway at the end of the hallway. The spatial layout of the second floor is much more intact, with two nearly square, communicating bedrooms to the left of the passage and a single formal room – the second best room in the house – likely used as the dining room, to the right. To the rear right of the second floor is a small space which would have housed the original stairway, and at the end of the longitudinal passage is a formal enclosed porch with a sheathed tray ceiling, sheathed walls, a base and a surbase, supported by turned columns below. To the rear left is a small room with exposed framing, which was likely used as a closet or pantry.

The enclosed porch at the end of the passage, known as a "cockpit", allowed the owner of the house to monitor movement through the house and activity in the rear yard. Yellow-brick, Flemish bond walls of a carriage house and a remodelled kitchen structure remain to suggest the organization of domestic support buildings located in the yard. This building suffered a major fire in the summer of 2014.

FIGURE T1.9. 7 Market Street rear elevation, drawn by Brian L. Cofrancesco, 2008.

NOTES

1. Edward Barrett to Rebecca Lake, 21 November 1775, Deeds, Island Record Office, volume 270, folio 120.
2. Thomas Reid to Rebecca Lake, 29 May 1771, Deeds, Island Record Office, volume 247, folio 162; Trelawny Estate Map T272, National Library of Jamaica.

Baptist Manse

9 Market Street (1798, 2004)

KRISTIN ROURKE AND BRIAN L. COFRANCESCO

Now known as the Baptist Manse, the building on the corner of Market and Trelawny Streets was built as a Masonic Temple in 1798. The Athol Union Masonic Lodge of the Scottish Constitution formed in that year and arranged for the construction of one of the first Masonic halls in Jamaica. Records from 8 October 1798 indicate that the lodge was meeting in the courthouse, then at the corner of Market and Duke Streets, while their building was under construction: "the Right Worshipful Master and Wardens and brethren of Lodge No. II . . . have the use of the Court House for their meetings on their agreeing to make good any injury that the building may sustain in consequence of their Lodge being held therein".[1]

The four corner stones of their own lodge building were laid in an elaborate ceremony with Scottish and English Masons present in great regalia. The corner stones were placed east to west, symbolizing the Masonic belief in the movement of wisdom from the East to the West. Details on the interior and exterior reflect the order's teachings and philosophies, although they are unrecognizable to the uninitiated. When completed, the Masons met on the second storey and used the first floor as a dining hall. In 1832, the Athol Union Lodge, deeply in debt, was forced to foreclose on the property and relocate to another building. The temple was auctioned to the local Baptist church to settle the lodge's debt.[2] It is likely that this house served as a manse for William Knibb, the great advocate for emancipation, while he was the pastor of Falmouth's Baptist church.

The building façade is symmetrical with rusticated quoins at the corners, grounded by a projecting water table. The windows are surrounded by projecting frames surmounted by keystones, an ashlar belt course separates the first and second stories, and an early classical cornice appears on the porch pediment. Two hipped roofs of differing sizes interrupt the building's classical symmetry; a large hip spans the two left bays, and a smaller hip covers the right bay. It is likely that the larger roof covered the main meeting space upstairs, while the smaller roof covered space with an unknown original use. Curious are the six-over-six windows surmounted by pointed arches on the second floor, an early Gothic element. Gothic windows might have been used to emphasize the mystical and exotic nature of the Masonic meetings held on the second floor. Gothic architecture was not common in the Caribbean at the end of the eighteenth century, and so the presence of these windows, along with the

---

This entry depends on an extensive on-site field report and analysis of surviving historic fabric written by Edward A. Chappell in the summer of 2002

FIGURE T1.10. 9 Market Street, 2002.

FIGURE T1.11. 9 Market Street, Baptist Manse, drawn by Kate Brady, 2009.

early use of cut stone, make the Baptist Manse an unusual building in Falmouth.

The interiors of the Baptist Manse have been altered significantly. The downstairs is now one open space with entrances in the centre of the front and back of the room; a partition wall may have divided the space following the spatial divisions suggested by the two hipped roofs. The original staircase is in the northwest corner of the building. There is evidence of framing members, flooring and wall plaster on the first floor, and the only original doors are the three-panel cedar doors on the front of the building.

Behind the manse is an ancillary building, which was likely a kitchen, workspace, or worker's quarters. The outbuilding features the same cut-stone as the main structure, but with a rougher treatment of the masonry, suggesting that it was built along with the temple and intended as a more utilitarian space. The building has had many alterations including an addition and removal of a chimney on the long south wall. This building, along with the main house, was stuccoed at some point.

Falmouth Heritage Renewal began rehabilitating the structure in October 2002 and, in 2004, leased the building from the William Knibb Trust; the downstairs is their restoration workshop, with lodging for visiting scholars upstairs.

NOTES

1. Daniel L. Ogilvie, "History of the Parish of Trelawny" (manuscript, 1954), ch. 9. Available at http://www.jamaicanfamilysearch.com/Samples/histre.htm.
2. Ibid., ch. 9.

Post Office

17 Market Street (*c.* 1832)

JUSTIN GREVING

Located in a prominent position on Market Street, the building that now serves as the Falmouth post office is one of the finest examples of a merchant storehouse in town. Thomas Robert Vermont, a senior resident magistrate of the parish, built the storehouse sometime after he purchased this lot in September 1832.[1] Vermont died in 1865 and left this Falmouth house to Mrs Mary Atkinson and her daughter Wilhemina [*sic*], who tended to the house when Vermont was away in England.[2] Two stories of brick with bold architectural detailing, this building differs from earlier masonry and frame merchant storehouses like the Moulton Barrett House down the street. The building is remarkable for its decorative details, such as the well-articulated classical door, the rough faceted masonry panels below smaller windows, and the quoins that emulate heavy stone blocks defining the building's corners.

The loggia contains two conventional windows flanking a flush-panel double door with an iron-barred transom. Of note are the diagonal iron bars used to close the window shutters (typical of the nineteenth century) and the means by which a wrought-iron staple and bracket could bar the door; both iron features indicate the necessity to secure the building from outside elements and protect the store's contents.

The double door opens to a wide sales/storage space extending the width of the building, and the ceiling framing in this room is substantial. Two doors punctuate the rear wall of the room: a central double door leads to a stairway located at the northwest corner of the building, while a smaller single door to the south (left) opens to a storage room, which may have originally functioned as a counting room. The central door has the same iron-barred transom as the front door, indicating a desire to protect the room from the rear quarters of the house as well as from the outside.

Upstairs, a large room extends over the loggia, lit by three windows on the Market Street façade, one of which is a large three-part window, a signal of the best, most formal living space in a Falmouth residence of this period (see figure 2.15 for the second-floor plan of 17 Market Street). The existing tray ceiling may not be original, even though a small hatch reveals that roof rafters and shingle lath remain unfinished, indicating this room likely had a finished ceiling. A single passage leads to this main room from the northwest stairway with chambers on either side.

The building contains a nearly complete set of iron rim locks with oval brass plates cast with "V & R BLAKEMORE, BIRMINGHAM", likely dating to the 1840s.

This entry depends on an extensive on-site field report and analysis of surviving historic fabric written by Edward A. Chappell in the summer of 2002.

FIGURE T1.12. 17 Market Street, 2009.

INLAND
OVERSEAS

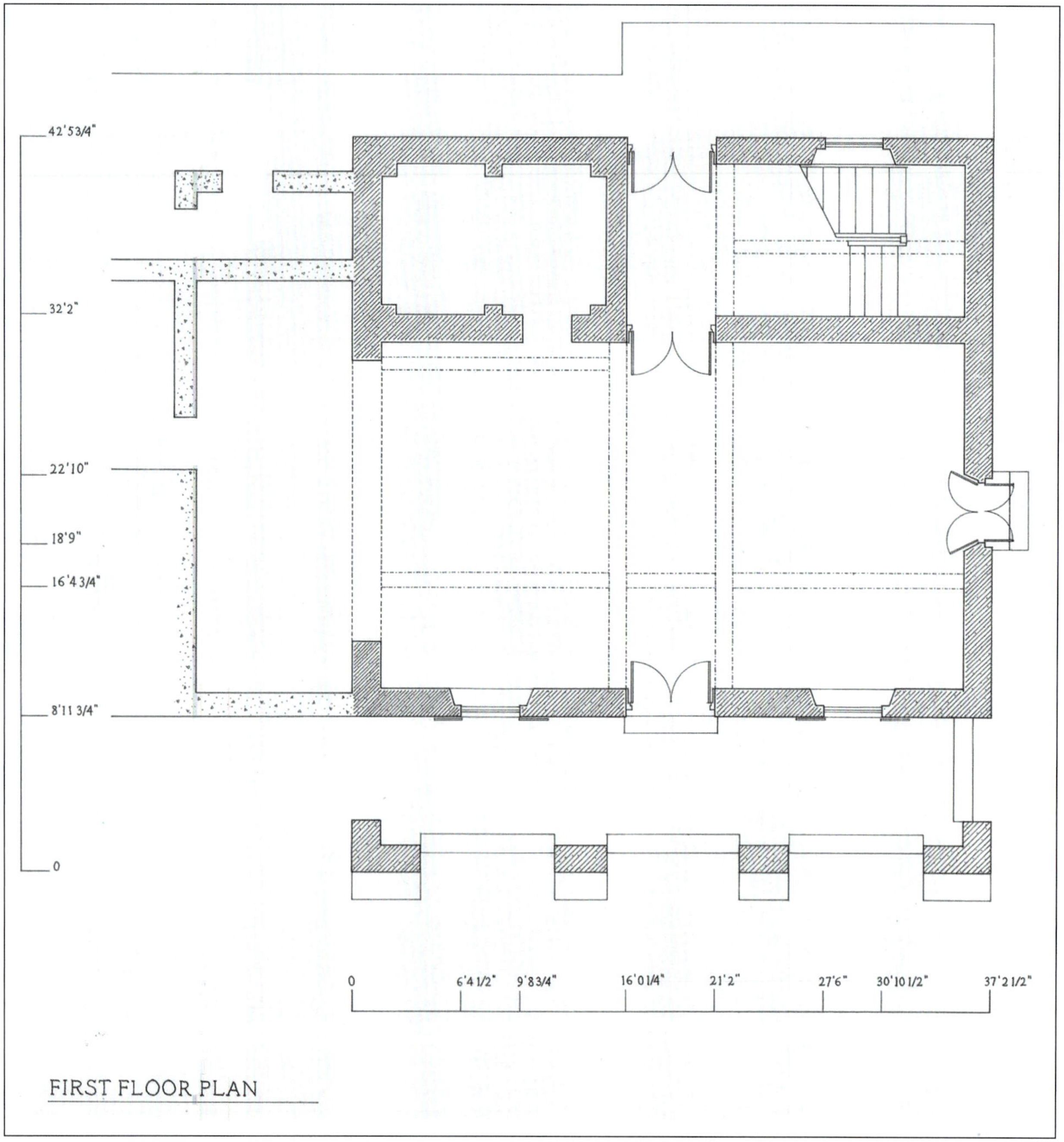

FIGURE T1.13. 17 Market Street, first-floor plan, drawn by Kevin Riddle and Elizabeth Milnarik, 2004.

In 2003, Falmouth Heritage Renewal removed exterior latex paint and Portland cement and replaced the mortar in the masonry walls with a historically accurate lime-based substance. The exterior was then painted a yellow-ochre lime wash. Window sashes and frames badly damaged by termites were either salvaged or replaced with materials to match the original mouldings.

A Trelawny company, King Pepper Products, Limited, uses the Falmouth post office on the label of their Eaton's line of sauces, chutneys and jams, which are sold throughout Jamaica. Clearly, the image of a two-storey merchant's storehouse from mid-nineteenth-century Falmouth possesses an associational marketing purpose for the manufacturers of this modern day product.

NOTES

1. Estate Map T98, Special Collections, National Library of Jamaica.
2. Thomas Robert Vermont Will, 14 January 1865, Island Record Office, volume 130, folio 28.

18 Market Street

(*c.*1775–1811)

LOUIS P. NELSON AND EMILIE JOHNSON

Eighteen Market Street is a building unlike any other in town. Its one-storey mass is constructed of tightly laid ashlar stone masonry. Still largely in its original condition, the building was built as two large, communicating lateral chambers set front to back. These chambers are lit through large splayed windows on the front and rear elevations. The tall exterior walls become parapets at their upper edge that mask the double masonry vaults that soar over each of the two chambers. The building also has a full cellar, a relatively unusual feature in Falmouth, clearly intended for storage.

The building's original function is not entirely clear, although its substantial masonry construction and stone vaulting offer some clues. The quality of its stone masonry certainly suggests a late eighteenth- or early nineteenth-century construction date. Edward and Judith Barrett first sold a 60-foot-square lot bounding on Cornwall Street, Market Street and on other Barrett property in 1775, to Edward Davis of Trelawny. Davis paid £35 Jamaican currency for it.[1] The size of the lot is odd; almost all Falmouth lots measure 120 feet by 60 feet. Between 1775 and 1811, the lot passed back to the Barrett family; in 1811, Samuel Barrett Moulton Barrett sold it to Adam Steele, a significant investor in the Falmouth Water Company, for £250 Jamaican currency, suggesting the lot had a building on it.[2] In 1822, Steele sold this property to John Kelly, a merchant, for the very large sum of £700 Jamaican.[3] This sale almost certainly includes the masonry building. Curiously, in 1828, Adam Steele and Catherine Harris Steele, the widow of John Steele, a carpenter, who was likely Adam Steele's brother, sold the portion of lot 66 facing Market Street to John Kelly for an unknown sum.[4] Even though the exact subdivision of the lot is unclear, the sums paid at purchase in the first decades of the nineteenth century indicate that a large, solid, expensive masonry building was in situ before 1811.

It certainly predates 1844, when it appears in the Duperly lithograph of Water Square. In that view, this building's north elevation faces Water Square unobstructed by other buildings, sheltered by a shingled gable roof and a small bell cupola at the front end of the roof. In this way, the building is unlike its neighbours; its substantial, vaulted, stone fabric closely aligns this building with the military installations of Fort Balcarres, rather than the domestic and commercial architecture seen elsewhere on Market Street, the prime commercial thoroughfare of Falmouth. And, in fact, one historian has ventured to suggest that this building might be part of the military installation of Fort Balcarres when the first still occupied the centre of town, the site of the current courthouse, before its removal in the first years of the nineteenth century. In his history of Fort Balcarres, Christoph Wilhelm suggests that this build-

FIGURE T1.14. 18 Market Street, 2009.

ing might have been the barracks for the fort, which his research indicates was close to but not within the eighteenth-century fortification.[5] While not definitive, the building's material qualities do offer the real possibility that this building was associated with the earlier, in-town iteration of the fort.

NOTES

1. Edward and Judith Barrett to Edward Davis, 22 April 1775, Deeds, Island Record Office, volume 277, folio 68.
2. Samuel Barrett Moulton Barrett to Adam Steele, 30 September 1811, Deeds, Island Record Office, volume 607, folio 208.
3. Adam Steele to John Kelly, 14 November 1822, MSS 966, National Library of Jamaica Special Collections.
4. Adam Steele and Catherine Harris Steele to John Kelly, September 1828, MSS 967, National Library of Jamaica Special Collections.
5. Christoph K. Wilhelm, "Fort Balcarres and the Town of Falmouth, Jamaica: An Analysis of the Fortification and the Relationship to the Town through Time" (undergraduate thesis, University of Virginia, 2010), 28–29.

FIGURE T1.15. 18 Market Street, drawn by Burgess Rice, 2010.

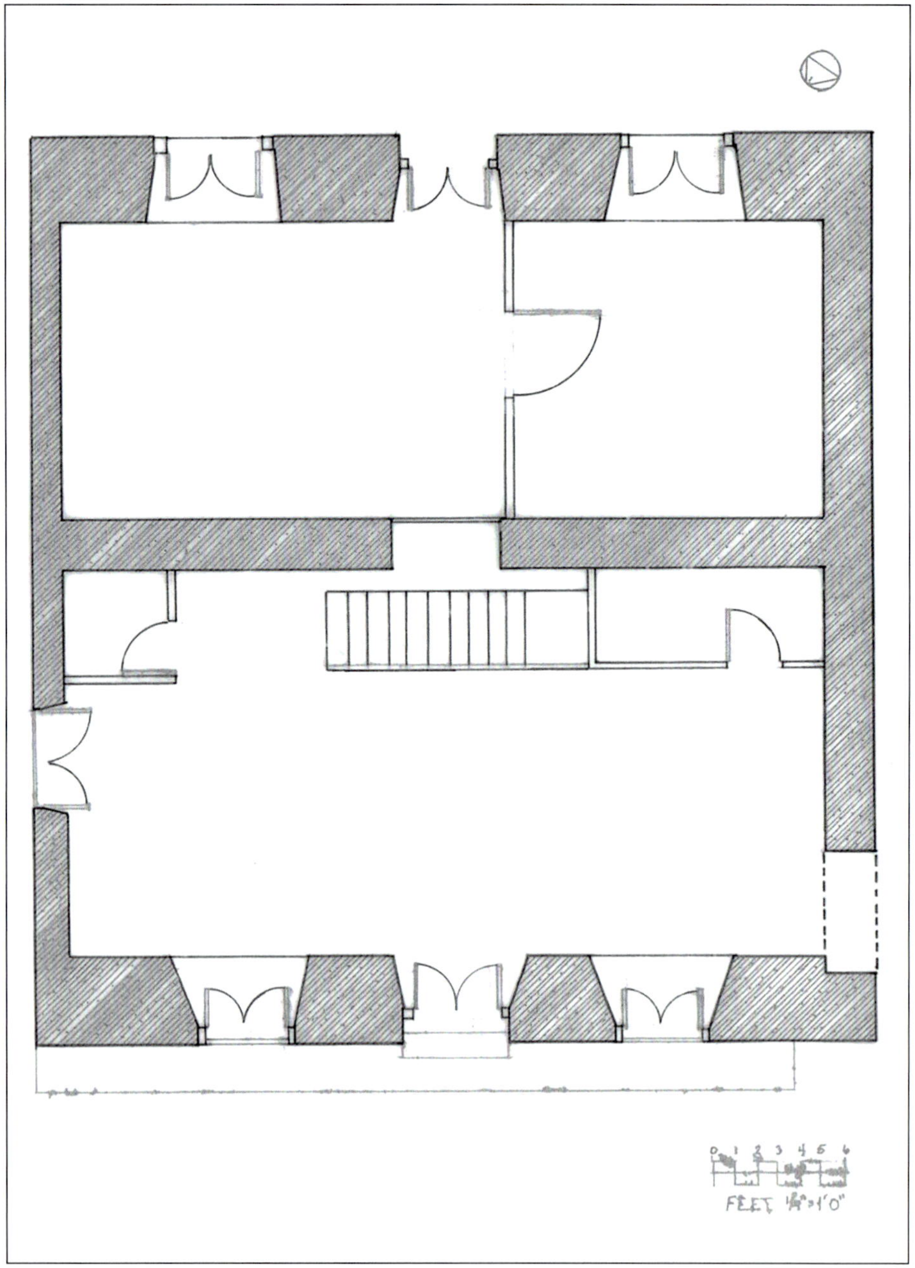

FIGURE T1.16. 18 Market Street, ground-level plan, drawn by Laurin Goad, 2010.

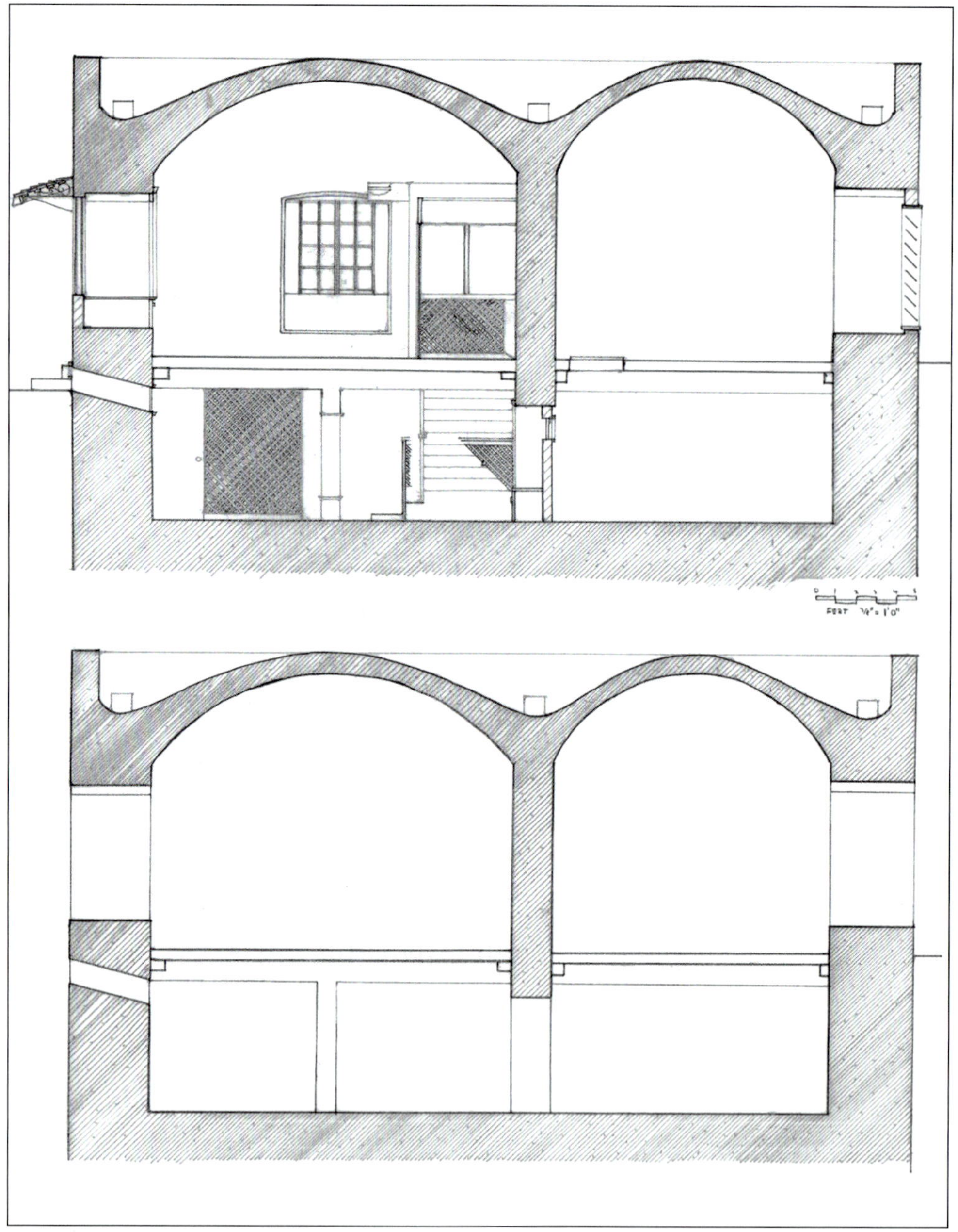

FIGURE T1.17. 18 Market Street, sections, drawn by Eduardo Diaz-Etchevehere, 2010.

21 Market Street

(1810–1830, 1900–1910, 1980)

KATHERINE H. SPICER

One of the most intact merchant storehouses in Falmouth, 21 Market Street is two stories tall with a full cellar under the building. The ground-floor walls are primarily stone; a wood-frame structure at the back has been renovated with Portland cement. The second floor is wood frame, covered by a single hipped roof, likely a replacement for three hipped roofs, corresponding with the front-to-back spatial division of the plan.

The typical merchant storehouse loggia is articulated by six columns. The symmetrical, five-bay-wide façade of well-executed masonry includes two doors flanked by windows at the building corners and in the centre.

The right entry door leads to two rooms, one behind the other, in the right two bays of the house, with access to a cellar bulkhead in the wood-frame portion at the back of the building. The rest of the ground level is one large room, occupying the three leftmost bays of the house and extending the full depth. A floor hatch with an early keyhole opens into the cellar. There is no direct access to the upper level from this room; a door on the left side leads into an alley, from which one can enter the rear wood-frame portion of the building, which contains the stair to the second floor.

The plan of the upper level has seen many changes over time. Doors were replaced and rooms have been subdivided even before the stair was moved to its present location. As the uses of the building have changed throughout the nineteenth and twentieth centuries, the plan has altered to meet new needs.

The reworked stairs lead to a small reception area that opens into a central passage dividing the plan in half. Three well-lit and well-ventilated chambers flank either side of this central passage. While the upstairs was likely open to the roof originally, matchboard ceilings from circa 1900–1910 are visible in the passage and lobby. The other spaces have plywood ceilings from around 1980, which is also when jalousie windows replaced all the windows on the right (north) façade upstairs, as well as most of the rear (west) façade.

Both ends of the passage have arched openings with double architraves, over piers with recessed panels. Moulding details on these archways, along with chair-rail mouldings, heavy classical bases and double architraves on some windows on this floor, suggest a construction date of 1810–1830.

The reception area at the top of the stairs, the passage itself and the front room feature smooth, planed and beaded sheathing. Planed and beaded studs, braces, and door and window frames visible on the insides of the chambers. The chambers, however, feature large, three-part windows, usually found in the most formal interior spaces.

FIGURE T1.18. 21 Market Street side elevation, drawn by Maggie Hansen, 2007.

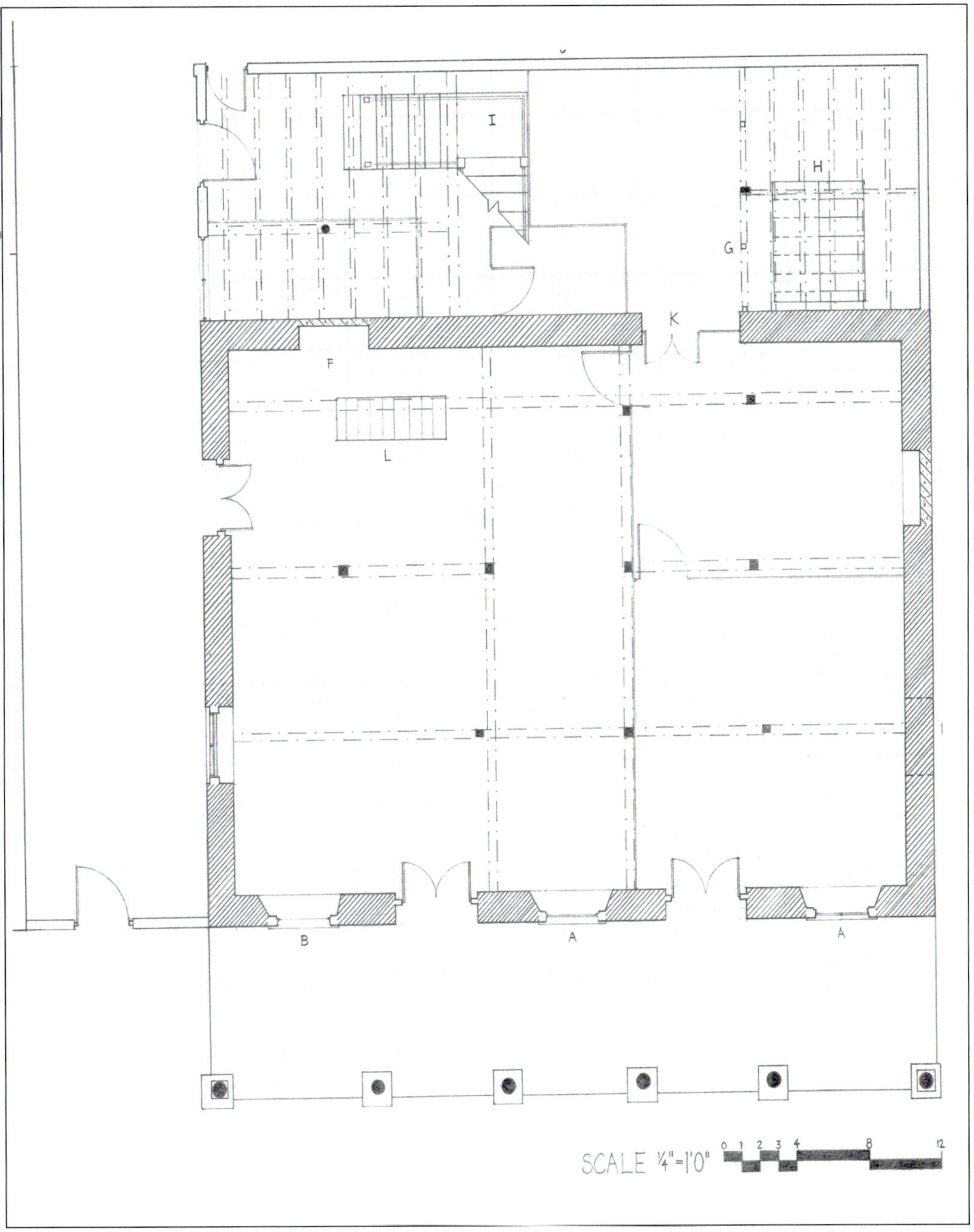

FIGURE T1.19. 21 Market Street, first-floor plan, drawn by Thomas Schaperkotter, 2007.

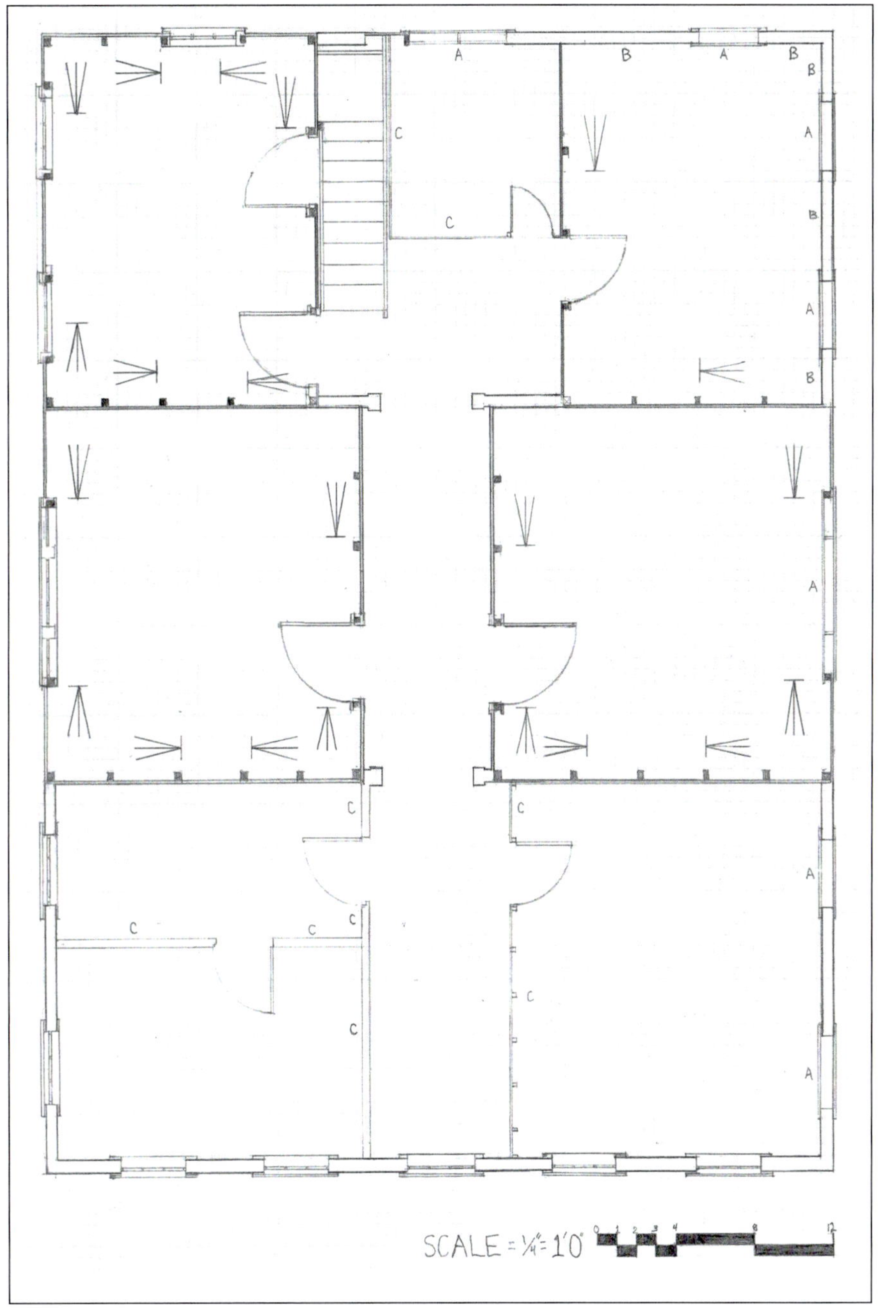

FIGURE T1.20. 21 Market Street, second-floor plan, drawn by Sarah Eissler, 2007.

23 Market Street

(*c.* 1825)

D.P. SEFTON AND BRIAN L. COFRANCESCO

The two-storey masonry building at 23 Market Street is among Falmouth's more imposing and intriguing structures. The lot on which this building stands was bought by Archibald Galbraith, a carpenter, and James Somervail, a butcher, from Edward Barrett in 1776, early in Falmouth's development.[1] Evidence suggests this building was built around 1825, probably by a subsequent owner, and appears in the far right foreground of Adolphe Duperly's 1844 coloured lithograph of Market Street (see figure 1.4). Clad in whitish-grey stucco, it appears taller and more massive than its frame neighbours, but bears no signs or other visual suggestions of its use.

The building appears today much as it did in Duperly's image. Its exterior walls are stucco-covered brick; a modern photograph showed exposed brickwork where the cornice separated from the front façade. On the upper storey, the walls are approximately 1 foot 3 inches thick, too thick to be a nogged frame. Duperly's image shows a portion of the building's colonnade of six substantial masonry Tuscan columns beneath a protruding upper storey. The bulk and diameter of these columns contrast markedly with the spindly turned wood columns that support the upper stories of the building's frame neighbours. They are spaced symmetrically in groups of three at either end of the first floor, with a wider space separating the innermost columns. Duperly's image depicts this central gap, which suggests a central entrance to this commercial building.

The lower-storey façade is roughly symmetrical. Framed by the middle and innermost column of each set of three columns is a pair of matching doors each with twelve lights and a rectangular panel below. Today, the central space framed by the innermost columns is filled by three asymmetrically placed sash windows, which reflect changes of an unknown date.

The building's protruding upper-storey façade is more rigidly symmetrical. It consists of six bays in a fenestration pattern of A-AA-A A-AA-A, with doubled six-over-six sash windows flanked by single, conventional six-over-six windows. According to the Duperly view, the doubled windows were originally triple sash, running floor to ceiling with six lights per sash.

In 2007 the interior of this building was substantially renovated without documentation; the original layout must be inferred through clues from the exterior. One theory is that the strong axiality of the façade suggested an arrangement of two three-room apartments separated by a central partition. Another theory is that the upstairs was intended as

---

This entry depends on an extensive on-site field report and analysis of surviving historic fabric written by Edward A. Chappell in the summer of 2009.

FIGURE T1.21. 23 Market Street elevation, drawn by Katherine Cullinan, 2010.

a single residence, with four side rooms, the two at the rear slightly larger than those at the front, with a large central room more than 18 feet wide by 39 feet deep. The former is what the fenestration suggests, while the latter seems more logical, although this plan differs significantly from others observed in Falmouth.

The second storey is covered by two hipped roofs running parallel to the front façade. An external staircase on the right side of the building now provides access to the upper storey; there is no indication of the original method of access. Structurally, the building receives support from piers about 1 foot thick at its corners, as well as at the corners of the second-storey rooms. Tray ceilings span the upper rooms; although no original fabric survives, their placement on the support piers suggests they are original.

NOTE

1. Edward Barrett to Archibald Galbraith and James Somervail, 7 February 1776, Deeds, Island Record Office, volume 276, folio 215.

37 Market Street

(*c.* 1842)

JUSTIN GREVING

Thirty-seven Market Street is one of four similar east-facing merchant storehouse-style residences on the west side of Falmouth's primary commercial street. Located on Barrett lot 125, Thomas Walker, identified in the deed as a schoolmaster, purchased the property from Edward Barrett for £70 Jamaican currency on 20 February 1775.[1] When the block was surveyed in August 1842, the lot was labelled as the property of William Green, although the date of the property transfer has not been securely identified.[2]

This two-storey building is three bays wide with nogging or Spanish-wall framing on the first floor topped by timber framing on the second. In the style of similar merchant storehouse buildings along Market Street and elsewhere in the Caribbean, the second floor is cantilevered to create a covered sidewalk. The 7-foot-deep overhang is supported on the exterior by four evenly spaced twentieth-century masonry piers which replaced the original columns. On the ground floor, exterior walls have a smooth stucco finish, with two shuttered windows flanking a 6-foot 6-inch-wide door. The door leaves suggest an early construction date and swing on strap hinges in a tenoned and pegged frame. Ground-floor windows retain pairs of early double-sheathed shutters with exterior diagonal sheathing, which extend outwards and can be secured with diagonal wrought-iron bars. The interior of the ground floor was likely a large open space with one or two posts supporting a summer beam, an ideal layout for a large warehouse space in this storehouse.

The upper storey is sheathed in wood clapboard siding; its façade features a large central window flanked by two smaller ones. The central window contains three nine-light sashes with nearly square panes and adjoining vertical sidelights. In lieu of a balcony, the two upper sashes drop directly to the floor. The two flanking windows, although not identical, are approximately the same shape and size, with nearly square panes and side louvres. The right sash appears to be the older of the two windows.

The three-part hipped roof indicates three divisions of space: the street-fronting hip spans a full-width reception room, while two back hips cover an axial passage with two chambers to the left, each lit by three-part windows, and two corresponding spaces on the right. The plan of the upper storey is very similar to that found in the house at 7 Market Street, which also has a front reception room that occupies the full width of the building, with an axial hallway and four chambers

---

This site report was completed using a variety of source material, including photographs, field drawings and an on-site building description by Edward Chappell, dated 9 June 2009.

FIGURE T1.22. 37 Market Street, 2009.

behind. Like the house at 7 Market Street, the central window on the second floor is on axis with an arched passage doorway (another arched doorway is located deeper within the building, although its exact location is unclear).

NOTES

1. Edward Barrett to Thomas Walker, 20 February 1775, Deeds, Island Record Office, volume 306, folio 147.
2. T 463, National Library of Jamaica, Estate Maps, Trelawny.

FIGURE T1.23. 39, 37, 35 Market Street, 2006.

FIGURE T1.24. 37 Market Street elevation, drawn by Sarah Thomas, 2009.

Water Square

(*c.* 1800)

EMILIE JOHNSON

As early as 1800, Water Square was the central commercial district in Falmouth (see figure 1.3). Located close to the wharves and warehouses that housed merchandise and supplies from England, the square was surrounded by shops and businesses. As early as 1800, the town constructed a frame market building primarily for use by slaves and free blacks and dedicated first to the sale of fish, then both fish and beef. An extremely public place, Water Square was the site for brutal punishments and humiliations; the newspaper reported that a slave would be whipped in Water Square before and after serving three months in the workhouse.[1] Water Square also featured a substantial stone building called the cage built in 1803 to detain "all sailors found in Grog shops or loitering about the streets of Falmouth" after their 6:00 p.m. curfew. Both the "Negro" market and the cage were demolished in 1894 to make way for the Albert George Arcade. The food markets abutted the square on its southeastern edge, close to the present-day Albert George Market.[2]

The parish seat of Trelawny moved from Martha Brae, its original location, to Falmouth in about 1795, in large part due to Falmouth's position as a port town and centre of commerce. At this time, every resident who could afford one had a well on their private property. Given the proximity of the sea, these wells were very shallow and provided less than pristine water. The water requirements of the town greatly surpassed the amount that could be drawn from private wells. Growing rapidly, Falmouth was a location for ships to resupply food and water stores, and the constant threat of fire made the complete reliance on private water sources untenable.[3]

The Falmouth Water Company, an organization composed of wealthy Falmouth residents and Trelawny plantation owners, formed in 1799 to address water issues for the bustling town. Under its charter, the Falmouth Water Company could raise capital, purchase land, and build aqueducts to bring potable water from the Martha Brae River into the heart of Falmouth. The sale of shares in the company and the water usage duty levied against every ship that entered Falmouth Harbour financed the programme. The company bought land at Martha Brae, about a mile from Falmouth, and built a diversion canal, rubble dam, water wheel and sluice gate, which fed water from the river into Falmouth through a series of aqueducts and mains. In Falmouth, water was stored at a masonry tank in the middle of Water Square. The company purchased land in the square over the span of the water system's development between 1799 and 1805, built the reservoir, then sold the extra land back to the parish vestry for commercial development.[4]

Water Square received its name by being the terminus of the famed Falmouth water system; the tank filled with available water for the

FIGURE T1.25. A view of Water Square with large circular stone reservoir (Courtesy of the National Library of Jamaica).

citizens of Falmouth and visiting ships was located in the square. Even though Falmouth had a municipal water source earlier than New York City did, the system was not without problems. Only a few residences were allowed to have a "service pipe" to connect to the main supply, and the water levels and quality were directly affected by the condition of the Martha Brae River; during a dry season, the river did not have enough volume to force water through the system to Falmouth. Later in the nineteenth century, a steam engine and pump were installed to provide a reliable flow of water to town. In the 1950s, the old reservoir was demolished and replaced with the garden and fountain that now sits in the middle of Water Square.[5]

NOTES

1. Cornwall Correspondent, *Gossip*, no. 30, 13 September 1826, National Library of Jamaica.
2. Daniel L. Ogilvie, "History of the Parish of Trelawny" (manuscript, 1954), ch. 5. Available at http://www.jamaicanfamilysearch.com/Samples/histre.htm.
3. Ibid.
4. Ibid., ch. 9.
5. Ibid.

Albert George Market

(1894)

EDWARD BARNES

Built in 1894, the Albert George Market is the most prominent landmark of Falmouth's Water Square. It was erected to provide permanent shelter to an activity that has presumably taken place on this site since the town's founding or soon thereafter. Located on the southeast edge of the square, the structure has two distinct portions. The first of these is a single-storey masonry gatehouse structure with a three-storey masonry and wood-frame tower rising from the centre. Designed as the building's main façade, the gatehouse faces Upper Harbour Street – the main commercial artery heading out of town to the east – rather than the square itself. In keeping with the town's Georgian character, familiar architectural forms of Caribbean neoclassicism are present in the gatehouse façade. The building's corners and window surrounds are enlivened with quoins, while the gateway arch is crowned with a pediment at its centre. Clock faces alternate with arched windows in the octagonal tower. The one-storey wings on either side of the gateway arch each contain a single room accessed by doors in the rear wall.

Three panels positioned at the sides of the gate record the building's construction. The upper panel to the east of the gate is engraved with the name of the building and its date of erection flanked by two Stars of David. Below is a panel listing the name of the Kingston-based construction firm that undertook the project, Purdon and Cox. To the west of the gate, a panel records the names of two local men, the Honourable L.C. Shirley, chairman of the Trelawny Parish Council, and A.M. Solomon, Esq., chairman of the Market Commission. Judging by the number of Solomons buried in the Jewish cemetery, A.M. Solomon was probably a member of Falmouth's sizeable Jewish community.

The second portion of the building is a large open-air market arcade. Twenty-six columns support a two-part hipped roof that shelters what was once a large and empty market floor, intended to be occupied by vendors. The columns, and the roof-framing system they support, are constructed of cast iron, a technologically advanced material in the late nineteenth century. During the second half of the twentieth century, changing shopping habits resulted in four-frame, free-standing shop buildings, built in the open areas of the market floor. A number of businesses now occupy these buildings, in what was intended to be a shared commercial space. The Albert George Market is a polished example of an architectural type for commercial spaces located at the centre of a town in the late nineteenth century. Brown's Town, located inland on the border of Trelawny and St Ann parishes, has a similar market structure that appears to date from the same period.

As a result, the architecture of the building is remarkably complex. The cast-iron sheds to the rear emulate those behind contemporary

FIGURE T1.25. Albert George Market, 2009.

FIGURE T1.26. Albert George Arcade elevation, Drawn by Lawrence Lazarides, May 2009.

English train stations, technologically modern and sublime. Conversely, the clock tower enlists architectural details from the prevailing Georgian tradition – the quoins at the corners of the masonry front and around the windows, and the arched entryway with the pediment above – well over a half-century after that style had fallen out of favour. In this way the building connected with both the future – modernism and technology – and the past, the period of Falmouth's economic zenith.

FIGURE T1.27. Albert George Arcade detail, drawn by Stephanie Burcham and Jennifer Pack, May 2009.

FIGURE T2.1. Map of the Wharf District.

TOUR 2

Wharf District

EMILIE JOHNSON

The wharves into Falmouth Harbour were the features that most closely linked Falmouth's economy to that of the greater Atlantic world. Through the wharves, Jamaican planters exported sugar, molasses, coffee and rum, destined for Europe or the United States. From the wharves came goods from England, the necessary accessories for fashionable life in a colonial outpost. For example, a 1794 inventory of goods arriving in Falmouth on the Martha Brae lists, among many other goods, violet hair powder, refined white sugar, sherry, soap, tobacco, lamp oil, culinary spices, superfine bombazine (black, blue and yellow Durants for men's clothes) and split peas. These goods, in turn, were sold by local merchants in the shops of the merchant storehouses found on Market Street.

From the town's founding, private individuals developed their own wharves. Plantation owner John Tharp had a wharf which extended into the harbour in front of his town house, now entirely land-locked by the cruise ship wharf. Tharp's Wharf managed the exports and imports of sugar and sugar-related commodities, generated by his almost twenty-five hundred slaves from his multiple properties. Tharp probably shipped goods and received imports for other Trelawny planters. John Stogdon, a wealthy merchant in Falmouth in the late eighteenth century, also had his own wharf next to Tharp's. The Martha Brae inventory mentioned above is a record of one of Stogdon's shipments. An 1844 map of Falmouth identifies Jarrett's and Lyons's wharves next to Tharp's, and Barrett's Wharf around the bend of the harbour, closer to Fort Balcarres.

RADA Building

9 Seaboard Street (*c.*1775–1815, 1900–1925)

BRIAN L. COFRANCESCO AND EMILIE JOHNSON

Nine Seaboard Street, formerly the office of the Rural Agricultural Development Authority and known to locals as the RADA building, was one of the oldest extant structures in the wharf district. Presumably dating to the late eighteenth or early nineteenth century, it reputedly was the residence and office of Dr S.T. Vine, whom local lore proclaims as Jamaica's first surgeon and a college friend of Sir Arthur Conan Doyle, of Sherlock Holmes fame.

Although it saw significant alterations and modifications, the RADA building appeared to share the merchant storehouse form seen throughout Falmouth. The masonry first floor maintained the traditional Falmouth floor plan, with a large public room occupying nearly half of the first floor, and a rear hallway – marked by a substantial mahogany archway – providing access to smaller chambers on either side. The rear chambers had exposed framing members, in contrast to the panelled walls of the public room, suggesting that they were private rooms. The first floor also featured unique mahogany cabinets built into the wall, which seemed to be early twentieth-century additions and may have been used by Dr Vine to store medical supplies for his office.

Three staircases provided access to the second floor, however the stair to the east of the main public space (inside the easternmost addition) was the most elaborate, made of mahogany and featuring turned balusters, decorative newel posts and panelled walls. Based on the presence of nails in the joinery, the stair may have been from the early twentieth century, possibly part of a larger Georgian-revival renovation that also included the mahogany cabinets in the large downstairs room. As seen in prominent homes all over Falmouth, the upper storey featured a full-width reception room overlooking Seaboard Street. The most refined space in the house, this room had plastered and sheathed walls, decorative wainscot, a tray ceiling and an abbreviated entablature with a dentil cornice. Two wide mahogany doors opened into the two back chambers, which also featured tray ceilings. Tripartite windows, each with two six-light sashes flanked by horizontal louvres, lit the rear chambers. To the far west of the house was a two-storey, shed-roof addition with an entrance space and a stair to the second floor; this may have been a double-height verandah, and was probably the primary access to the upstairs living quarters.

In October 2010, 9 Seaboard Street was subjected to severe vandalism in which the roof and walls were destroyed. Original fabric and fenestration, tray ceilings, and first-floor medicinal cabinets were removed or defaced by unknown looters. The building remained unstable and was later demolished.

This entry depends on an extensive on-site field report and analysis of surviving historic fabric written by Edward A. Chappell in the summer of 2010.

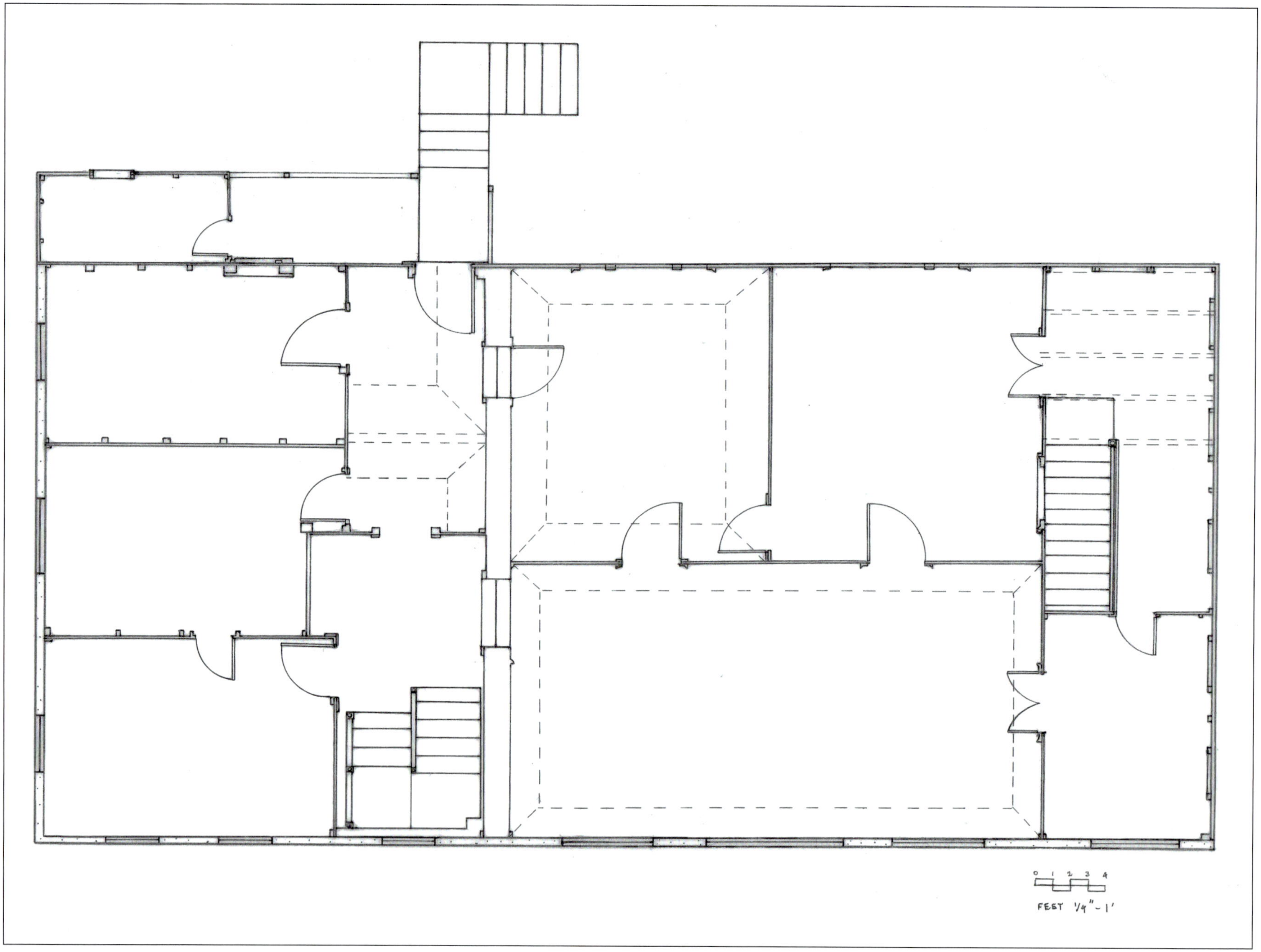

FIGURE T2.2. 9 Seaboard Street second-floor plan, drawn by Meagan McFadden, 2010.

FIGURE T2.3. 9 Seaboard Street staircase elevation, drawn by Marilyn Moedinger, 2010.

Tharp House

(*c.*1790–1795, 1988)

BRIAN L. COFRANCESCO WITH EDWARD A. CHAPPELL AND EMILIE JOHNSON

In April 1778, John Tharp (d. 1804) purchased a plot of land along the harbour in Falmouth from Edward Barrett.[1] Tharp was a merchant and planter who specialized in sugar production, and he developed the shore-side parcel into a wharf – Tharp's Wharf – to serve as the shipping arm of his plantation at Good Hope (approximately eight miles inland along the Martha Brae River). With thousands of acres of land, he oversaw one of the largest sugar operations in northern Jamaica and owned approximately twenty-five hundred slaves, making him the largest individual slave owner in Jamaica in the early nineteenth century.[2] In the early 1790s, Tharp began constructing a house on his wharf property to serve as both a residence and office for his sugar industry; the house was likely built at the same time as the great house at Good Hope. The Tharp House was the urban face of John Tharp and his business.

The Tharp House is a single-storey, five-bay house with a masonry foundation and brick-nogged and rendered first-floor walls. Bearing a close resemblance to eighteenth-century plantation houses in Jamaica, it has one principal floor with rooms dispersed beneath a series of hipped roofs. It follows the principles of Georgian architecture with a symmetrical façade of evenly dispersed fenestration, a system of organizing bays, a central door, a classical cornice along the roofline and a symmetrical interior plan. The house is distinguished from contemporary plantation houses, however, in that it does not utilize the traditional Jamaican and Caribbean louvred windows but common sash windows. The house includes a cellar, however it is built at-grade rather than below ground. Tharp's town house ignored the form of the typical merchant storehouse type in Falmouth of a masonry ground level and a wood-frame upper storey overhanging a covered walkway. Tharp also avoided building a high-style urban townhouse. It appears that he intended his town residence to bear resemblance to his buildings at Good Hope, a case of architectural branding for the Tharp name.

The stairs on the front façade form an "L" and are original to the house. The steps have torus-edged platforms and unmoulded steps constructed of high-quality limestone; iron cramps are not used. The concrete balustrades date to 1988 and replaced an early wrought-iron railing. The protruding aedicule porch is an addition, but boasts a classical cornice and solid turned wooden columns 11 inches in diameter. The central door provides access into a main entrance hall, and the short windows on either side of the door provide light in the room. The hall once led to a short front-to-rear passage, giving access to two rooms on the

This entry depends on an extensive on-site field report and analysis of surviving historic fabric written by Edward A. Chappell in the summer of 2006 and 2009.

FIGURE T2.4. Tharp House, north façade.

back end of the house. Two of the four hipped roofs covered these spaces – those with their broad sides facing the harbour – one covering the entrance hall, and the other covering the two rooms in the back.

The two outer bays on the front façade feature slightly taller windows that light narrow but deep side reception rooms. Each of these rooms has a single window on the front wall and two windows on the side wall. Evidence shows the scar of a doorway originally on the exterior wall of the front right reception room, which would have opened to an exterior staircase down to the water. An early doorway exists in the corresponding position in the front left room, which perhaps gave access to a work yard

FIGURE T2.5. Tharp House existing north elevation, drawn by Queenie Lin, 2006.

or lane beside the house and was the route for food to enter the dining room from the service wing at the rear. The two reception rooms open up to respective rear chambers on each side; each pair of front and rear rooms is covered by a longitudinal hipped roof running perpendicular to the roofs covering the central bays of the house (they run front to back with gables facing the harbour).

The cellar below the principal storey is an open space and runs beneath the entire house. The walls on the left, facing the side lane, are of smooth ashlar and include full-size windows with proper keystones, lintels and stone sills. Two doors into the cellar flanked the L-shaped stairway and another door was centred on the left end wall. On the front right, however, the stones are roughly squared – perhaps due to the construction of a warehouse in front – and the cellar wall on the right, which abutted the shoreline, is of stone rubble. A carefully carved stone cavetto moulding runs along the exterior and corresponds with the top of the cellar ceiling; it is the only carved classical masonry at the house.

Until a fire in 2005, a wing extended from the right rear of the house. Sitting 5 feet atop a mixed material foundation of masonry to the left and

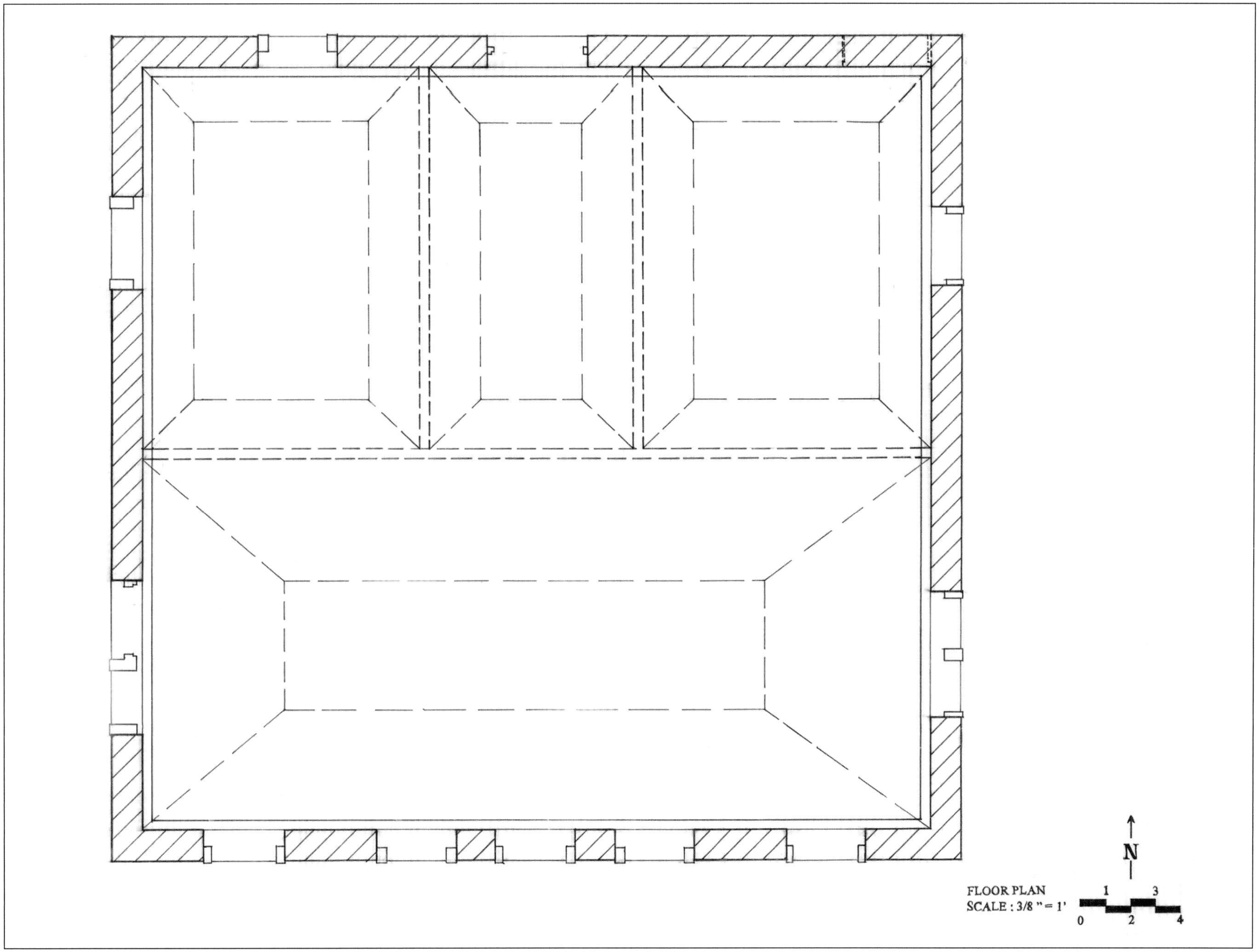

FIGURE T2.6. Tharp House warehouse plan, drawn by Sara Anderson, 2004.

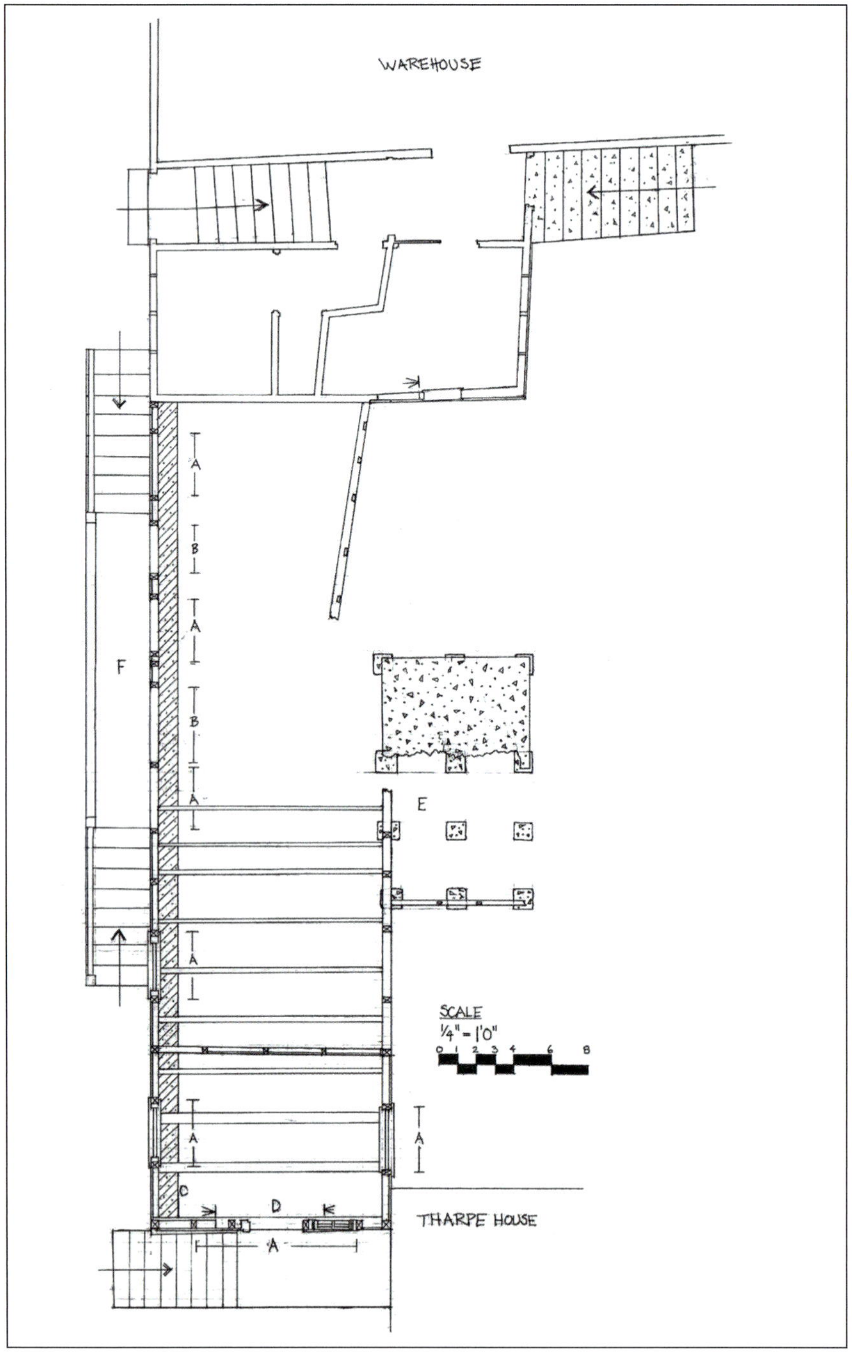

FIGURE T2.7. Tharp House service buildings and slave quarters, drawn by Thomas Schaperkotter, 2006.

earthfast wood posts to the right, the building was a framed structure of mortise-and-tenon pegged studs with six-over-six double-sash windows for lighting. There is no evidence of doorways on the lane/work yard-facing wall; a door must have opened onto the yard at the rear of the house, suggesting – along with the absence of chimneys – that this was a servants' hall or slave quarter. The wing was divided into two rooms, the first 23 feet by 12 feet 5 inches and the second 23 feet 8 inches by 12 feet 5 inches.

Southwest of the wing in the corner of the lot is a 34-foot by 33-foot masonry shell that may have been an auxiliary house and a warehouse. The ground-floor walls are masonry, accessed through a round-vaulted entry, while the upper-storey walls are brick, laid in Flemish bond. Research into the building fabric in 2004 indicated that the upper storey was altered significantly during the twentieth century, but that the original layout had a room running the length of the southern front with five windows and a fancy tray ceiling. Two smaller chambers, bisected by a short hallway opening into all three rooms, occupied the northern half, facing the Tharp House.

After the death of John Tharp, the Tharp House stayed in the family as they continued to occupy Good Hope until it was converted into wharf offices in the 1860s. It has since served as a tax collector's office, and will be restored with the new wharf development project. The Tharp House is an example of Caribbean Georgian architecture and an important monument to the sugar industry along the northern coast of Jamaica. In particular, it represents the wealth of eighteenth- and nineteenth-century Falmouth and the Tharp family, and the slave labour that brought the family – and industry – such success.

NOTES

1. Edward Barrett to John Tharp, 7 April 1778, Deeds, Island Record Office volume 291, folio 102.
2. John Tharp Inventory, 23 December 1824, Inventories, Jamaica Archives volume 148, folio 151–69. For more information, see entry on Good Hope plantation.

The Dome

(*c.*1810)

IVOR C. CONNOLLEY

The Dome and foundry yard was the location of a nineteenth-century multifunctional industrial site in Falmouth, Jamaica. Traditionally, the property referred to as "The Dome" had been known as a foundry constructed in 1810 by Mr Field. Tradition held that the building slate-roofed was used for the repairs of machinery from nearby sugar estates and associated with shipping interests.[1] Initially constructed as a bottle kiln to manufacture ceramics and possibly glass products, the Dome only operated as such for a limited period. Archaeology and architectural study of the structure reveals the various uses experienced by the building.

The unusual structure of the Dome indicates that the original plan was to use the building as a glass or ceramic kiln, supporting a vibrant market for these products that acted as an incentive for their manufacture. Furthermore, the presence of a furnace in one of the archways suggests that the building was used as a kiln. Furnaces along the perimeter provided heat for annealing glass products.

Evidence of ceramic manufacture is not as strong, although an unusual imprinted sherd has been found on the site showing the top section of a coconut palm.[2] If this piece is unique to Jamaica, it may be evidence of a new type of ceramic design which could have been manufactured at this facility as it represented palms endemic to the islands of the Caribbean. Further research ought to be undertaken to determine if such pieces were manufactured in England or in other colonies.

Given the acknowledged wealth of Jamaica in the eighteenth and nineteenth centuries it would not be surprising to find that ceramics and glass were being produced on the island.[3] It would have to be shown, however, that clay of the type which produced such pottery was either available in Jamaica or was imported from England. Given that stones and bricks often came to Jamaica as ballast in ships plying the route from England to the Caribbean, it is likely that clay necessary for the manufacture of ceramics also could be imported. Additionally, coal – a material unavailable in Jamaica – was found in the ground beneath the Dome. This find demonstrated that this material and possibly others needed for kiln operations were sourced from England for use in this facility.

FIGURE T2.9. British ceramics.

FIGURE T2.8. Dome site, Falmouth, Jamaica (n.d.).

Proof of the Dome's use as a glass kiln from artefacts and structural remains is rather weak. Remnants of unblown glass were not found on the site to support an interpretation as a glass kiln. A quantity of glass sherds of various colours and types were collected from the site, which may indicate a limited level of glass production.

It was soon adapted to function as a foundry. In August 1837, a report mentions Jonathan Smithers kept a coke foundry in Upper Harbour Street, likely this building.[4] In this phase, the structure added bellows to the outside of the structure with air ducts leading to the central furnace and permanently blocking a number of the archways. Smelting of iron and manufacture of iron products for shipping interests and sugar factories would have been their primary business activities. They also manufactured copper products such as nails and other household and factory prerequisites.

As business deteriorated from the demise of numerous sugar estates, and with fewer ships in the harbour after emancipation, the foundry eventually ceased operations.

Fill and a new floor may have been laid down after the roof collapsed and the building deteriorated. Possibly some of the equipment was salvaged. Subsequently, the site became a visitors' centre for a limited period and eventually even this activity was abandoned. By the twentieth century, the building was in ruins, becoming a curiosity piece for passing tourists. The Dome site is currently the only such structure known in Jamaica. Additional study of this structure and the associated yard is critical to understanding of the level of industrial advances and development in Jamaica during the early nineteenth century.

NOTES

1. Both authors Daniel Ogilvie and Ray Fremmer agree on the date and the name of the founder. Daniel L. Ogilvie, "History of the Parish of Trelawny" (manuscript, 1954), ch. 6, available at http://www.jamaicanfamilysearch.com/Samples/histre.htm; Ray Fremmer, "History of Trelawny" (manuscript, n.d.).
2. The fronds also resemble those of a banana plant.
3. E.H. Carter, G.W. Digby and R.N. Murray, *History of the West Indian People: Eighteenth Century to Modern Times* (London: Thomas Nelson and Sons, 1967), 8, 27.
4. Ogilvie, "History", ch. 11.

7 Upper Harbour Street

(*c.* 1815–1835, 1835–1860, 1970)

KRISTIN ROURKE

Even though 7 Upper Harbour Street is located in Reid Town, the section of Falmouth laid out by Thomas Reid in 1769, its construction date between 1815 and 1835 renders it one of the earliest surviving buildings in this part of town. The two-storey structure originally had residential space on the upper floor with a commercial store space on the ground floor; an exterior stair in the northwest side yard led to the second-floor apartment, insulating the residence from the more public lower level. Unlike the merchant storehouse on Market Street, there is no columned overhang across the front entrance to shelter shoppers. There are, however, two formal street-front façades, one facing Upper Harbour Street and one facing Jarrett Street, both with symmetrically fenestrated façades. The structure was originally stuccoed, unifying the appearance of framed and nogged west and south walls and brick north and east walls. There is only one hipped roof, compared with the tradition of multiple roofs as seen on other early Falmouth buildings such as the Baptist Manse.

The interior plan remains relatively intact. The commercial space would have been completely open with the exception of one small room in the rear, which would have functioned as an office or counting room. Three posts carry a longitudinal summer beam, only one of which might be original, although it is partially imbedded in a later partition wall. Most of the fenestration was rebuilt in the twentieth century with the exception of the front doorway and rear southeast window. The front room is partitioned off now as feed store and a space where men gather to play dominos.

The upper storey is also largely intact with nineteenth-century fabric. The framing of the upper storey is pit-sawn while the woodwork is sash-sawn. Some of the partition walls are frame with nogging while others are brick, and the floor is mahogany secured with cut nails. A lobby or circulation space opens into a larger public reception room covered by an elaborate tray ceiling and neoclassical cornice, while the other rooms are exposed to the rafters of the hipped roof. The lobby also opens into two chambers, which were not originally communicating spaces, but later, around 1835–60, were connected by a door. Additionally, there is a service or storage room in the northwest back corner, which may have been where children or servants slept.

In the mid-twentieth century, a kitchen space was added to the back of the rear chamber, and a bathroom was added into the service room. Around 1970, the circulation space was partitioned to add another space which is now used as a bedroom. An outbuilding, which functioned as a kitchen (although this may not have been its original purpose), is set behind the main structure, although only a few courses of the original brick remain, and the rest was rebuilt around 1950–60.

This entry depends on an extensive on-site field report and analysis of surviving historic fabric written by Edward A. Chappell in the summer of 2009.

FIGURE T2.10. 7 Upper Harbour Street, 2009.

FIGURE T2.11. 7 Upper Harbour Street first-floor plan, drawn by Erin McGinley, 2009.

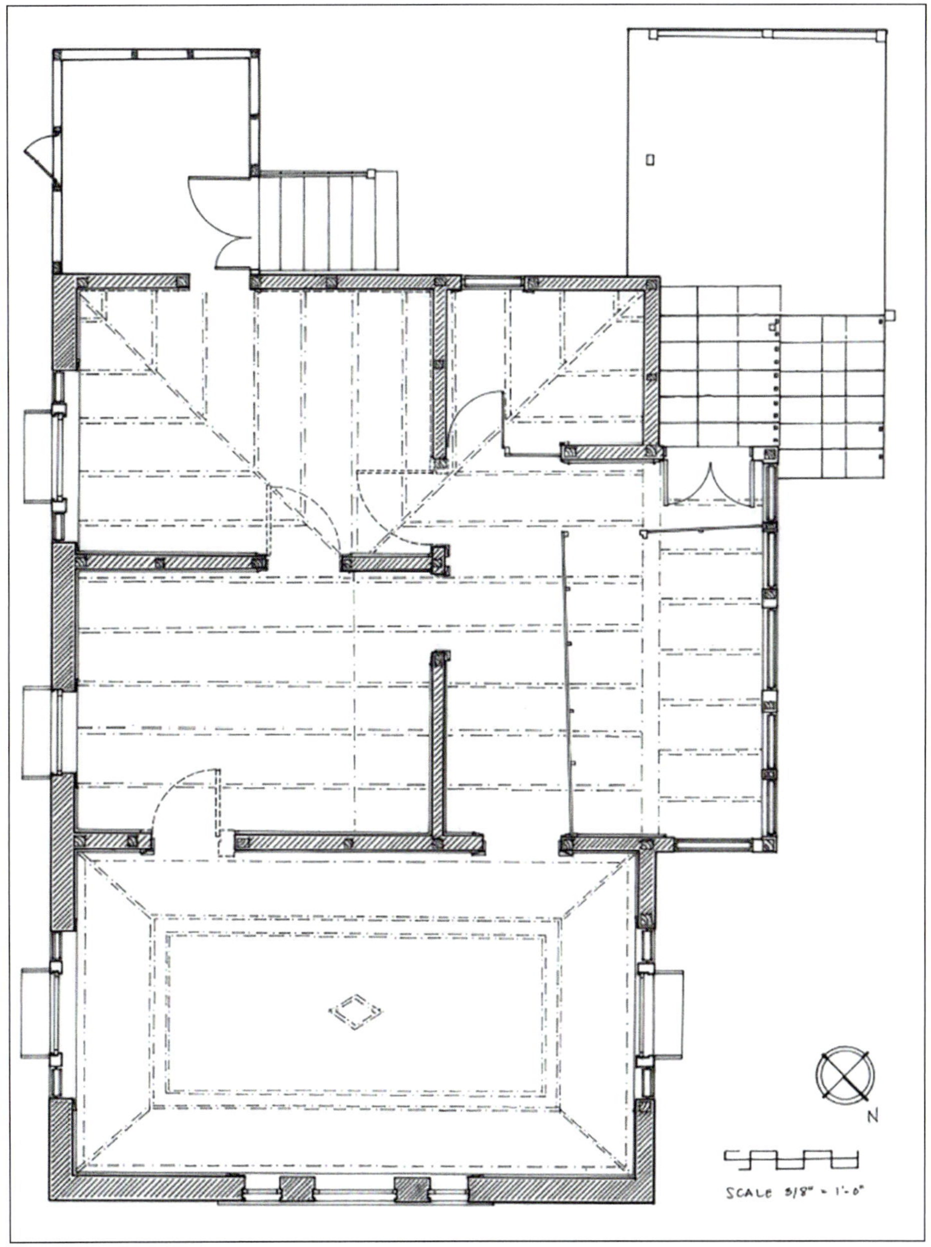

FIGURE T2.12. 7 Upper Harbour Street second-floor plan, drawn by Alison Ross, 2009.

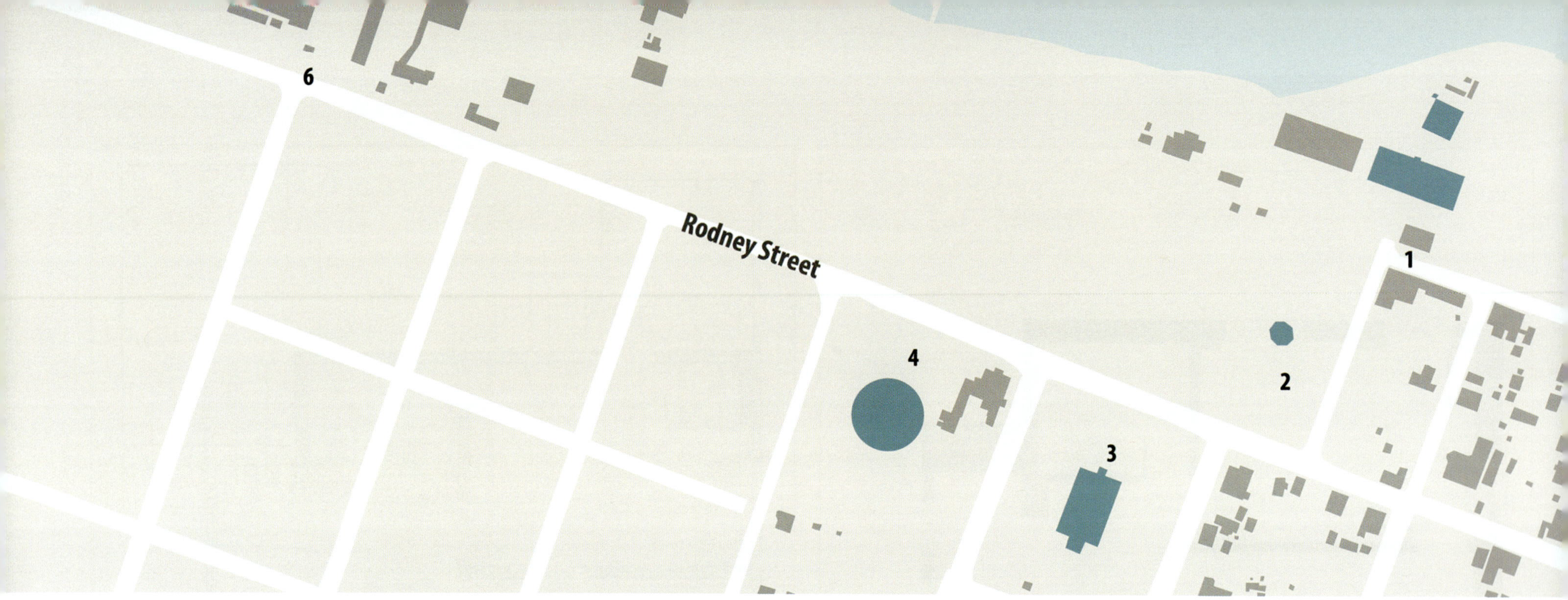

FIGURE T3.1. Map of Rodney Street.

TOUR 3

Rodney Street

EMILIE JOHNSON

Rodney Street is, with Duke Street, the primary east–west artery into and out of Falmouth. Stretching along the northern boundary of the town and paralleling the sea, Rodney Street is the location of the town's civic institutions, some churches and a few residences. The blocks of Rodney Street closest to Falmouth's harbour developed first, primarily as residential buildings. Historically, as one moved west, churches, the jail or gaol, mariners' hospital and poor house occupied the street; today, many civic institutions remain on Rodney Street.

Edward Barrett, the patriarch of the Barrett family, who developed the western half of Falmouth in the 1770s, specifically held a parcel of land out of subdivision into lots. He gave this land, described as "from the high water mark 100 feet inland, from Tharp's Wharf as far as Half Moon Bay", to his grandson, Samuel Barrett Moulton Barrett, when the grandson reached his majority at twenty-one years of age. Edward Barrett's will delineated the land on the north side of Rodney Street; the south side was divided into lots, very few of which sold. At some point between 1810, when Samuel Barrett Moulton Barrett claimed his inheritance, and 1820, the parish vestry purchased the land.

Two of Falmouth's prominent churches stand on the south side of Rodney Street. What is now the United Church was built in 1834 for Scotch Presbyterians. Farther to the west stands Falmouth's Catholic church, the town's most important twentieth-century building. Built in 1966 under the beneficence of Father Joseph R.N. Maxwell, a former president of Boston College, the concrete church is an extraordinary experiment in tropical modernism.

At the eastern end of Rodney Street and one block north was the site of Fort Balcarres, the British military post built to protect the valuable shipping interests of Falmouth's harbour around 1802. In 1902, the former military barracks became the all-age school, and it remains the town's elementary school today. Proceeding farther west, one comes to the police barracks, the jail and the site of the poor house on the north side of Rodney. The police barracks shares a wall with the jail, suggesting a later construction date for the barracks, probably 1820–30. The Falmouth workhouse, which housed a treadmill for grinding corn, was located in the complex with the present-day police barracks. The five-bay, double-pile masonry jail was built in 1814, probably housing jailers in two apartments on the second level with detention cells beneath. According to an 1844 map, the poor house was across Rodney Street from the jail and police barracks, although little information on the poor house remains.

Moving farther west, one comes to Falmouth's football (soccer) stadium, a field with seats for spectators behind a high, concrete wall. Beyond the stadium is Falmouth's hospital, a large complex on the left side of the road, a centre for medical care in the community.

Fort Balcarres/Falmouth All-Age School

Charlotte Street (*c.*1803–1804, 1811, 1986)

LOUIS P. NELSON AND D.P. SEFTON

Signalling its anticipated significance as a port city, Falmouth had a fort almost immediately after its founding. Writing in 1774, Edward Long mentions "a small fort placed on Point Mangrove, which projects into the sea on the West side". He continues by cautioning that the site will not likely be very healthy since it is "altogether swamp".[1] This site – likely the same site as the fort today – was quickly determined to be unsuitable because within just a few years, the fort was moved into the centre of town, occupying the oddly shaped triangular spot resulting from the intersection of the town's two different grid patterns. As described in its new location by 1787, "the fort, which was situated so as to overlook the harbour, and prevent ships going to sea whose captains had omitted to pay the harbour dues".[2] The 1793 plan of Falmouth shows the fort situated in the midst of the city, a square block with two corner towers not unlike the plan of the near contemporary fortified house at Stewart's Castle just east of town (see figure 1.1 for the 1793 plan of Martha Brae [Falmouth]). This in-town fort was named for the Earl of Balcarres, Royal governor of Jamaica from 1795 to 1801 and the leader of British troops in the Second Maroon War.[3]

But by 1803, the Jamaican House of Assembly once again moved the fort, this time back to its original location. The assembly gave two reasons for the move. First, they argued that the new location rendered the fort "almost useless, from its situation". And, more importantly, "Falmouth is in danger of being set on fire whenever the guns of the said fort are fired, the same being nearly in the centre of town". As a result, an alternative site on Palmetto Point was selected "for erecting a fort, barracks, and other necessary buildings for the protection of the town".[4] The proximity of the fort and its guns to the town was even a cause for anxiety for those most closely connected to the fort. One Scottish visitor reported in 1787 that "Mr. Baillie [commander of the fort] caused preparations to be made to fire a salute on the arrival of his excellency [the royal governor] which occasioned much alarm to Miss Baillie [his sister] for the safety of the windows in her brother's house, several of which were glazed – a very unusual comfort at that time in Jamaica, except in Kingston".[5]

The critical source for historical information on Fort Balcarres is Christoph K. Wilhelm, "Fort Balcarres and the Town of Falmouth, Jamaica: An Analysis of the Fortification and the Relationship to the Town through Time" (undergraduate thesis, University of Virginia, 2010)

FIGURE T3.2. Falmouth All-Age School, modern addition, 2008.

By 1804, the fort was well under construction on its new site as it appears on a map of that year in its new location. An 1844 map of Falmouth represents the new site of the fort. Just as the all-age school does today, the fort occupied all the point of land to the north of Charlotte Street. Defending the mouth of the harbour, a small fortification with two circular bastions stands at the very tip of the site. One of those bastions survives on the site today. In the midst of the large, triangular tract is a long, rectangular building that served as the barracks building for the soldiers stationed at the fort. This is the large two-storey historic masonry building, which was under construction in 1811, which dominates the site today.[6] One report from 1824 identifies seven hundred men stationed on this site, most of whom would have resided in the two floors of this building.[7] The 1844 map also shows one other large building in the midst of the site, probably an officer's quarters. The map also delineates a long string of buildings erected directly along Charlotte Street, at least some of which were certainly stores and shops. An 1816 newspaper announcement of work to be completed at the fort lists an officers' quarters, officers' kitchen and soldiers' barracks. Lastly, the map illustrates the four privies which were "removed back into the sea, twelve feet at low water mark, upon hardwood piles, with a gangway planked upon piles to the land".[8]

The map also identifies the powder magazine, a remarkable survival

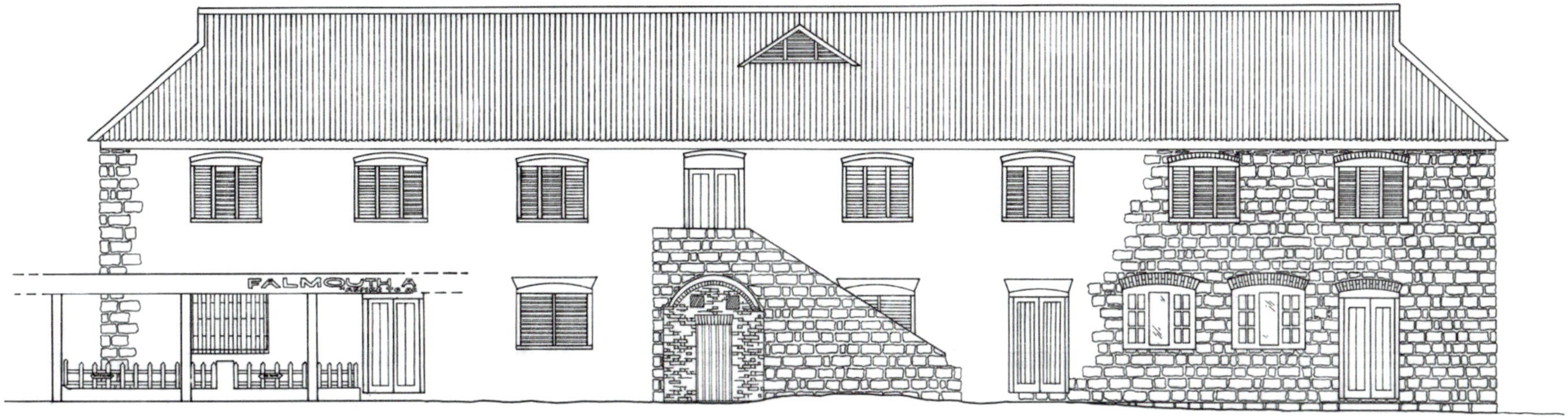

FIGURE T3.3. Fort Balcarres Barracks/Falmouth All-Age School, drawn by Colin Curley, 2008.

built by William Danny and completed in 1803 for a sum of £1,500. The magazine provided a storage space where powder and shot could be protected from fire, safe from detonation during earthquakes or hurricanes, a concern even a century after the devastating earthquake at Port Royal in which explosions from unsecured munitions caused further damage.[9] The magazine must be built strong enough to contain the force of explosions and thus minimize damage and casualties in the surrounding area.

To accomplish these functions, the magazine is built with inner and outer shells of squared stone. Its outer shell is 23 feet 9 inches square, with outer walls that rise 13 feet 10 inches to a corbelled cap course. Including both inner and outer shells, the walls are 4 feet 6 inches thick. A south-facing doorway, bridged by a yellow-pine lintel, and a pair of parallel tall and narrow vent slots, vertically aligned on the side (east and west) walls pierce the otherwise solid masonry. The vents allow limited study of the interior of the walls, which reveals that the magazine's seemingly solid walls are actually built in three layers. The vault supports a low pyramidal roof, whose upper surface is covered with cobble-size stones stuccoed together to form a smooth surface.

The garrison at Fort Balcarres was intended to serve as a military defence of the port, a responsibility that came to the fore in the "French scare" of 1804, when Jamaicans feared a French naval attack. The garrison was also useful in helping the city to combat city fires, two of which burned large sections of the city in 1808 and 1809. But one of the other

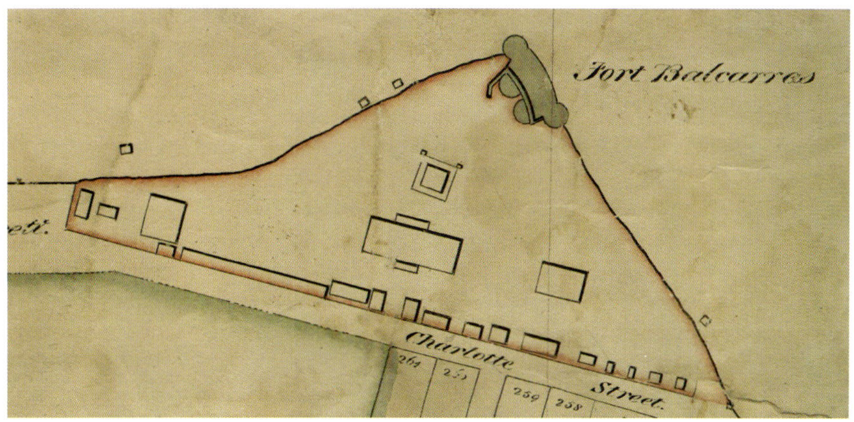

FIGURE T3.4. Fort Balcarres, from a plan of the town of Falmouth in the parish of Trelawny (n.d.). Courtesy of the National Library of Jamaica.

major fears that gripped city residents was the threat of slave insurrection. While white Jamaicans did not frequently express this anxiety in writing, we get a sense of this anxiety from this 1835 report from the second year of apprenticeship:

> Riots in Jamaica – From a letter received in town yesterday, dated at Kingston, (Ja.) June 22d, we learn that the whole island has been kept in a state of alarm and feverish agitation in consequence of the insurrection of the manumitted slaves, (or apprentices, as they are now called.) Not a day passes but one or more of the murderers are brought up for trial. The Governor at present is very unpopular, in consequence of his taking part with the apprentices and favouring their cause. It is expected daily that a general insurrection will take place throughout the island. Who will be the conquerors, time only will disclose.[10]

After emancipation, the perceived need for a military to defend the city began to wane. By the 1850s, the British government began to actively withdraw troops from their West Indies colonies, and by 1864, Fort Balcarres is described as "in ruins".[11] By 1882, the site was taken over by the town constabulary and rehabilitated slightly.[12] In 1902, the site took on a function as the town's free all-age school. In that year, the town's denominational schools – Church of England, Wesleyan and Baptist – were amalgamated and the government school inaugurated in the barracks and old Fort Balcarres.[13] In 1986, the school was finally able to expand with the addition of the large concrete wing, more than doubling the size of the school.[14] The school has now occupied this site for more than a century, longer than it was a military installation.

NOTES

1. Edward Long, *History of Jamaica* (1770), 2:220–21.
2. Phillip Barrington Ainslie, *Reminiscences of a Scottish Gentleman* (1787), 169.
3. Daniel L. Ogilvie, "History of the Parish of Trelawny" (manuscript, 1954), ch. 5. Available at http://www.jamaicanfamilysearch.com/Samples/histre.htm.
4. *The Laws of Jamaica, 1799–1803* (A. Aikman, 1812), 293.
5. Ainslie, *Reminiscences*, 169.
6. Ogilvie, "History", ch. 2.
7. *The Laws of Jamaica: A table of the titles of the Public and Private Acts passed during that time* (A. Aikman, 1824), 77.
8. "Falmouth Barracks", *Cornwall Chronicle*, 13 January 1816.
9. James Robertson, "Jamaican Architectures before Georgian", *Winterthur Portfolio* 36, nos. 2–3 (Summer–Autumn, 2001): 73–95. (Published by the University of Chicago Press on behalf of the Henry Francis du Pont Winterthur Museum.)
10. *Cornwall Chronicle*, 16 September 1835.
11. Christoph K. Wilhelm, "Fort Balcarres and the Town of Falmouth, Jamaica: An Analysis of the Fortification and the Relationship to the Town through Time", 109, 112.
12. Ibid., 110.
13. Ibid.
14. Ibid., 8.

Victoria Park/Uriah Rowe Park

Rodney Street (*c.* 1808, 1811)

EMILIE JOHNSON

The site of Victoria Park, or Uriah Rowe Park, in front of the Falmouth All-Age School, on land that fronts the sea, has been used as recreational space throughout its history. Historically known as the "grass piece", the parish vestry purchased a little over five acres from the estate of Edward Barrett in 1808.[1] The parish negotiated for the rest of the land in the grass piece in 1811, shifting Falmouth's seaside boundary from private to civic ownership.[2] The western end of the property was developed in the 1820s and 1830s as the site for the house of correction, workhouse, jail and hospital, but it appears that the eastern end always has been left open for recreation.

In the nineteenth and early twentieth centuries, the cricket field that adjoined the park was the site for highly contested matches between the soldiers at Fort Balcarres and townspeople, although, in reports, it seems that the soldiers usually won. The park was set aside, planted, and the concert pavilion, constructed in the nineteenth century, named in honour of England's Queen Victoria. Over the years, particular Falmouth residents have adopted the park, devoting hours to its maintenance and upkeep.

In 1977, the park was renamed to honour Uriah Rowe, the first mayor of Falmouth, who served from 1972 until his death in 1975. In 2001, the Jamaica *Gleaner* reported plans to transform an unfinished building on the site to an amphitheatre, in hope that Uriah Rowe Park will become a venue for cultural events.[3] The status of these plans is not clear. More recently, Falmouth Heritage Renewal has renovated the masonry walls and the pavilion, rendering the space more inviting to residents of the town and students of the school.

NOTES

1. Daniel L. Ogilvie, "History of the Parish of Trelawny" (manuscript, 1954), ch. 5. Available at http://www.jamaicanfamilysearch.com/Samples/histre.htm.
2. Ibid., ch 11.
3. *Gleaner*, 4 August 2001.

FIGURE T3.5. Victoria Park/Uriah Rowe Park, 2009.

Unity Church

Rodney Street (1834)

EMILIE JOHNSON

Now part of the denomination of the United Church in Jamaica and the Cayman Islands, the Unity Church historically was the Falmouth home of the Presbyterian Church. The Presbyterian Church in Jamaica and the Cayman Islands and the Congregational Church in Jamaica combined to form Unity Church in 1965; the Disciples of Christ in Jamaica joined in 1992.[1] Originally called St Andrews Kirk or the Scots Kirk, the building was completed in 1834.

A group of seven Scottish immigrants to Jamaica formed a committee to establish the church and purchased the lot in 1830 for £300 from the Trelawny parish vestry. The vestry acquired the land from the executors of Edward Barrett in 1808 and held it for twenty-two years. One of the church elders was a saddle maker named Alexander Simpson. He bought a lot in Falmouth from Samuel Barrett Moulton Barrett in 1812, paying £70 for a 50-foot by 120-foot lot on the corner of George Street and Princess Street. Simpson's grave remains visible in the churchyard.

Money for the church's construction must have been tight. The parish vestry gave a grant of £700 for the building's completion in 1832. The vestry gave the Committee of St Andrew's Kirk another donation of £300 for the minister in 1834, and another £300 in aid to the church in 1836. Members of St Andrew's Kirk asked for an additional grant to help satisfy the church's debt in 1838, but the vestry determined that it could no longer legally use public funds to support religious institutions.[2]

The church occupies an entire city block, facing Rodney Street and bounded by Princess, Lower Harbour and Newton Street, a location that has been called one of the coolest in the city. In keeping with the denomination's Calvinist history, and partially because of limited finances, the church is a relatively austere red-brick box with little architectural detailing, although the original pews were boxed in with doors.[3]

When completed in 1834, the primary entrance was the double door topped by a fanlight centred on the north façade, facing the ocean. The door is flanked by vertical four-panel, six-light windows that open on a pivot through the muntins, topped by fanlights. Of the fourteen windows lighting the building, seven appear to have their 1834 fanlights intact. The remaining seven were replaced in the twentieth century. Along the western façade, four of the five windows have original window shutters, with later repairs. A door was cut into one of the windows on the eastern façade after the original construction phase and is now the main access point into the church.

The bell tower, incorporated into the porch that shelters the door on the north façade, is supported by four thin cast-iron columns. These were originally used in the interior of the church to support a gallery with additional seating and the roofing system.

FIGURE T3.7. Unity Church elevation, drawn by Catherine Redfearn, 2009.

FIGURE T3.6. Unity Church north façade, 2009.

FIGURE T3.8. Unity Church east façade, 2009.

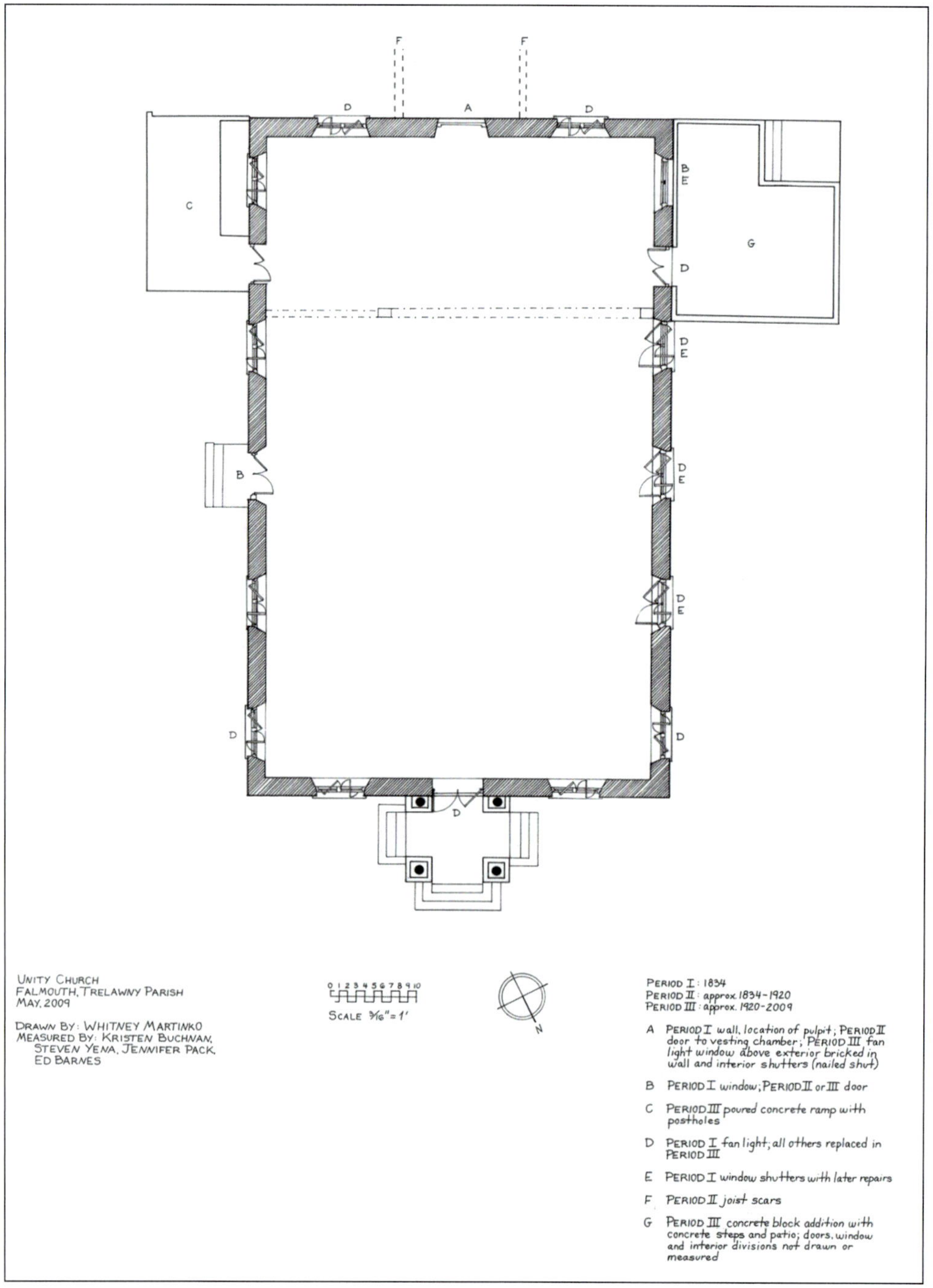

FIGURE T3.9. Unity Church plan, drawn by Whitney Martinko, 2009.

NOTES

1. United Church in Jamaica and the Cayman Islands, http://www.unitedchurch.org.ky.
2. Daniel L. Ogilvie, "History of the Parish of Trelawny" (manuscript, 1954), ch. 8. Available at http://www.jamaicanfamilysearch.com/Samples/histre.htm.
3. Ibid.

St Joseph Roman Catholic Church

Rodney Street (1966)

BEN HAYS AND EMILIE JOHNSON

The Roman Catholic church named for St Joseph – the husband of Mary, mother of Jesus – is one of the most distinctive modernist buildings in Falmouth. Situated across the street from the ocean, its north entrance opens towards the water, with a front door of Italian copper. Its most distinctive features, eight curved and gabled roofs, can be interpreted as a reference to the tradition of building multi-pitched roofs in Falmouth, or more expressively, a series of irregular ocean waves or a collection of nuns' wimples.

Catholicism in Falmouth began in an organized fashion in the mid-nineteenth century. Charles Moulton Barrett, a member of the prominent family who developed much of Falmouth, converted to Catholicism in 1862. His sponsorship of Father Joseph Sidney Woollett, a Catholic missionary to St James, St Ann and Trelawny parishes, gave the faith a foothold in the area. Barrett invited Woollett to set up a mission on the grounds of his property in St Ann, the first Catholic chapel in the northern part of the island.[1] Father Woollett hoped to build a chapel in Falmouth in 1866, but the citizens were unable to raise sufficient funds for the building's construction. His ambitions remained unrealized for another century, dating the construction of St Joseph to 1966, the year the church was dedicated.[2]

Jesuits from New England became deeply involved with Catholic mission work in Jamaica in the twentieth century. After a career in educational administration as the president of Holy Cross College, rector of Cranwell School, and president of Boston College, Father Joseph R.N. Maxwell (1899–1971) turned to parish work in Jamaica. As the pastor of St Joseph in Falmouth, he initiated construction of "a church of his own designing adapted both to the new liturgy and age-old semi-tropical heat of Jamaica".[3] A. Benghiat of Kingston assisted with the building's engineering, though the design and plan, described as "the first of its kind in the Caribbean", is attributed to Father Maxwell. The Vaccino Brothers built the structure.[4]

St Joseph is constructed of cast-in-place concrete and is circular in plan. The exterior features an alternation of rock-faced walls and inset entrance porches to create a dynamic façade. The interior is flooded with light from multiple sources, including louvred vents on the lower level, a decoratively pierced concrete "breeze block" halfway up the wall and twenty-four louvred windows in the gabled clerestory above. On the interior, the altar is located opposite the entrance, raised on a platform. Rows of pews, capable of seating five hundred, face the altar. The circular plan of the church reflects changes to the liturgy made at the Second Vatican

FIGURE T3.10. St Joseph Catholic Church exterior, drawn by Tahinee Felix Marin, 2009.

FIGURE T3.11. St Joseph Catholic Church interior, 2009.

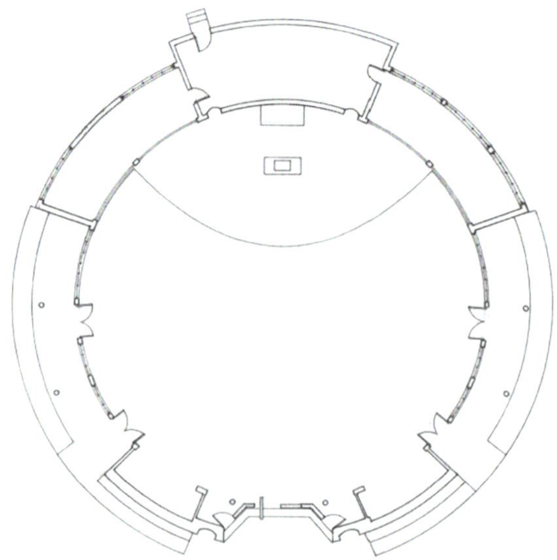

FIGURE T3.12. St Joseph Catholic Church plan, drawn by Jenni Pack, 2009.

FIGURE T3.13. St Joseph Catholic Church, 2007.

Council of 1963. A significant outcome of this council was the active rethinking of Catholic worship space and architecture. Churches adopted the circular plan with free-standing altars; spaces to encourage greater participation by the faithful during the celebration of the mass. St Joseph sits historically at the turning point of a Catholic rethinking of sacred space and simultaneously provided Falmouth with a significant modernist landmark.

NOTES

1. Francis J. Osborne, SJ, *History of the Catholic Church in Jamaica* (Chicago: Loyola University Press, 1988), 240.
2. Ibid., 242.
3. Francis W. Anderson, SJ, "Salute to a Veteran", *Jesuit*, New England ed., 44, no. 3 (Autumn 1969): 4.
4. *Catholic Opinion* 70 no.2 (14 January 1966): 1–2.

Police Barracks

Rodney Street (*c.* 1820–1830)

JAMIE FRIELING WITH BRIAN L. COFRANCESCO

The police barracks were built between 1820 and 1830 as a two-storey building, nine bays wide on the ground floor and eight bays wide on the second floor, with an exterior kitchen to the rear. The building was originally part of a complex called the house of correction, the property on which the Trelawny Workhouse with its punishing, corn-grinding treadmill was rebuilt in 1837.[1] The barracks are constructed primarily with light red brick laid in Flemish bond and locally harvested squared stone. Alterations to the brickwork made the façade appear less uniform, which perhaps encouraged the later application of lime wash with yellow-ochre pigment over the exterior brick.

There are four rooms on the first floor, although later partitions further subdivide these spaces. The largest room, at the centre of the first floor, served as the "Men's Ward" and "dormitory", as shown on an 1897 plan of the barracks. This room has several original windows – with square, diamond-set iron bars in an iron frame to protect from intrusion – on the western (rear) wall as well as window and door openings onto the eastern gallery porch. These windows date to the twentieth century, but the openings correspond with the 1897 building plan.

The northernmost room on the first floor is the second largest on the ground level. Strap hinges secured the heavy door into a beefy frame; this space was originally a lockup. The room was later transformed into a bathroom and is now used for equipment storage. An open concrete stairway with rails has been added in this room, supplementing the original exterior stair at the southernmost end of the building. Traditional finished joinery on this staircase – including rails that are tenoned and pegged to round-topped posts – suggests the persistence of older building techniques into the twentieth century. In the 1897 plan, the southernmost room on the first floor was called the "guard" and the adjacent room the "store"; the store was probably also used as a holding cell for prisoners, as indicated by the presence of another heavy door frame with a substantial lock.

There are three rooms on the second floor, all of which are two structural bays long. The largest is the one farthest to the north, labelled on the 1897 plan as the "chapel", generously lit by six windows.

The framing system of the fully exposed hipped roof includes principal and common rafters, a ridge beam, five trusses and tie beams, the original members being planed and beaded. Over the years, the roof has fallen into disrepair, which has caused the deterioration and destruction of the building's interior. Recent surveys have deemed the barracks building

This entry depends on an extensive on-site field report and analysis of surviving historic fabric written by Edward A. Chappell in the summer of 2008.

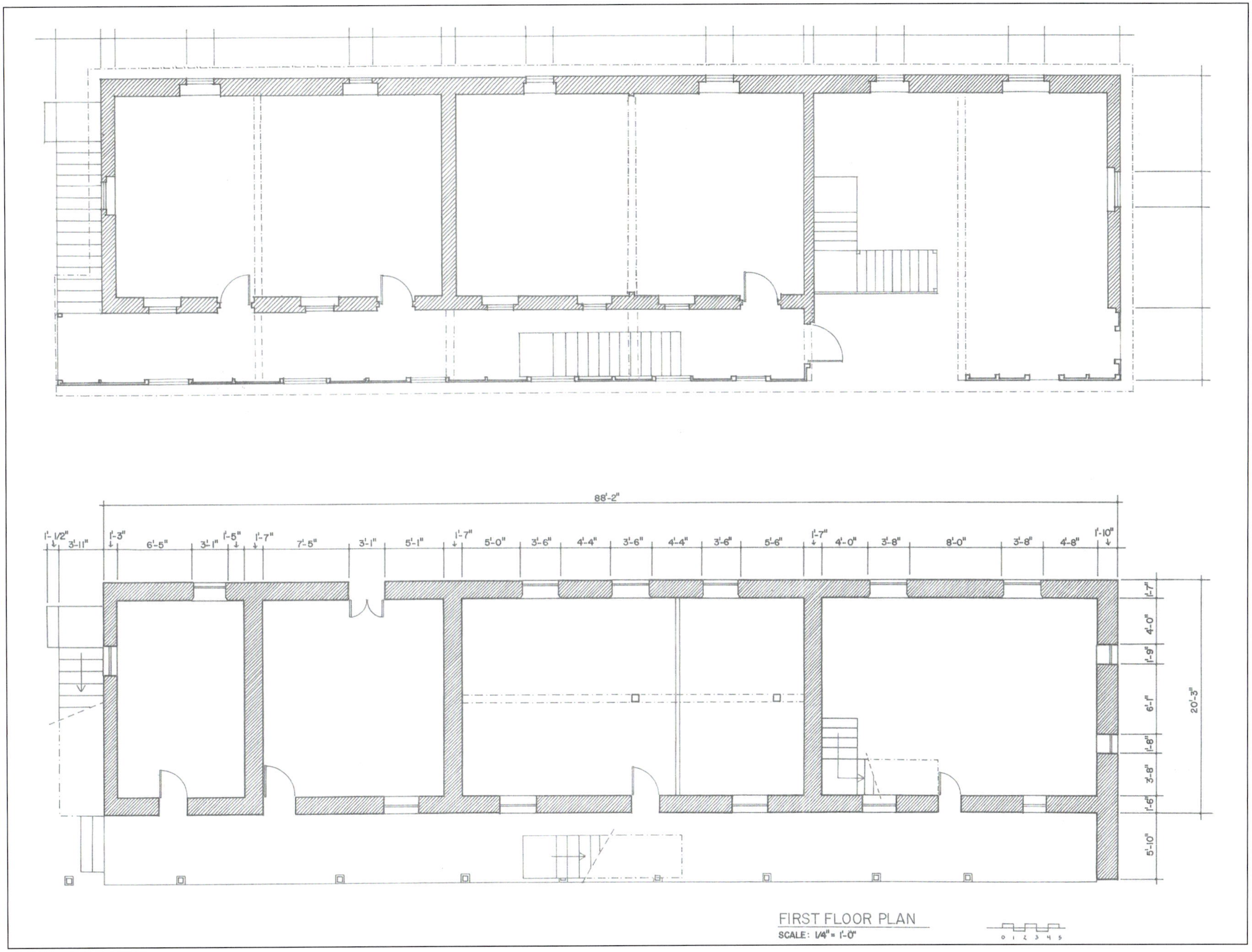

FIGURE T3.14. Police barracks plans, drawn by Patricia Slovinac (n.d.).

FIGURE T3.15. Police barracks, 2008.

too dangerous to restore, even though it remained in use for police changing stations and storage. Although the building will not be salvaged, its position as one of the important civic buildings in early Falmouth deserves recognition.

NOTE

1. Daniel L. Ogilvie, "History of the Parish of Trelawny" (manuscript, 1954), ch. 11. Available at http://www.jamaicanfamilysearch.com/Samples/histre.htm.

Trelawny Workhouse and House of Correction

Rodney Street (*c.* 1781)

EMILIE JOHNSON

During the late eighteenth and early nineteenth centuries, Falmouth was a bustling port town. It was the host of the weekly market and the urban centre of Trelawny, one of the most productive sugar parishes with one of the largest slave populations in Jamaica. Falmouth was home to wealthy merchants, planters, a significant population of free people of colour, soldiers, sailors, slaves and runaways. The relative anonymity offered by Falmouth's concentrated, and relatively fluid, population made the town a popular destination for runaway slaves, particularly escapees from nearby plantations.

English authorities established the workhouse to confine runaway slaves who had been captured until their masters could or would pay for their release back into plantation custody. The workhouse was also the destination for slaves convicted of crimes like stealing. In 1826, the newspaper reported that James Richards, a slave, would be incarcerated in the workhouse and sentenced to hard labour for three months; his crime: stealing imported crockery from a crate on one of the Falmouth wharves.[1]

In 1781, the parish vestry converted the hospital located at "the Point" into the workhouse. John Tharp, the wealthy proprietor of Good Hope plantation, was one of the commissioners, charged with inspecting the building and making recommendations for its repair. "The Point" is Palmetto Point, the current location of the Fort Balcarres complex.[2] In 1782, the *Cornwall Chronicle*, the major newspaper of the northwestern coast of Jamaica, advertised that twenty slaves moved from the jail in Martha Brae to the Trelawny Workhouse.[3] In 1794, slaves from the workhouse built a horse track at Cave Island, the old name for what is now the western half of Falmouth.[4]

The earliest workhouse left no architectural traces. Displaced by the construction of Fort Balcarres, in 1802, the vestry purchased land known as the Marl pit from Edward Barrett's executors and paid Walter Henry Birmingham, a carpenter, £2,487.7.5 to build the new workhouse in the complex where the police barracks now are located.[5] Prominent Falmouth residents held management positions over the workhouse; James Stewart, of Stewart Castle, was the president in 1816.[6]

In 1834, a nervous parish vestry authorized the construction of a new workhouse with an imported treadmill in the house of correction complex, and acknowledged the parish government's fears of social chaos

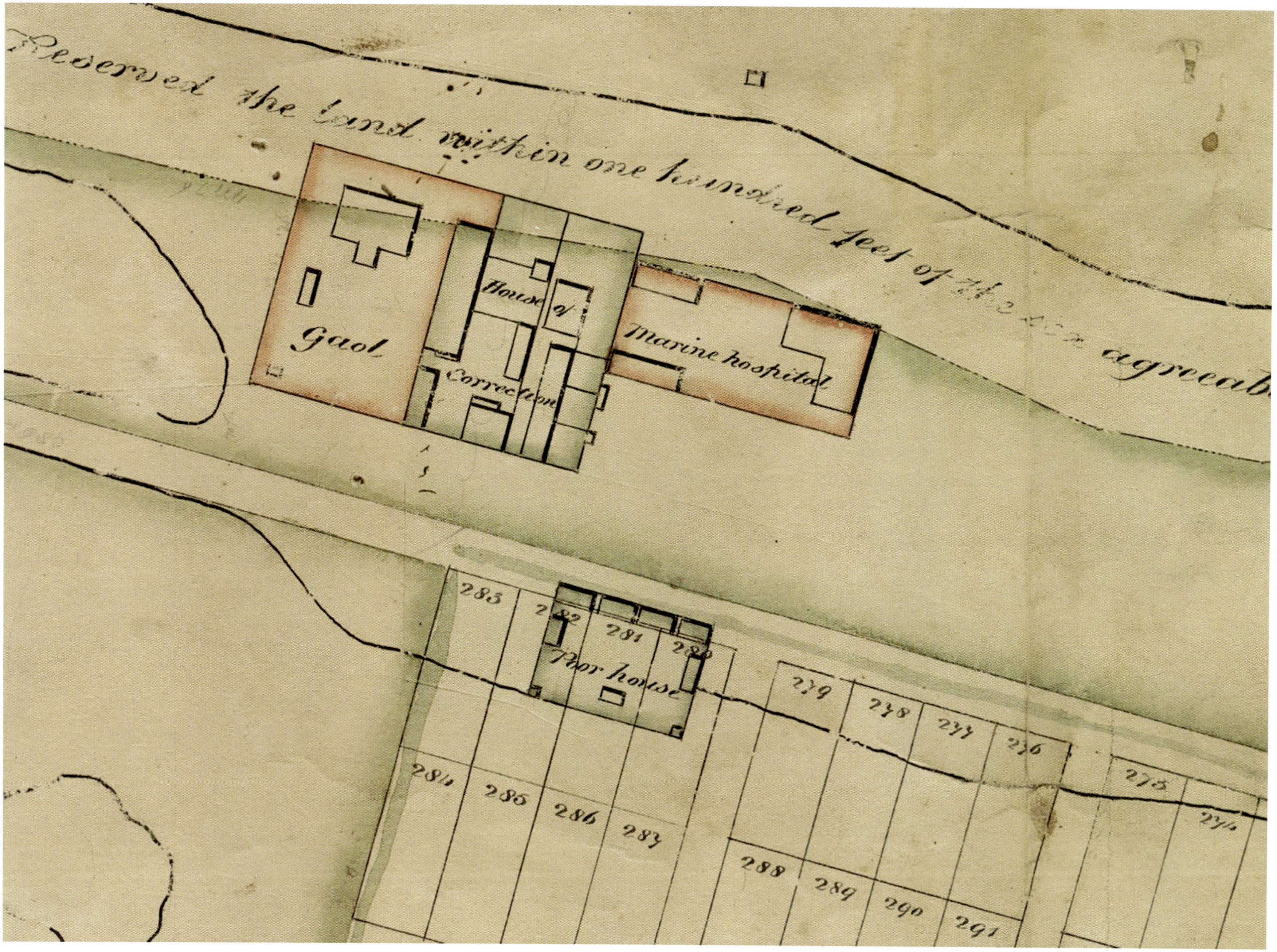

FIGURE T3.16. The jail, house of correction, marine hospital and poor house, from a plan of the town of Falmouth in the parish of Trelawny (n.d.). Courtesy of the National Library of Jamaica.

after emancipation. The treadmill in the new brick workhouse was a fearsome contraption. Described as two large wheels, "bladed across with steps", the prisoners used their body weight to revolve the wheel, which ground corn into meal, the basis of the workhouse diet (see figure 1.6). Injuries were common. The treadmill must have been used heavily; only a year later, the treadmill needed new wheels and new straps and had a clock installed.[7]

It is unknown how long the treadmill remained in operation, as it is not mentioned after 1838. By the end of the nineteenth century, prisoners worked on road construction and maintenance instead of the gruelling, corn-grinding apparatus.

NOTES

1. Cornwall Correspondent, *Gossip*, 13 September 1826, National Library of Jamaica.
2. Daniel L. Ogilvie, "History of the Parish of Trelawny" (manuscript, 1954), ch. 5. Available at http://www.jamaicanfamilysearch.com/Samples/histre.htm.
3. *Cornwall Chronicle, and Jamaica General Advertiser*, 2 March 1782.
4. Ogilvie, "History", ch. 1.
5. Ibid., ch. 5.
6. *Cornwall Chronicle*, 20 January 1816.
7. Ogilvie, "History", ch. 5.

Trelawny Gaol

Rodney Street (1814)

LAURIN GOAD

In 1814, the Trelawny parish vestry paid John Robey £2,349 to build a T-shaped stone jail.[1] The jail was at the centre of an open yard for male prisoners, with officers' quarters, a "dining shed", a bath house and a condemned cell surrounded by a stone wall 14 feet high at the front of the property and 20 feet high at the rear. Within the compound, a brick wall enclosed a separate "women's yard".

The exterior received the finish required of a public building, including cut-stone walls with raised mortar joints. The main stairs have lead-filled sockets for wrought-iron handrails. Even though the railings and the porch are twentieth-century replacements, they show traditional carpentry techniques, such as chamfers and mortised joints, indicating that traditional joinery remained in wide use into the twentieth century. The wooden porch at the entryway may have been an original feature as there is no evidence the iron rail extended onto the top landing.

Just beyond the wooden porch, the masonry entryway gives access to the main floor of the building, which is divided into two separate apartments, probably housing for the jailers (see figure 2.10 for the first-floor plan of the Trelawny Gaol). Each apartment has a similar layout to free-standing houses in Falmouth with one large front room and two smaller chambers. The left (eastern) apartment has an additional exit leading to an exterior staircase, indicated as stairs to the "Gallows" on the nineteenth-century plan. The interior spaces are plain, with exposed roof-framing systems that use a principal rafter truss with purlins and a ridge board with vertically set-sheathing, rather than common rafters. The main structure is covered by two large hipped roofs with a smaller, perpendicularly oriented hipped roof over the masonry entryway.

Flanking the entrance tower on the lower level, doors open into two corridors with four cells each; plans from the turn of the twentieth century label six cells for men and two for women. The three surviving leaves are fairly typical of eighteenth- and nineteenth-century jail and asylum doors with slide bolts secured by padlocks. Holes with cover plates pierce the leaves, which allowed the jailers to observe prisoners while maintaining a safe distance.

Other buildings in the jail yard include a "condemned cell", constructed in the late nineteenth century in the front right corner of the compound, away from the main cells. Built with concerns for high-security, the 13-foot 2-inch square masonry building has narrow, barred windows located immediately under the eaves of the gable roof. Small ground-level openings led to drains for cleaning and privy use.

During the early twentieth century, authorities tightened jail security by installing additional bars and screens and filling in portions of each

---

This entry depends on an extensive on-site field report and analysis of surviving historic fabric written by Edward A. Chappell in the summer of 2007.

FIGURE T3.17. Trelawny Gaol, 2008.

FIGURE T3.18. Trelawny Gaol elevation, drawn by Noel Makubwa, 2008.

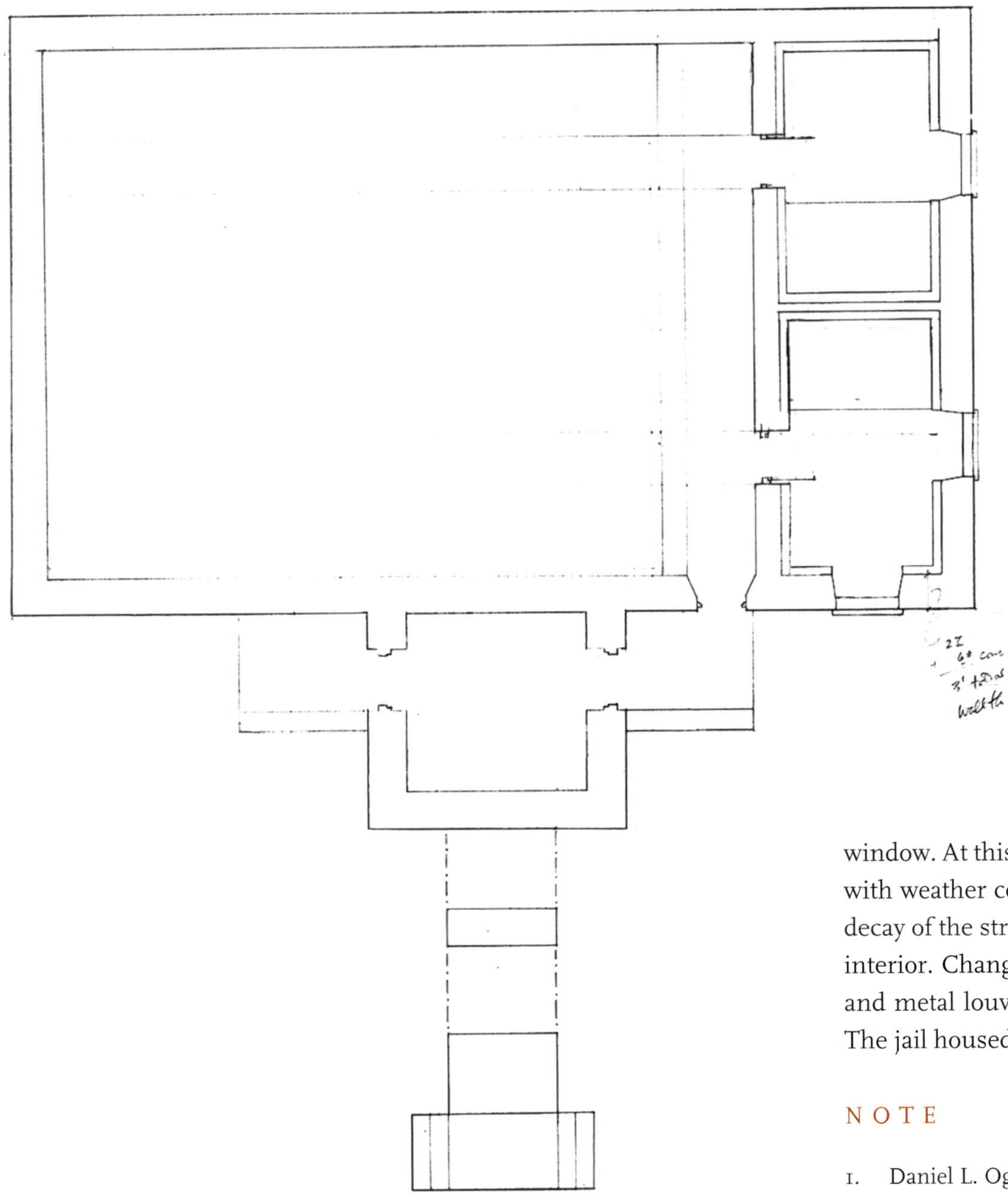

FIGURE T3.19. Trelawny Gaol basement, plan drawn by University of Virginia Falmouth Field School, 2007.

window. At this time, the walls were also thickened with concrete. Along with weather conditions, these changes have contributed to the current decay of the structure, blocking air circulation and thus creating a damp interior. Changes to the structure, including the addition of restrooms and metal louvred windows, continued through the twentieth century. The jail housed prisoners as recently as 2006.

NOTE

1. Daniel L. Ogilvie, "History of the Parish of Trelawny" (manuscript, 1954), ch. 11. Available at http://www.jamaicanfamilysearch.com/Samples/histre.htm.

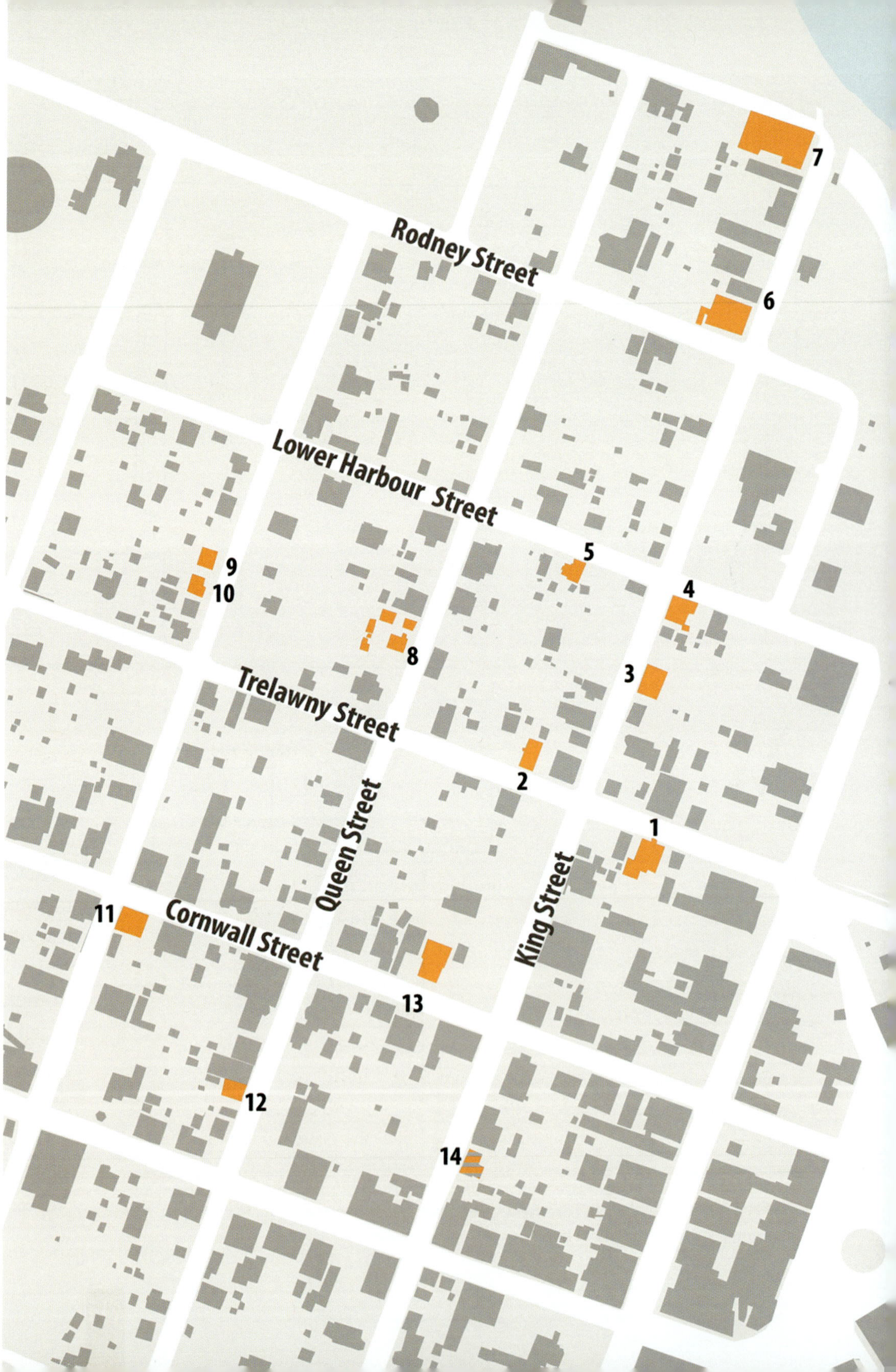

FIGURE T4.1. Map of the residential core.

TOUR 4

Residential Core

EMILIE JOHNSON

While Duke Street and Market Street have large merchant storehouses, stores and churches, and Rodney Street has many of the town's civic institutions, Trelawny, Cornwall, Lower Harbour, King, Queen, Princess, Newton and Pitt Streets make up the residential core of historic Falmouth. Even though these streets have some large residences, most of the building fabric is small two- and three-room houses, many of which exhibit traditional building techniques like nogging. These streets remain vibrant residential neighbourhoods; houses of different periods, materials and scales coexist, new houses next to old houses next to renovated ones. The diversity of the neighbourhood's built environment testifies to its long, stable existence.

There are three historic house types found in the residential core. The earliest, which probably date to the early and middle of the nineteenth century, had two rooms, often with the gable end towards the street and an entry from the side yard on one of the long sides of the building. Examples of this kind of building stand at 7 Lower Harbour and 8 Trelawny, and many of these two-room cores lie underneath accumulated layers of remodelling and expansion. Later in the nineteenth century, and into the twentieth, residents began building two-roomed houses organized like duplexes, with separate entrances from the front porch into each chamber.

Examples of these houses, which suggest a more American version of turn of the twentieth-century worker's housing, survive at 8 Princess Street and at 11 Queen. Also beginning near the turn of the twentieth century, residents introduced the next type, a three-room house. A rectangular footprint under a gable roof, one enters into the house from one of two doorways off a front porch, which spans about half of the front façade under the overhanging roof. A single room occupies the space behind the porch, while two rooms, front and back, span the depth of the house. Doors open into the single room and the front chamber. An excellent example is the ruinous building at 9 Princess, a nogged or Spanish walled building of a local tropical hardwood called bullet wood. A few other unremodelled examples of these buildings remain on lower King Street.

Even though unmodified examples of two-room, three-room and double-chambered buildings are few, many of these buildings survive as cores in houses continuously transformed by small additions. As you walk around the residential core, be sure to look at foundations, additions to buildings and changes in the roofline. Very often, a historic structure lurks underneath a veneer of cinderblock or sheet-metal roofing.

1 Trelawny Street

(*c.* 1781)

STEPHANIE LANGTON WITH BRIAN L. COFRANCESCO

The house at 1 Trelawny Street may have been built by Isaac Love, a mulatto mason, sometime after he bought this lot – Barrett lot 38 – in 1781 from Edward and Judith Barrett. Together with this property, Love purchased lot 126, located farther south at the corner of Duke Street and Crooked Street, from the Barretts and paid a total of £100 for the two properties.[1] The documentary record shows that Isaac Love was actively involved in Falmouth real estate. Before he bought Barrett lots 38 and 126, Love purchased lot 121, located on the southwestern corner of George Street and Market Street, in 1775.[2] Deeds show that Love was active in real estate into the nineteenth century; Isaac, his brother Thomas, sisters Elizabeth and Johanna, and six other free people of colour (who might be related to the Loves through marriage) sold another lot on Duke Street between King and Queen Streets, in 1804 to another artisan – a carpenter. The deeds give valuable information about the Loves and their associates, listing their occupations in skilled trades like masonry and chair-making and recording kinship ties between people in Trelawny and St Ann parishes.[3] The Loves' participation in the Falmouth real estate market suggests property speculation. During the Falmouth boom decades of the 1790s and 1800s, investment in real estate appears to have been a solid investment opportunity for a family of skilled free black artisans.

This house, located right on the street, is a two-storey brick house. The main entrance is centred on the symmetrical façade and is fronted by a much later lattice-screen exterior vestibule capped by a classical pediment form. Two six-over-six double-sash windows flank the entrance. Above the front door is a tripartite window composed of a triple-sash window flanked by louvres, a common arrangement seen across Falmouth signalling the "best room". An iron balcony – moved from another house – now sits in front of the window. The two-storey structure boasts a substantial hipped roof.

NOTES

1. Edward and Judith Barrett to Isaac Love, 29 June 1781, Deeds, Island Record Office, volume 333, folio 162.
2. Edward and Judith Barrett to Isaac Love, 22 April 1775, Deeds, Island Record Office, volume 289, folio 95.
3. Isaac Love, Thomas Love et al. to Walter Henry Birmingham, 12 January 1804, Deeds, Island Record Office, volume 560, folio 114.

FIGURE T4.3. 1 Trelawny Street front elevation, drawn by Eryn Brennan (n.d.

FIGURE T4.2. 1 Trelawny Street, 2005.

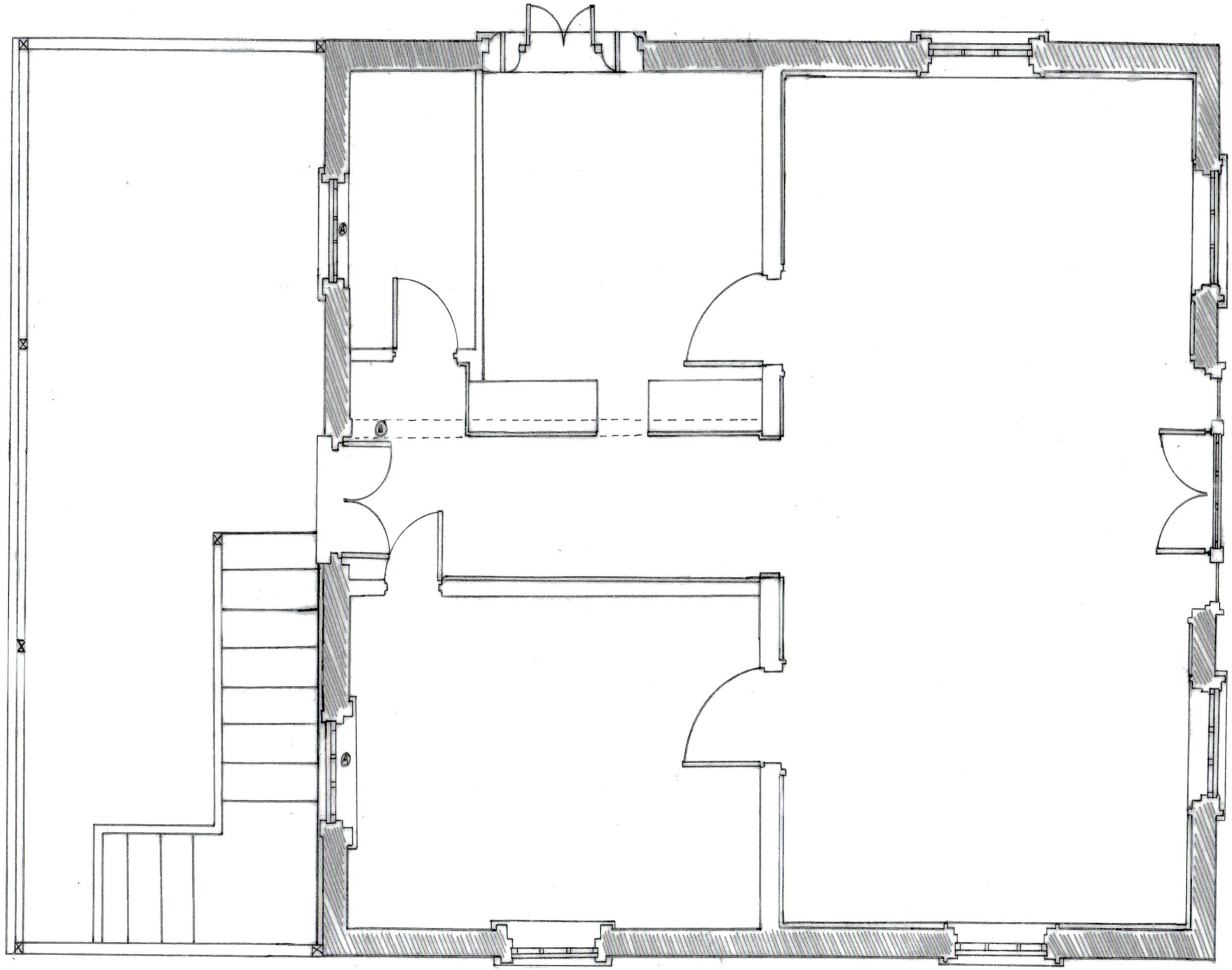

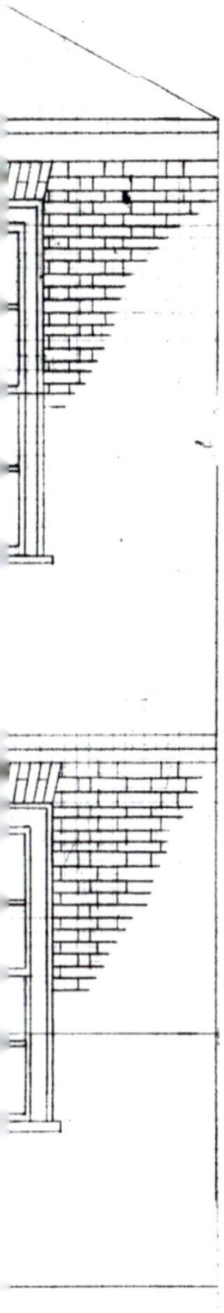

FIGURE T4.4. 1 Trelawny Street second-floor plan, drawn by Adam T. Erby, 2010.

Elizabeth Somerville House

8 Trelawny Street (*c.* 1836)

LOUIS P. NELSON

Elizabeth Somerville, probably a slave undergoing emancipation or a free woman of colour, purchased this unimproved 50-foot by 120-foot lot in 1836 from Samuel Barrett Moulton Barrett for £60. Little is known about Somerville, except that on the deed, she is noted as being from Trelawny, suggesting that she lived outside of Falmouth prior to purchasing her property. She probably erected the oldest, two-room portion of this house soon thereafter. In its earliest form, it was very similar to a number of other houses of its type in town. The original structure consisted of a front and a rear room of nearly identical dimensions, separated by a partition wall with a doorway. The front room is now used as a sitting room and bedroom, and the rear a sitting and waiting room. The framing of this original structure is entirely joined, with transverse plates tenoned into longitudinal plates, and rafter feet that bird-mouth out over outer wall plates. This two-room structure is still covered by its original hipped roof, still covered with lath and shingles now covered on the exterior by corrugated metal roofing.

Behind the main house stands a nog-walled kitchen building, suggesting that Somerville preferred to cook in the kitchen rather than in the yard. Few dedicated kitchen structures survive in Falmouth, partly due to changing culinary habits and neglect of unused buildings and partly to the nineteenth-century local preference to cook in the yard. The current owner remodelled this building into a beauty salon. A chimney or smoke hole divides the front cook room space in this building from a small rear space, which is now used as a privy and accessed through its own board door to the outside. The cook room is accessed by a door facing the front of the property.

Sometime after the construction of the house by Elizabeth Somerville in 1836, a later owner altered the front elevation by changing the front window into a double door, presumably transforming the front room into a shop. The open porch wrapped around from this eastern side of the house to the front, and features chamfered 4-inch posts, slotted with sloped sills below a lattice. The front doors have also been altered and now feature 3-foot-wide double doors with two-panel leaves hung on butt hinges, flanked by moveable louvres. In keeping with the traditional Jamaican manner, these doors are supported on a frame with beaded inner edges, and the louvres move on straight-sided rails without glazing.

In the early twentieth century, the house was expanded to the rear (north) along the full width of the rear façade and covered by a shed roof. Occupied by a new kitchen and dining room, the framing is exposed to the interior and features reused studs and beaded sheathing. Both the kitchen and dining room have their own exterior doors to the rear yard, and interior doors to the original rear room. While 8 Trelawny is of modest size, it reveals evidence of a rich architectural past, which might have included some of the commercial livelihood that it exhibits today.

FIGURE T4.5. 8 Trelawny Street, 2006.

FIGURE T4.6. 8 Trelawny Street elevation, drawn by Jordan Matthews, 2007.

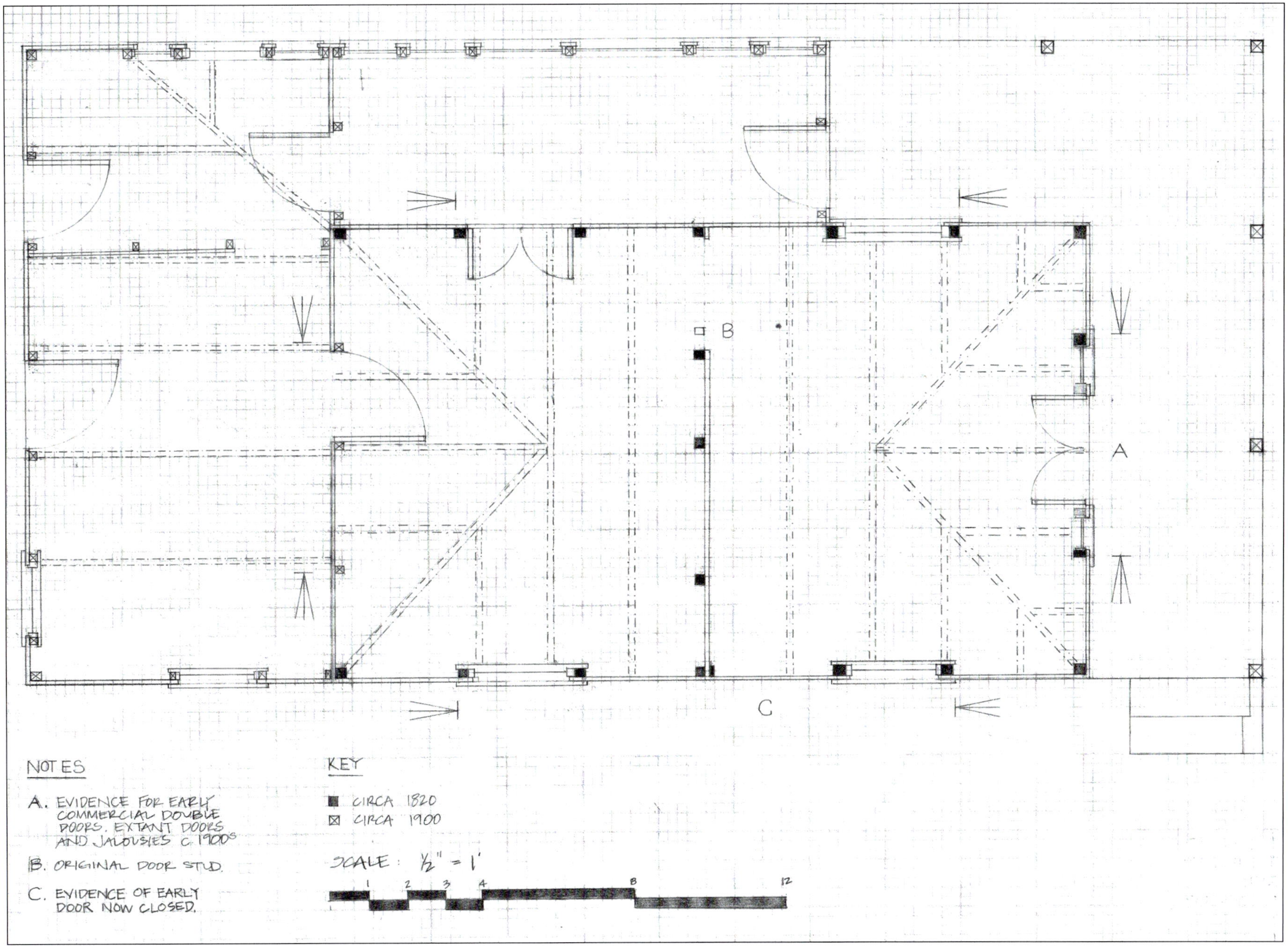

FIGURE T4.7. 8 Trelawny Street plan, drawn by Kristin Hennings, 2007.

6 King Street

(*c.* 1815–1835)

KATHRYN LASDOW

The house at 6 King Street is one of Falmouth's best-preserved pre-1835 buildings, a distinctive example of a four-over-four plan that does not adhere to a typical central-passage Georgian layout. The house is a two-bay, two-storey frame house, with a longitudinal hipped roof over the front (west) rooms and a narrower hipped roof that covers the two smaller rear (east) rooms. The exterior siding consists of flat boards, planed and beaded on both sides, although shingles now cover some of the street-facing façade. Based on material evidence, the house appears to date to 1815–35.

Further investigation suggests that the house was originally a single-pile structure, and the rear range of rooms was added shortly after. The original stud framing the door between the two left rooms was cut for a window head and there is evidence of unweathered sheathing on the back wall.

On the second storey, an original doorway allows access between the large front rooms. From each large room, a doorway communicates independently with the smaller back rooms, which also have a doorway between them, creating an internal circulation system. The interior frame is fully exposed, with beaded posts, studs, braces, lower edges of plates and joists. The transverse partition consists of unbeaded sheathing applied on the left side, so studs are visible in the smaller room. Rafters and shingle lath are exposed, planed and beaded. Interestingly, beaded boards of 8 inches by 1 inch are used instead of shingle lath at the ridge, to protect the roof at its most vulnerable point.

The first-floor plan virtually mirrors that of the second floor, except that what was probably the front entrance opens into one of the smaller rooms. The first-floor doorway that opens directly onto the street is of an uncertain date. Although there is no evidence for an interior stair, it is thought that the house was originally constructed as a single-family dwelling, with a stair possibly rising from one of the rooms.

After the addition, an exterior stair gave access to the upper level. The double-height porch runs the full depth of the structure, with a contemporary joined, beaded frame staircase with round-topped rails tenoned into chamfered posts. The stair rises from back to front, ending behind an original door flanked by moveable louvres and no glazing. The door features an all-beaded frame with cyma backbands on the outer edge, reminiscent of doorways that face side yards in Charleston, South Carolina.

Access to the second-storey on the opposite, southern façade, is reached by a modest stair and platform added when tenants divided the upper floor. This door has early trim, heavy stiles and rails, and four panels nailed on with handmade rails.

This entry depends on an extensive on-site field report and analysis of surviving historic fabric written by Edward A. Chappell in the summer of 2003.

FIGURE T4.8. 6 King Street, 2005.

FIGURE T4.9. 6 King Street elevation, drawn by Molly McDonald, 2008.

3 Lower Harbour Street

(*c.*1810–1820)

LAURIN GOAD

Three Lower Harbour Street, consisting of a house, shop and the remains of a kitchen chimney, is better described as a domestic complex rather than an individual house. Joseph Matthews, a cooper, purchased this lot from Edward Barrett on 3 November 1780 for £50.[1] This purchase was probably a real estate investment as he did not build on his lot.[2] This complex and the house at 6 King Street sit on Matthews's original lot, demonstrating that the large 50-foot by 20-foot lots standard in Falmouth were subdivided early. Materials and finishes suggest a construction date around 1810 to 1820 for the house, which was originally a double-pile structure with the largest room overlooking Lower Harbour Street and two smaller rooms behind. Like other Jamaican houses of its time, the primary entrance to the house was from the courtyard, rather than from the street. Another door on the southern face was probably more private, permitting communication between the house and the shop.

The interior of 3 Lower Harbour Street features an interesting juxtaposition of high-style details with rougher finishes. On the interior, only the shingle lath and some of the rafters are beaded; the framing is entirely exposed and unbeaded. The best room is not sheathed, but boasts a tripartite window with deep neoclassical muntins, fenestration found lighting the best rooms of fine homes all over town. Surviving interior door leaves on the door between the north room and back chamber, crafted to suggest a six-panelled door facing into the best room, designate a more formal space, as does a large neoclassical double architrave around the door. In the chamber, a single architrave surrounds the doors, supporting a reading of the north room as the formal entertaining space in the house.

To the right of the house, facing King Street, is a small, well-lit outbuilding. Currently a tailor shop, the single room structure exhibits traditional building form and practice in Falmouth. Much of the lower frame is original with joists lapped into the sills, which sit on brick piers. Originally, one accessed the shop from the courtyard, an opening that conforms to the stud spacing of the building. Empty slots for windowsills and the spacing of the studs suggests that the building originally had four six-light casement windows in addition to the courtyard door. The door opening to the street is likely a twentieth-century alteration.

A portion of the brick foundations and the yellow-brick chimney of the kitchen still survive. Within the foundations, three square stones seem to mark the location of the kitchen door.

This entry depends on an extensive on-site field report and analysis of surviving historic fabric written by Edward A. Chappell in the summer of 2004.

FIGURE T4.10. 3 Lower Harbour Street north elevation, drawn by Jennifer Lindstrom, 2010.

FIGURE T4.11. 3 Lower Harbour Street west elevation, drawn by Anna Danz, 2010.

This complex of buildings forms the necessary buildings for the household – house, kitchen and shop. While only vestiges of the kitchen remain, much of the original fabric remains in the house and shop.

NOTES

1. Edward Barrett to Joseph Matthews, 23 November 1780, Deeds, Island Record Office, volume 324, folio 193.
2. Joseph Matthews, 24 July 1787, Inventories, Jamaica Archives, volume 72, folio 8.

7 Lower Harbour Street

(*c.* 1812, 1900–1925)

MARILYN W. MOEDINGER

Seven Lower Harbour Street is now a four-room timber-frame house on a brick pier foundation (see figure 2.13). John Harris, a gentleman of Trelawny, bought the lot from Samuel Barrett Moulton Barrett in 1812, and it is possible that he built the original two-room structure; it might have served either as his residence or as a rental property.[1] If so, this example offers further evidence that the social station of house builders in Falmouth should be read in terms of architectural elements and finishes, rather than size of house. The narrow, one-bay-wide house faces the street and, as is typical for houses of this type, the entrance to the building faces the side yard.

The entrance door on the west wall and an adjacent louvred panel open directly into the north room, which faces the street and contains generally superior finishes compared to the rest of the house. The three-part window on the north wall is a well-crafted, six-over-six window with decorative trim and is flanked by louvred panels. A twentieth-century six-light casement window occupies an early opening on the east wall, while the door to the rear room is located in the southeast corner.

Aside from the front window, other subtle examples of superior finishes in this room include the partition wall and the exterior doors. Planed sheathing on the north side of the partition wall presents a finished surface to the front room, leaving exposed studs in the rear room. Two of the best doors in the house are in the front room, their applied stiles and rails giving the appearance of a six-panel door, oriented to the more important space: the front door towards the exterior, the partition door towards the front room. The rear exterior door, which now opens into a later addition, features three bevelled battens and no applied stiles and rails. The twentieth-century door to the west addition matches the early, best doors.

The rear room is less well lit and less intact than the front room, with a louvred window, part of a twentieth-century renovation, on the east wall. The west wall was also replaced and a narrow door added to access the addition to the west. Presumably the east and west walls originally had windows, but the south wall shows no evidence of a window.

To the west is a one-room addition constructed in the early twentieth century. Connected to the rear room of the first-period house, the addition has a finished tray ceiling and was probably added to serve as a public space. It is now used for sleeping and dining.

All of the interior framing is exposed, though only some of the framing members are beaded. The sill plates and joists have all been replaced, some with reused beaded timbers. The early studs and posts may have been beaded (some studs have survived behind the casing around open-

This entry depends on an extensive on-site field report and analysis of surviving historic fabric written by Edward A. Chappell in the summer of 2009.

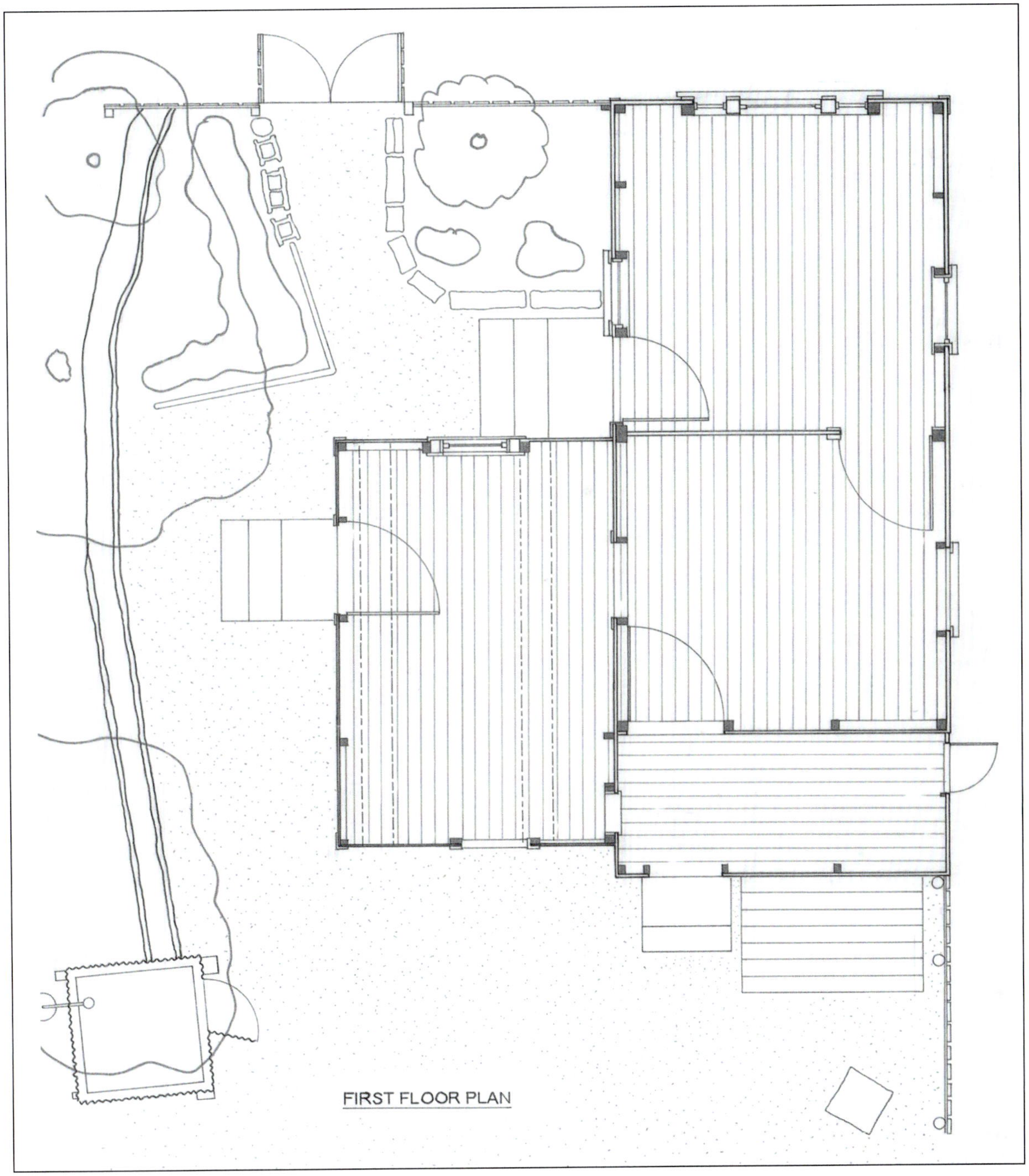

FIGURE T4.12. Lower Harbour Street elevations, drawn by Elizabeth Milnarik, 2004.

FIGURE T4.13. 7 Lower Harbour Street, 2007.

ings), though there is at least one post that is only planed and not beaded. All plates and rafters are hand-planed and beaded, as are the partition boards and lath supporting the shingles. The roof lath is replaced with beaded boards at the ends of the rafters as well as at the ridge.

The original structure has a hipped roof, while the rear addition has a shed roof and the west addition a gable roof, oriented along a north–south axis. The roof is currently clad in corrugated, painted steel, installed over the original wood shingles.

NOTE

1. Samuel Barrett Moulton Barrett to John Harris, 29 May 1812, Deeds, Island Record Office, volume 638, folio 160.

9 King Street

(*c.*1844, 1900)

SOPHIE JOHNSON

Richard Barrett Waite was a wealthy mason in Falmouth in the 1780s. He owned four enslaved masons, five carpenters and an additional labour force of fifteen men, among his sixty-seven slaves. Documentary evidence suggests that he interacted with, and probably was related to, the powerful Barrett family.[1] Waite purchased five lots of land for £70 apiece in Falmouth from Edward Barrett in 1782. Three of those lots stretched the entire block of Lower Harbour Street between King and Queen Streets; the other two were at the corner of King and Rodney Streets.[2] Yet, this house was not likely built by Waite. The house at 9 King Street was built in the first half of the nineteenth century, but certainly before 1844, when the parcel was subdivided and Mrs Mary Garth and A.J. Preston bought the portion occupied by the house.[3] This single-storey, timber-frame house is significant to Falmouth's architectural tradition as a compact version of a domestic form used in larger houses, such as those in the merchant storehouses on Market Street. With the exception of some twentieth-century renovations to the building, 9 King Street's structure, ornamentation and layout are characteristic of Jamaican domestic building practices. The house is distinguished by its three hipped roofs and the gallery which wraps around the north and east elevations.

Much of the structure is original. The most formal space in the house is a front chamber under the easternmost roof, connected to two smaller chambers divided by a central passage beneath the second hip. Openness is achieved in the principal chamber with three double exterior doors and two six-over-six windows. A pair of doors flanks a central front window on the eastern wall, while the second door, centred on the north end, directly opposite the south window, provides a second entry and allows cross ventilation. The ornamentation on the interior of the principal chamber speaks to its importance as the primary entertaining space in the house. The walls are sheathed with flush, unbeaded, horizontal boards and the ceiling is lined with a substantially restored dentil cornice detailed with thin neoclassical mouldings. The tray ceiling, with early twentieth-century matchboard lining, is not original to the structure and hides the original beaded timber roof frame.

Three original doorways, which lead into private chambers beneath the middle hipped roof, pierce the room's western wall. The arched central opening features panelled pilasters and opens into a central passage, while two flanking four-panelled doors give access to the two chambers on either side of the passage. Originally unlit, the passage now receives

This entry depends on an extensive on-site field report and analysis of surviving historic fabric written by Edward A. Chappell in the summer of 2007.

FIGURE T4.14. 9 King Street, 2004.

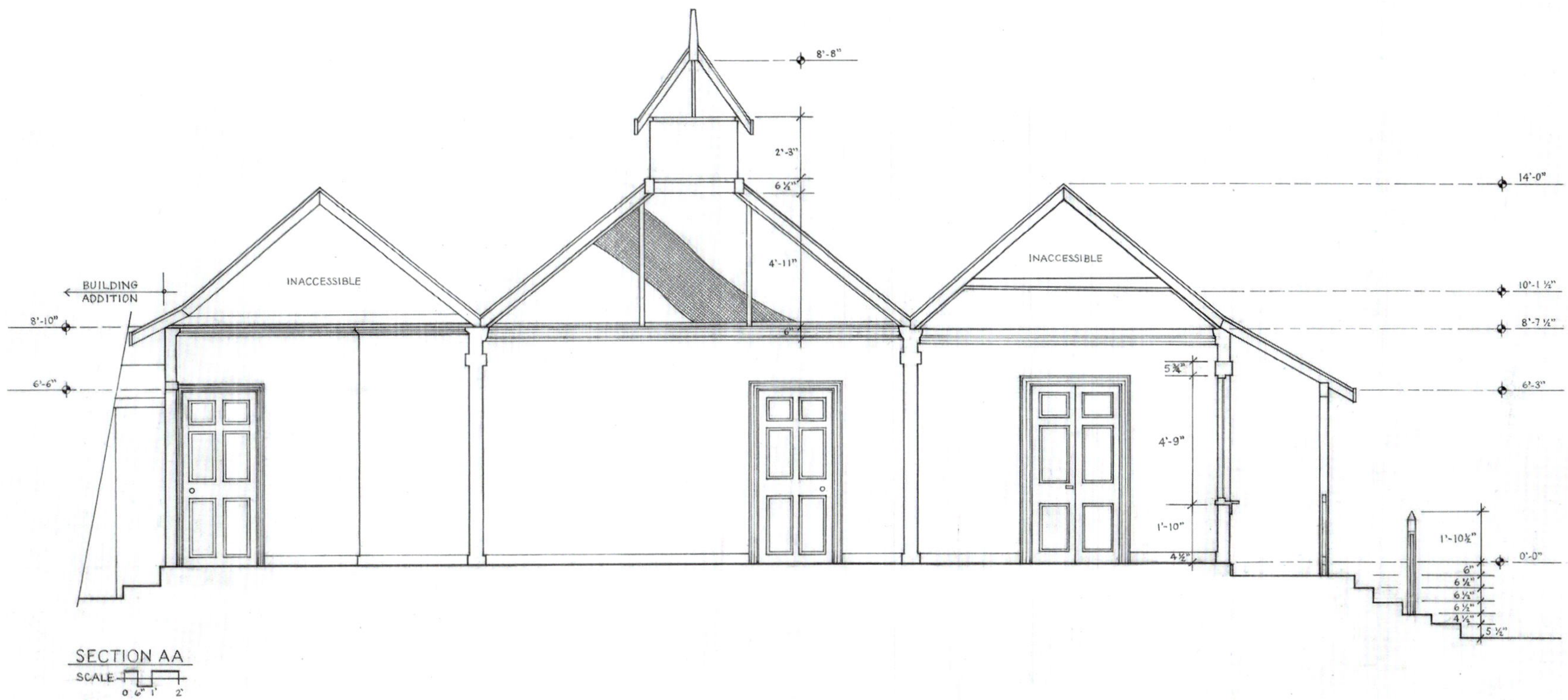

FIGURE T4.15. 9 King Street section, drawn by Ahn Thai, 2006.

natural light and air through a central louvred cupola, added circa 1900. Along with the fretwork on the gallery, this cupola contributes to the house's Victorian appearance.

The plan of the house offers numerous circulation patterns, but also exhibits a concern for privacy (see figure 2.14 for a plan drawing of 9 King Street). The chamber doorways to the central passage are staggered to increase privacy in a narrow space, even though the wall partitions between thc passage and adjacent chambers only rise to the eaves, leaving an open space beneath the hip. Unlike the sheathed central passage, the central chambers have exposed framing members, planed and beaded in the typical Falmouth manner.

Beneath the third hipped roof, exposed framing of the partition wall reveals beaded timbers and suggests that the rear section of the house always consisted of two spaces. A circa 1900 shed-roofed addition on the north side of the back room is an additional bedroom. The attached bath, which can also be accessed from the northern chamber under the middle hip, may have been enclosed from the gallery.

Around 1900, a rear door on axis with the passage was cut into

FIGURE T4.16. 9 King Street eastern interior elevation, drawn by Kosova Kreka, 2010.

FIGURE T4.17. 9 King Street western interior elevation, drawn by Marilyn Moedinger, 2010.

the back room, which opens onto a narrow porch that connects to the twentieth-century kitchen, a shed attached to an adjacent house that faces Rodney Street. A 2007 survey of 9 King Street speculates that the neighbouring house was always a separate dwelling, a suspicion supported by the 1844 subdivision of the lot. The original 50-foot by 120-foot property was divided into eastern and western halves, and 9 King Street stands on the eastern portion while the house facing Rodney Street occupies the western part.

NOTES

1. Richard Barrett Waite, 13 June 1789, Inventories, Jamaica Archives, volume 74, folio 84.
2. Edward Barrett to Richard Barrett Waite, 20 August and 10 December 1782, Deeds, Island Record Office, volume 318, folio 42–43.
3. Deeds, Island Record Office, volume 1288, folio 372. Transcript of deed received from Elaine Melbourne (purchased land in 1996), former owner of 9 King Street.

FIGURE T4.18. 9 King Street western interior elevation, centre door, 2004.

Thomas Davidson House

1 King Street (*c.* 1822–1837, 1838, 1875–1900)

LAURIN GOAD AND EMILIE JOHNSON

Long assumed to have housed unmarried officers from the adjacent Fort Balcarres, recent documentary research tells a very different tale about the two-storey galleried house overlooking the harbour at the corner of Charlotte and King Streets. In 1822, William Wray and John Gairdner, merchants and partners, purchased an unimproved lot from Samuel Barrett Moulton Barrett for £100.[1] Presumably John Gairdner took control of the property and then died, because the next reference to the property is in the 1837 will of Mary Gairdner, a free woman of colour who was probably John's wife. To a Mr John Finney, who was away from Jamaica, Mary Gairdner gave "my Bay Creole House". If Finney did not return, the house reverted to her son, Thomas Davidson, who also inherited her residence and furnishings.[2] Apparently illiterate, Mary Gairdner signed her will with an "X" rather than with her name.

Like a number of free women of colour in town, Mary Gairdner was an extensive landowner in Falmouth. In October 1800, Mary Gardner [*sic*], purchased a part of lot 55 on Upper Parade Street in the Reid Town section from John Baillie for £150.[3] Her will provided for each of her four children to remain in the houses where they were living at the time of her death in 1837.[4]

Today, the "bay" lot includes the large house, a two-storey, U-shaped structure facing the harbour, and two service buildings. A keystone over the east doorway bears the inscription August 1838, suggesting that whoever took control of the house after Mary Gairdner's death, either John Finney or Thomas Davidson, embarked on a significant remodelling or reconstruction campaign. Compared to other homes in Falmouth, this house is large; at 64 feet long with a 25-foot-deep central block and wings that extend an additional 13 feet, it occupies a significant percentage of the 50-foot by 120-foot lot. Much of the house was constructed of light red brick laid in Flemish bond, with several yellow-brick jack-arches. Portions of the brickwork were lime washed twice, first with ochre then a lighter ochre or white. The brick was then covered with lime stucco and scored to resemble ashlar stone. The upper stories of the two wings that project from the core of the house towards the south are frame and a portion of the east wing retains early beaded horizontal flush sheathing. The hipped roofs have a traditional roof crown, seen on buildings throughout Falmouth. A gallery surrounds the house on three sides. The balustrade on the upper level gallery features a decorative punched design and thin posts and appears to date to the late Victorian era; examples of the same

This entry depends on an extensive on-site field report and analysis of surviving historic fabric written by Edward A. Chappell in the summer of 2008.

pattern can be observed on buildings all over town. The interior of the house has not been documented; however there is an account of a grand stair curving up to the second storey from near the front door.

At the back of the property is a long, shallow service building measuring 64 feet 8½ inches by 12 feet 6 inches (see figure 2.32). A masonry partition divided the building into a 27-foot-long space and a second space that was 34 feet 9 inches. Currently, no evidence of a chimney is visible, though one could have been removed. It is also possible that the structure never had a chimney and cooking was done in smaller buildings previously on the site. One of these, a small service building, remains. Though also gutted and rendered with stucco, enough has fallen away to see rough masonry of yellow and red brick, laid primarily as headers.

NOTES

1. Samuel Barrett Moulton Barrett to William Wray and John Gairdner, 20 March 1822, Deeds, Island Record Office, volume 712, folio 108.
2. Mary Gairdner Will, 3 March 1837, Wills, Island Record Office, volume 117, folio 143.
3. John Baillie to Mary Gardner, 1 October 1800, Deeds, Island Record Office, volume 505, folio 154.
4. Mary Gairdner Will, 3 March 1837, Wills, Island Record Office, volume 117, folio 143.

FIGURE T4.19. Thomas Davidson House from Charlotte Street, 2009.

FIGURE T4.20. Thomas Davidson House, in Georgian Society of Jamaica, *Falmouth, 1791–1970* (Kingston: Georgian Society of Jamaica, 1970). Private collection.

11 Queen Street
(*c.* 1900–1925)

JUSTIN GREVING

Eleven Queen Street is a compound of four buildings, organized around a central courtyard. Although most of the buildings date to the early twentieth century, they retain the overall grammar and construction of earlier buildings and continue the tradition of carefully crafted small houses in Falmouth. An 1844 plat suggests that 11 Queen Street was a subdivision of an original Falmouth lot, a common practice throughout the nineteenth and into the twentieth century. The buildings are identified as Building A (house) at the front of the lot and left (south) of the main gate; Building B (toilet and kitchen) in the back of the lot; Building C (house) to the right (north) of Building B; and Building D (shop) in the front of the lot and right (north) of the main gate.

Building A opens onto the courtyard and contains a side-gabled roof over the house and shed roof over the porch. X-latticed rails and chamfered posts define the porch, with two doorways and attached casement windows centred on the façade of this small, symmetrical, refined house. Building A is likely the oldest of the four buildings and was in the worst condition when the entire courtyard was rehabilitated. The sills and floor were on the ground and suffered considerable termite damage. The house was taken apart and reassembled using any intact framing and trim and is now elevated on concrete blocks. Walls were nogged using salvaged materials from the original building.

Building B is a small concrete block building built during the third quarter of the twentieth-century with two doors that open onto the courtyard. This building houses a small cooking space while an adjacent concrete block building contains a shower/bath.

The second house, located towards the rear of the lot, has the same roofline and the same two-chambered plan with a central partition as Building A; its porch shares the same decorative features as the porch on Building A. Two centred doors punctuate the main façade while four windows, one on each side and two on the rear, illuminate the interior. The house is clad in hand-planed, straight-sawn, bevel-edged horizontal boards and is raised on concrete blocks like the other two wood-framed buildings. The studs and down-braces (and possibly corner posts) are butted and toe-nailed rather than joined, suggesting a construction date between 1890 and 1910.

To the right (north) of the main gate, Building D contains a front gabled room and adjoining shed-roofed side room. This building was most likely a shop built sometime during the early twentieth century. Both rooms open onto the courtyard and are lit from the sides and the

This entry depends on an extensive on-site field report and analysis of surviving historic fabric written by Edward A. Chappell in the summer of 2006.

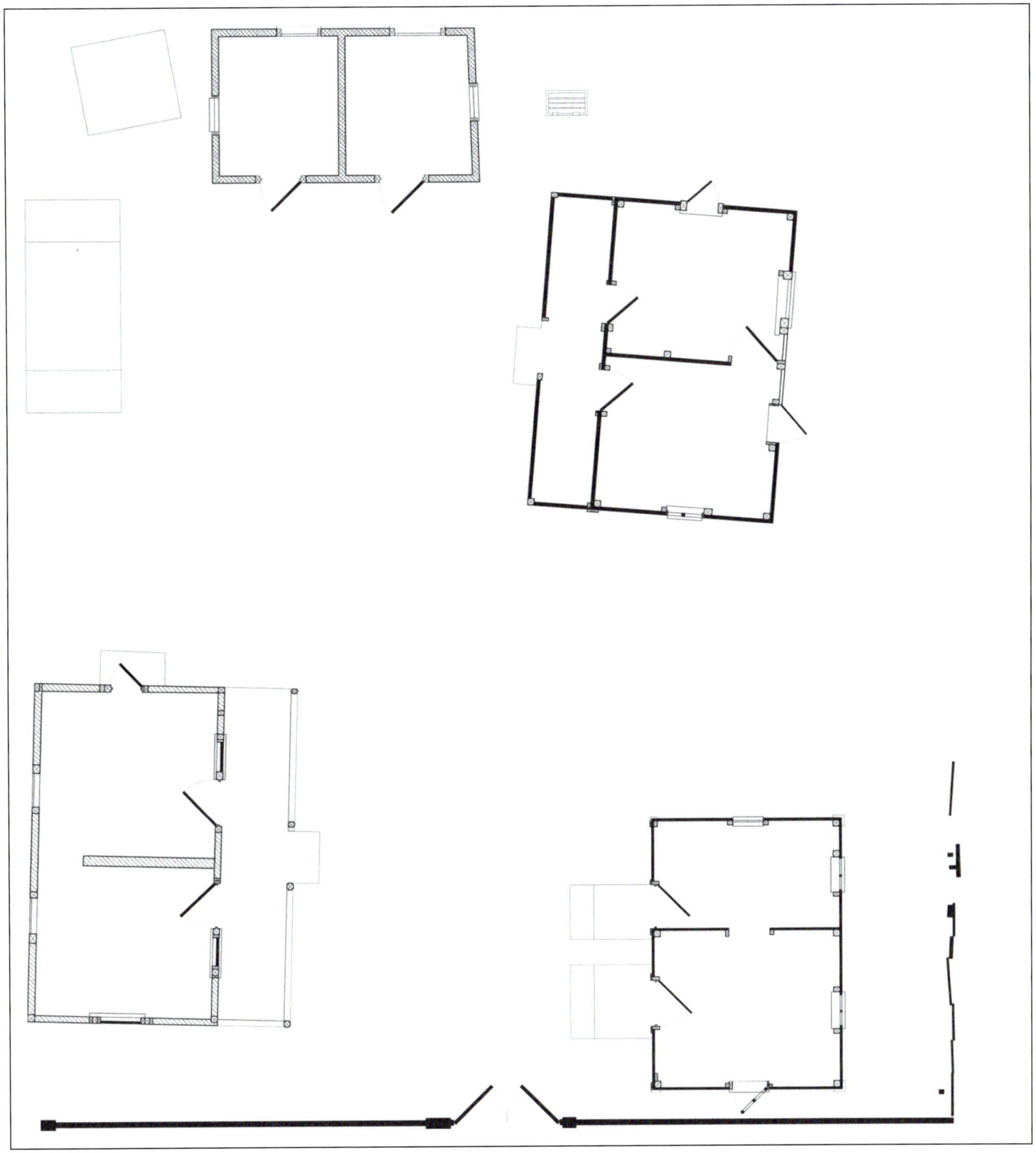

FIGURE T4.21. 11 Queen Street site plan (n.d.).

FIGURE T4.22. 11 Queen Street, 2005.

rear by casement windows; a doorway centred on the partition provides internal access between the spaces. Unlike the houses, mill-planed lumber frames the interiors; posts are butted and nailed to the sill and board plate on four sides, indicating a later construction date. The building is clad in a variety of hand-planed, likely recycled, bevel-edged siding. As the lower portion of the frame was termite ridden, the entire building was taken apart and reassembled using salvageable framing and wood finishes.

9 Princess Street

(*c.*1890–1930)

LEEANN DICKERSON

Nine Princess Street, located on the west side of Princess between Trelawny and Lower Harbour Streets, is a classic nogged (also called Spanish walled) middling house built between 1890 and 1930. While nogging – masonry used to infill a timber frame – was used in elite houses at the turn of the nineteenth century, it was widely used in all construction by the turn of the twentieth century. Compared with historic plats of Falmouth, it appears that this property sits on a subdivision of a lot, an example of changes in land use and domestic organization in Falmouth at the turn of the twentieth century. The house is set back from the street to create a small front yard, and rests on cast-in-place concrete piers. The framing members of each interior wall are joined together, showing that the house was originally built as the three-room dwelling that stands today.

A timber-frame building, the sills, corner posts, plates and studs have been secured with lap joints and cut nails. The down-braces, however, are simply butted and nailed together. All of the horizontal members, with the exception of the rear plate, are composed of short pieces, flat scarfed together and secured by pegs. The rear plate is a single large timber most likely recycled from an earlier house, mortised to allow for studs and posts, and slightly decorated on the interior with paint and beading. Other exposed wooden elements (door, window and wall trims) on the house's interior are also beaded, showing the continuation of this traditional finish into the twentieth century. Roof-framing members, however, are undecorated and left exposed on the house's interior. The original roof was shingled, but is now covered with corrugated metal.

The plan – typical for turn-of-the-century houses in Falmouth – consists of two large, adjacent rooms, approximately 9 feet 10 inches square, and a smaller room at the front right. A covered porch occupies the front left corner of the footprint and gives access to both the small front room and the large left room. Single doors connect each of the rooms on the interior and the large right room has a door to the outside at the rear. Windows in the larger rooms are six-over-six frame windows while the small front room features three-light casement sash windows, which may have been altered or replaced. The sidewalk to the house's north leads to a newer, occupied and well-maintained house directly behind the older structure.

This entry depends on an extensive on-site field report and analysis of surviving historic fabric written by Edward A. Chappell in the summer of 2008.

FIGURE T4.23. 9 Princess Street, 2006.

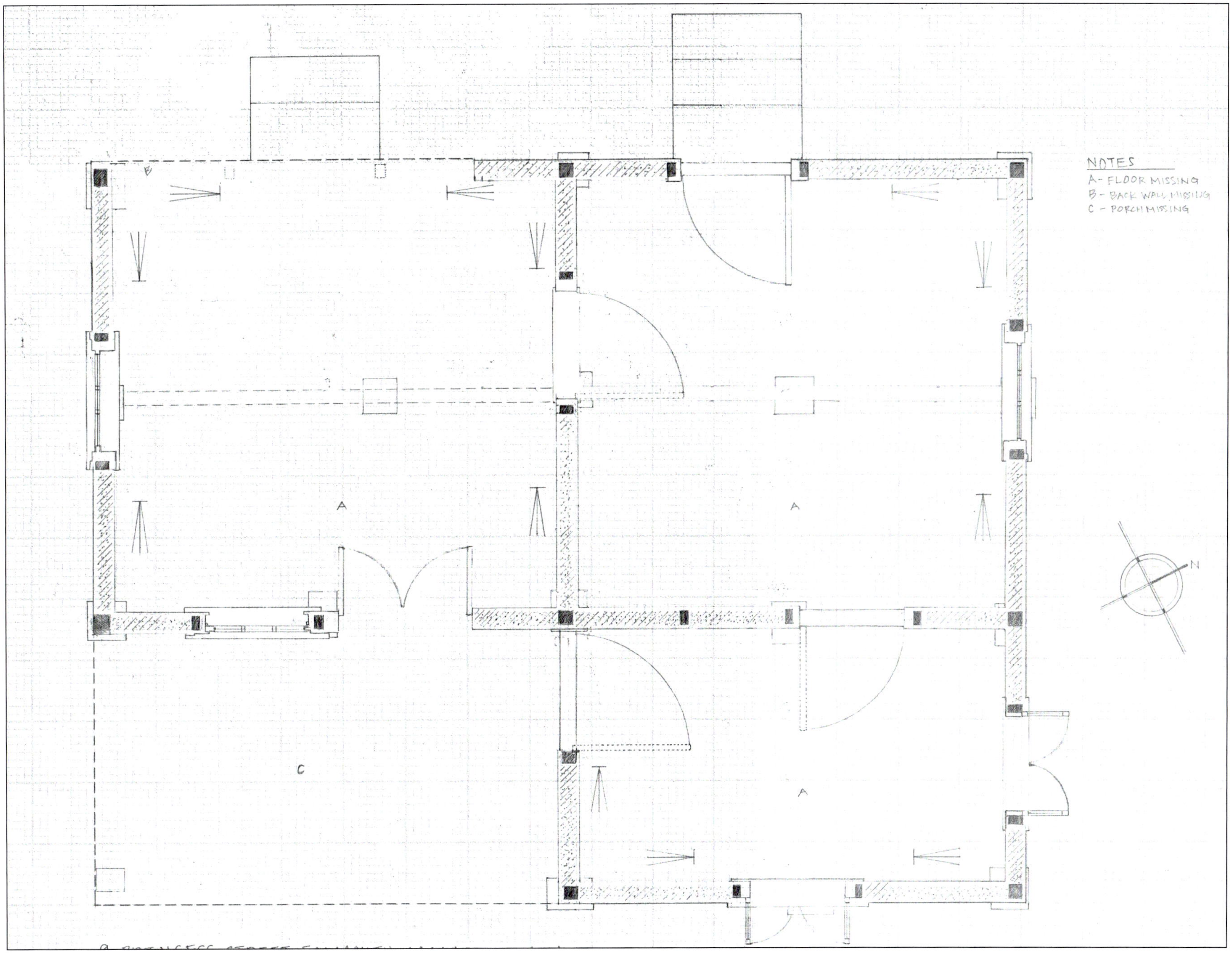

FIGURE T4.24. 9 Princess Street plan, drawn by Rachel Robinson, 2007.

8 Princess Street

(*c.* 1900–1925)

BRIAN L. COFRANCESCO AND EMILIE JOHNSON

The house at 8 Princess Street is an important survival of an early twentieth-century type of board house in Falmouth's historic district. Rather compact, it is approximately 20 feet wide by 12 feet deep. The house is a two-room building with front and rear entry into each room, with a communicating door between the chambers. Similar in size and materials to earlier Falmouth board houses, the situation of this house on its lot differentiates it from other examples. Earlier board houses tend to put their narrow ends towards the street with the primary doorway on the side façade, entered from a side yard. This house is oriented with the long side parallel to the street, with the front doors opening directly from the street. The shift in building orientation suggests a movement away from traditional building forms around the turn of the twentieth century; in fact, this house resembles standardized industrial housing found throughout the United States more than it does a traditional Falmouth house.

The front façade features two central doors, each with three panels of vertical beaded members. A shed-roofed porch, supported by concrete blocks, protects the doors from sun and rain. A railing surrounded the porch originally, however only a fragment to the right, a simple railing of undecorated horizontal members and vertical slats, remains.

Two six-light casement windows flank the doors, creating a symmetrical, four-bay façade. The structure is raised on cement block pillars, a common feature of many Falmouth houses, which allowed the house to be lifted and moved to a new site if rent became too expensive or relocation became necessary. The house is sheathed in horizontal clapboard siding with substantial beading, topped by a single hipped roof covered with corrugated tin.

The two interior rooms communicate via an off-centre, rear opening in the dividing wall. In addition to the casement windows on the front façade, sash windows on each side wall provide additional light into each room. A partition has been erected at the rear of the left chamber, which creates a narrow entrance space from the back door. A set of cement stairs leads from the back doors to a rear yard and work space where an outdoor cooking area remains.

FIGURE T4.25. 8 Princess Street elevation, drawn by Thomas Schaperkotter, 2007.

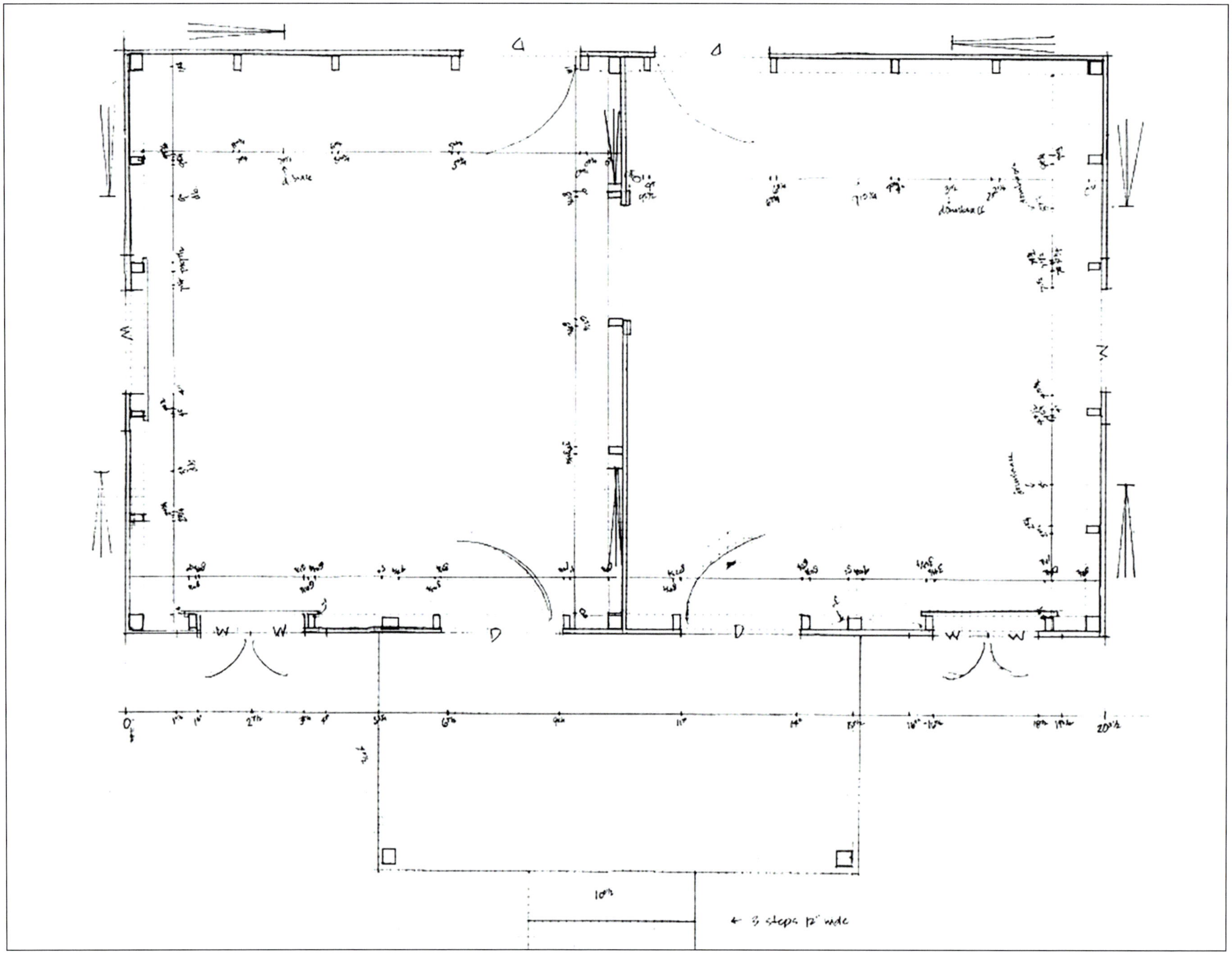

FIGURE T4.26. 8 Princess Street plan, drawn by Kristin Hennings, 2007.

29 Cornwall Street

(*c.*1800–1825)

KRISTIN ROURKE AND BRIAN L. COFRANCESCO

Two carpenters, Robert and William Hunter of Trelawny, purchased three lots on Cornwall Street from Edward and Judith Barrett on 22 September 1797, paying £280 Jamaican currency for the extensive property. A two-storey, double-pile house, 29 Cornwall Street was constructed in the first quarter of the nineteenth century and much of the original building fabric remains (see figure 2.27). The interior framing is planed, beaded and exposed, and most of the doors appear to be from the first period of construction. The building sits on a cut-stone foundation with fragments of raised mortar joints similar to those at the Baptist Manse on Market Street. The façade disregards traditional Georgian-style symmetrical fenestration by not having a central third opening on the upper floor. Instead, two three-part windows with early nineteenth-century louvres in the sidelights are evenly spaced across this storey.

Field studies estimate that alterations to the plan of the house were made in the second half of the nineteenth century. Prior to the alterations, the front door opened into a large front room in the northeastern corner of the house. A partition wall subdivided this room sometime in the later nineteenth century to create a central passage to the rear stair. Two chambers, a larger one in the northwest corner of the building with a smaller room behind, complete the ground-floor plan. The first-floor rooms do not have sheathed ceilings, however, the undersides of the second-storey floorboards have been planed and beaded for a more finished look.

The stairway rises to a large second-storey room which appears to have become the most formal public space after the renovations, when a partition was removed to create a space spanning the entire length of the east side of the house. The room boasts a tray ceiling and cornice, compared to exposed rafters in the other second-floor spaces. The presence of the two three-part windows on the upper storey suggests that these were the finest spaces in the house.

Behind 29 Cornwall is a small service structure, likely a kitchen, which has been greatly altered over time. The west wall is of yellow brick laid in Flemish bond and is contemporary with the main house; a framed north wall and a post in the southwest wall of the structure may also date to the early nineteenth century. The east and south walls are now cast concrete with the only fenestration being on the east wall (three windows and two doors).

The main house at 29 Cornwall is currently used as a daycare centre and the service building employed as a classroom. The home of a retired teacher in the late 1990s, the housc was repaired with funding from the Environmental Foundation of Jamaica.

This entry depends on an extensive on-site field report and analysis of surviving historic fabric written by Edward A. Chappell in the summer of 2002.

FIGURE T4.27. 29 Cornwall Street north elevation, drawn by Julie Robert, 2009.

23 Queen Street

(*c.* 1800–1825)

KATHRYN LASDOW AND KEVIN RIDDLE

Despite its present appearance as a modern concrete house, this building was once a small historic frame house. After the Falmouth Field School recorded the historic building in 2004, the structure was rebuilt in approximately the same massing, but entirely in concrete block. The site is an example of the loss of historic fabric that will slowly erode Falmouth's historic district unless the regulations of the district are more stridently enforced.

Originally, the structure contained two rooms, the larger common room later altered with partitions. Based on the building's placement on the property, it was evident that principal access to the interior was always located on the north side of the building facing the yard rather than from the street.

The northern façade was comprised of three bays defined by two doors and one window. It was fronted by a concrete porch which replaced an original wooden porch as evidenced by cuts in the sill that held the joists and planks of the porch floor. The eastern and southern façades were comprised of two bays – both with windows – atop a cut limestone foundation with original yellow-brick piers. The windows on both sides of the house demonstrated change from the original building period – the street-facing windows were taller and wider, while the easternmost window on the southern elevation was shortened. The western façade had an original window, but a door was later added.

The interior had an exposed roof-framing system with corner bracing in the wall frame in the building's interior. Mortise-and-tenon joints were used throughout the framing system, and were visible between the rafter pairs that met over the middle of the large common room. Beaded, first-period rafters, posts, studs and down-braces were on display in the two corners facing into the room.

Entrance into the interior was through a door on the north side of the structure. During the first-period, this door led into a large common room of approximately 15 feet by 22 feet. This large space led to two smaller chambers separated by a first-period partition wall with doorways allowing access into each back room. The first-period interior was sheathed by exposed planks of varying types. Although the planks on the lower walls were replaced, first-period boards survived higher near the plate, and showed evidence of distress from a jack plane. The sill on the northern wall and several of its mating members were chiselled with roman numerals to indicate their correct placement during the first building period. No evidence existed for original sashes or louvres, although several doors may have been first period. Both doors on the northern elevation had box locks in 2004. First-period tongue-and-groove floorboards were present in the southeast and northwest portions of the house.

FIGURE T4.28. 23 Queen Street (n.d.).

FIGURE T4.29. 23 Queen Street, 2005.

FIGURE T4.30. 23 Queen Street from the church tower, 2007.

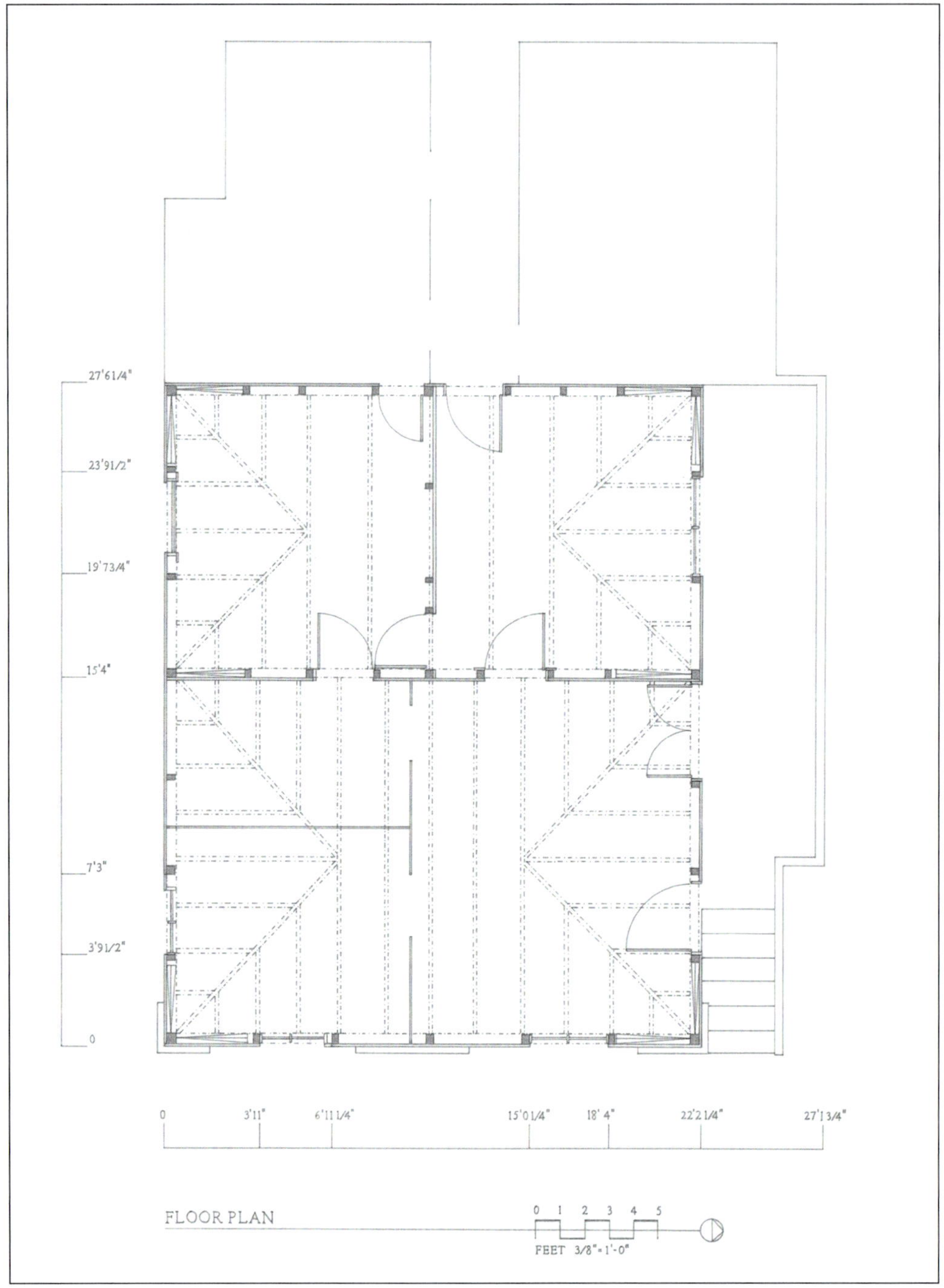

FIGURE T4.31. 23 Queen Street plan, drawn by Kevin Riddle, 2004.

16 Cornwall Street

(post-1820–1830, 1880–1920)

ANN PFUNTER AND EMILIE JOHNSON

Sixteen Cornwall Street is the result of three distinctive building phases over the course of the nineteenth and twentieth centuries. The oldest block is a now-buried south-facing, two-room house with a gable roof. Its situation deeply set within the lot is unusual and suggests that it might have been moved; small, early houses were usually constructed much closer to the street. While some large houses are recessed from the street, it is likely that this oldest portion of the house was at one point moved back from the street to its present location.

The framing finish suggests that this portion's original construction postdates 1820–30. Framing members are fully planed, but posts, braces and studs remain unbeaded, while the plates, central joist, upper stud in the partition, and rafters are all beaded. Posts and studs are tenoned and pegged, while braces are not visibly pegged. Particle board now covers the rafters, which remain unpainted.

Entry into the oldest portion of the house was likely through a door centred on the south wall of the east room and hung on small HL hinges. The door's superiority is evident from the rails and battens moulded with thin, Greek-inflected cymas and angled fillets. This original principal door gives entry to the best room, to the east, or right, in the original structure. A beaded board door hung on small HL hinges at the north end of the partition opened into the lesser room, to the west in the two-room core. The superior room had a window on what is now the east short wall; in the west room, a sill slot in an early stud indicates the existence of a centred window on what was the south-facing wall. The core now has two north doorways with only the twentieth-century fabric exposed; the associated wall framing is hidden.

The house grew substantially with the addition of three rooms and a porch to the south between 1880 and 1920. The addition consists of two rooms directly adjoining the southern wall of the old block, a large entry room centred between the two and a Victorian-detailed porch, which surrounds the western, southern and eastern walls of the front room.

The main entry is a six-panel door, with panels raised inside and out. The door has a decorative sawn and unglazed transom within a beaded frame that incorporates the flanking windows. The front room is filled with light from six-over-six windows on the west and east walls and flanking the front door. The rear rooms are darker, lit only by one end window in each room. The three new rooms maximize circulation between each

This entry depends on an extensive on-site field report and analysis of surviving historic fabric written by Edward A. Chappell in the summer of 2008.

FIGURE T4.32. 16 Cornwall Street, 2007.

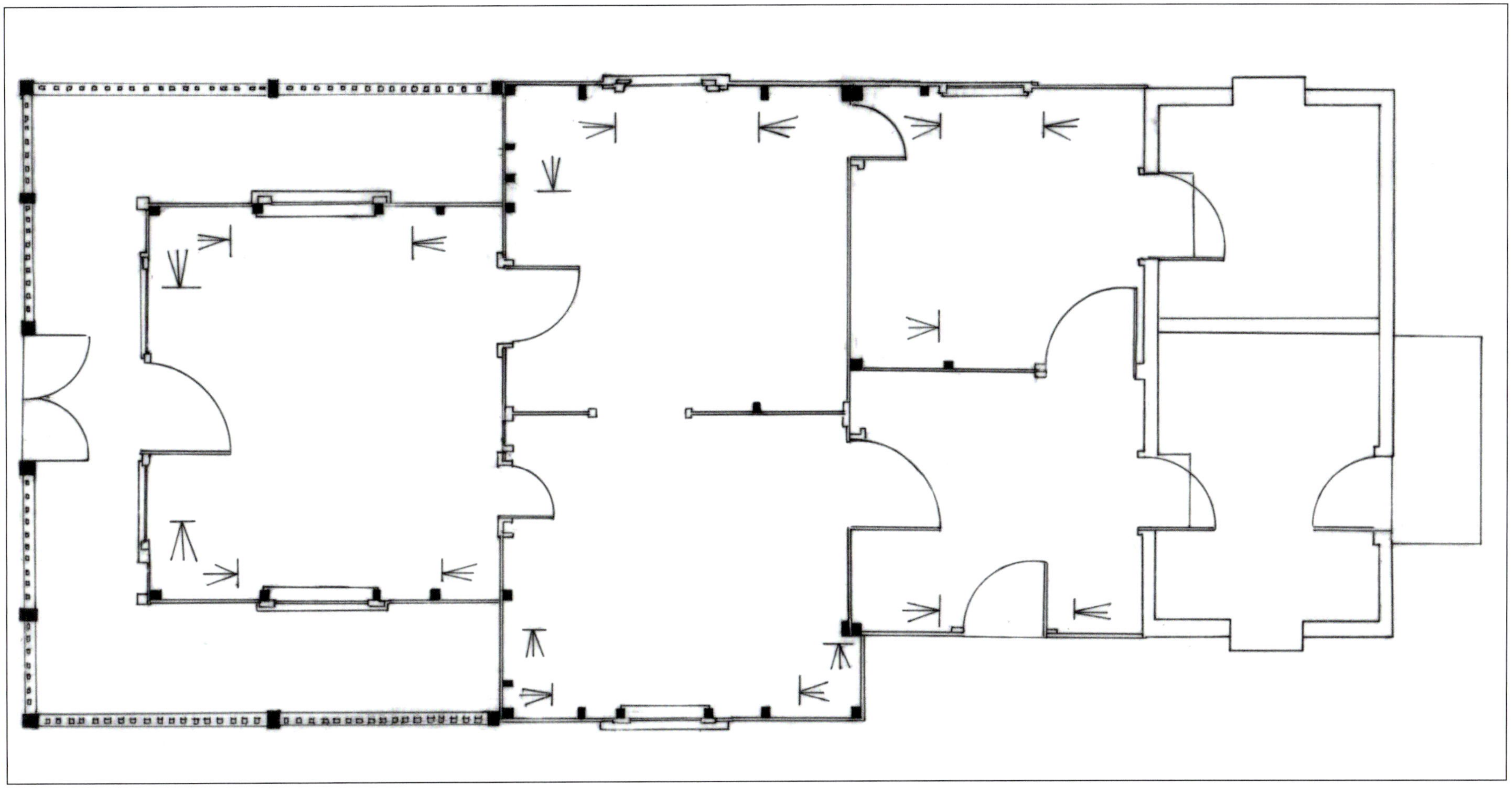

FIGURE T4.33. 16 Cornwall Street plan, drawn by Jacqueline Taylor, 2008.

other and between the new and old sections of the house. The front room opens into both of the new rooms, which open into each other and to the two old rooms.

The modern, two-room addition behind the core structure, adds two more chambers to the house. The smaller west room, has the most limited access of any room in the house. The room behind the original east room has a doorway to the yard in the back of the house. These spaces may have been added to accommodate kitchen and bathroom facilities.

18 King Street

(*c.*1790–1820)

LAURIN GOAD

In 1778, Samuel Smith, a merchant, purchased lots 63 and 64 from Edward Barrett for £100.[1] Lot 63 is the property that extended up to Duke Street that was later subdivided into at least three lots; lot 64 extended to Cornwall Street. As a result, Smith and another merchant owned the entire block of King Street between Cornwall and Duke Streets. Probably completed between 1790 and 1820, this house represents a subdivision of lot 63 and shares basic spatial distributions with Falmouth's typical merchant storehouses, with commercial space on the lower level and residential quarters above. The materials and plan, however, offer striking distinctions from the norm. Originally a double-pile building with two hipped roofs, only the front rooms survived to be documented by Falmouth Field School students in 2006. Fragments of the rear set of rooms indicate renovations to the building in the mid-nineteenth century. The abandoned building came down in a hurricane in 2008. It was a rare survival of a distinctive form, and its collapse and subsequent looting of materials was a significant loss.

Unlike the traditional Falmouth merchant storehouse, with masonry structure below and a framed upper storey, this building was framed on both levels. Its location off both Duke and Market Streets suggests that it probably housed the family and shop of a less prominent merchant, and may have been built as a rental property given a much-altered twin house in the adjacent lot. The foundation was yellow brick, laid in English bond, and the double stair from the street to the entrance level was brick and stone. Clapboards, secured with rose-headed nails, originally sheathed the building but were later covered with wood shingles. The clapboards provided evidence for the back rooms, as a few pieces continued past the corner of the building.

The lower floor was entered through double front doors, which suggested the commercial use of the space. Inside, the large storeroom opened into rear spaces that most likely functioned as an office and a smaller storeroom. The interior of the lower level had exposed framing and was simply planed.

According to locals, a U-shaped stair on the left side of the building gave access to the upper floor, into a smaller rear chamber before entering the front left room through an elaborate arched doorway. At some point, another stair was built, connecting the storeroom below to the smaller front room above. Originally, the framing of the upper rooms was exposed with planed and beaded rafters. Portions of the plate were painted, while the rafters were whitewashed. The second-floor interiors

This entry depends on an extensive on-site field report and analysis of surviving historic fabric written by Edward A. Chappell in the summer of 2006.

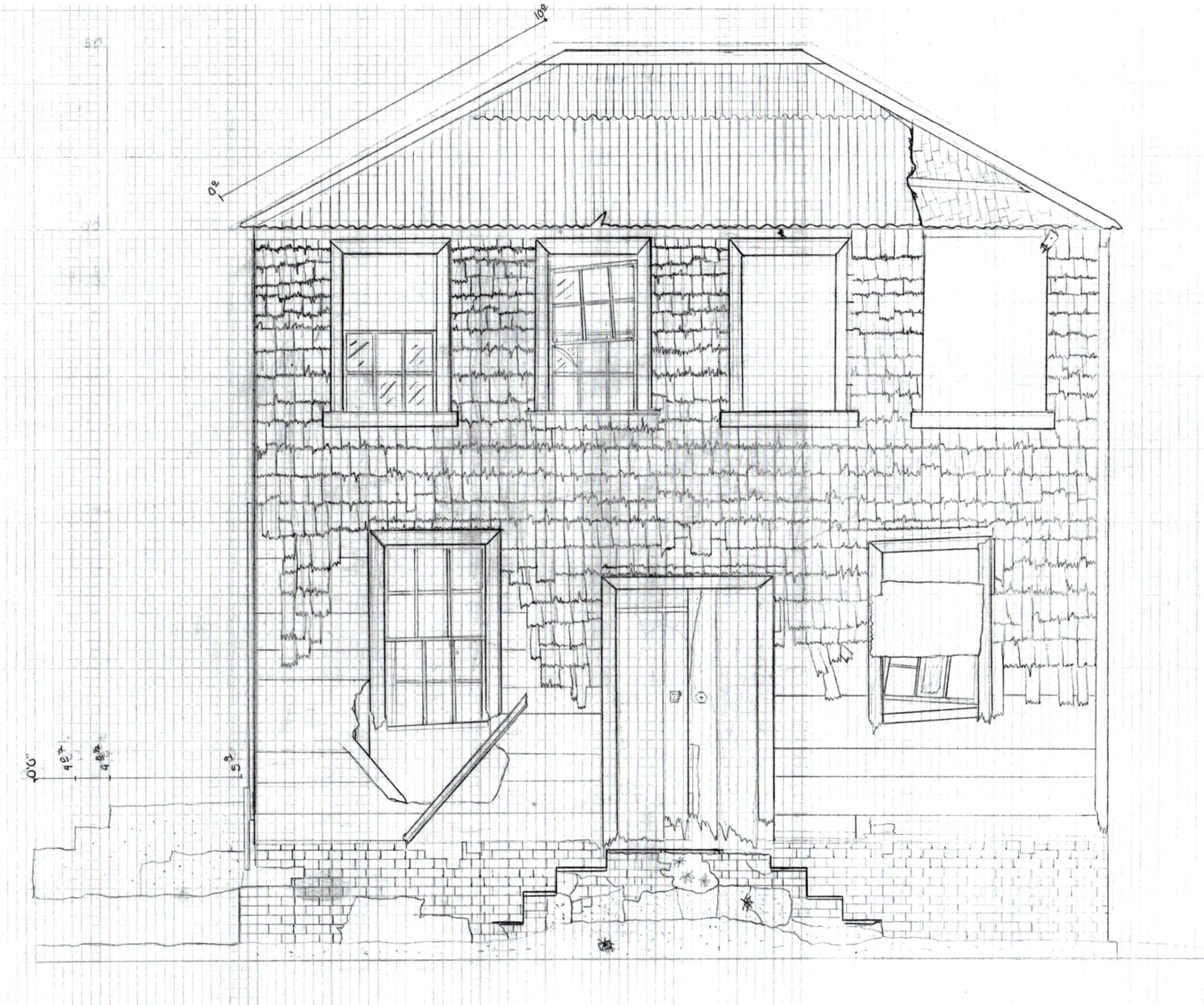

FIGURE T4.34. 18 King Street west elevation, drawn by K.D. Klepper, 2006.

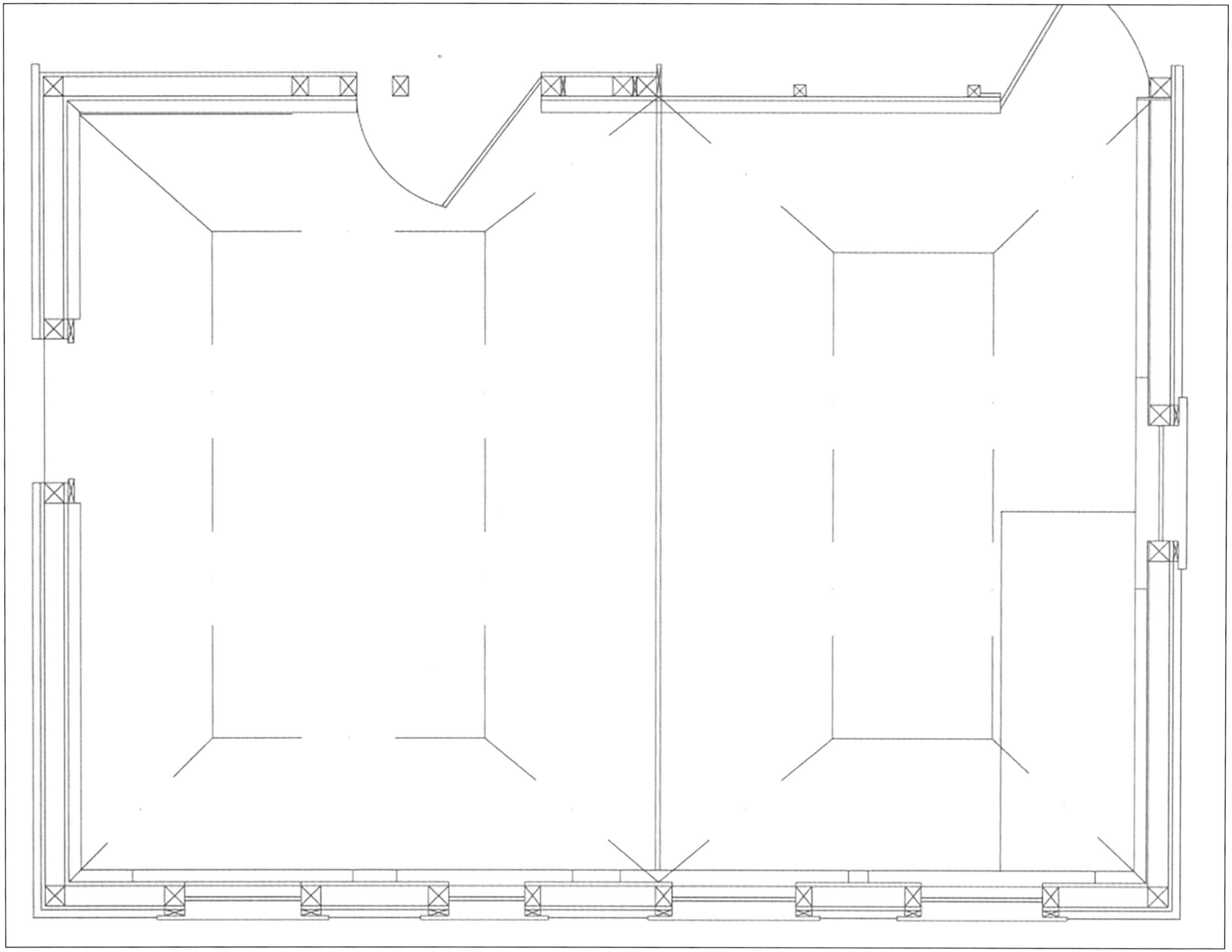

FIGURE T4.35. 18 King Street second-floor plan, drawn by Kristina Bookall, 2006.

FIGURE T4.36. 18 King Street, 2005.

dated to a renovation in about 1825, which included covering the framing and adding decorative details such as a wainscot and entablature. The roof framing was enclosed by tray ceilings over each of the front, upper rooms. The rear rooms of the upper floor were more simply sheathed.

NOTE

1. Edward Barrett to Samuel Smith, 1778, Deeds, Island Record Office, volume 304, folio 113.

FIGURE T5.1. Map of Duke Street.

TOUR 5

Duke Street

EMILIE JOHNSON

In addition to serving as the main coastal road into town from the west, Duke Street has always been one of the main commercial arteries in Falmouth. At the eastern end, closer to Market Street, refined two-storey buildings line the street. As one moves west, the landscape diversifies. One of the grandest houses of the late eighteenth century is 20 Duke Street, a striking example of a fashionable townhouse emulating urban English models. Duke Street also boasted the tavern owned by free black tavern-keeper Thomas Neale. But equally, if not more important, are the small, two- and three-room board houses that typify much of Falmouth housing in the early to mid-nineteenth century. The grand Anglican church with its soaring clock tower is on Duke Street, as well as the Jewish burial ground, located far to the west.

Duke Street had two distinctive periods of development. Edward and Judith Barrett sold lots in the blocks between Market Street and Princess Street from the 1770s through the 1790s, beginning with the lots surrounding the intersection of Duke and Market Streets and expanding westward in the ensuing decades. Again, in the 1810s, Samuel Barrett Moulton Barrett sold lots on Duke Street between Princess and Pitt Streets, with lots in the blocks between Pitt and Victoria Streets selling in the 1830s.

Historic deeds, especially the eighteenth-century lot sales of Duke Street, reveal a racially and socially integrated urban landscape. In the three blocks along Duke Street between Market and Princess Streets, most of which sold between 1775 and 1785, there were four carpenters, three gentlemen, two spinsters, a merchant, a planter, a tavern-keeper, a butcher, a mason, a free mulatto woman and three free mulatto men. While some of these people built on their lots and others purchased them as investments, the diversity of ownership offers a more representative mix of the town's population than did Market Street at the turn of the nineteenth century.

Duke Street was and remains one of the most vibrant streets in town, with shops, services and restaurants on the ground floor of many of its historic buildings and living quarters located on the upper stories. A testimony to Duke Street's continued importance is the presence of the newspaper sellers, purveying copies of the *Gleaner*, the most widely read Jamaican newspaper, from the corner of Duke and Market Streets.

William Knibb Memorial Baptist Church

King Street (*c.* 1944)

KATELYN CRAWFORD

The twentieth-century William Knibb Memorial Baptist Church stands on the site that has housed the Baptists in Falmouth since their first chapel, built in 1831 and destroyed in 1832. The church that replaced the chapel in 1836 was demolished by a hurricane in 1944, after which the present structure was built, incorporating material from the nineteenth-century church. Though no image survives of the first chapel, a lithograph of the second church betrays its sophisticated Greek Revival detailing.

The significance of William Knibb Memorial is largely historical, as these destroyed nineteenth-century buildings, their ministers, and the Baptist community engaged in the struggle for emancipation of Jamaica's enslaved population. Baptist missionary John Rowe was active in Falmouth and broader Trelawny by 1814 and received a permit from the parish vestry to open a Nonconformist (non-Anglican) school in April of that year. He died in 1816, leaving Falmouth without a Baptist minister. In 1827, Thomas Burchell arrived in Falmouth to found the congregation. He and his successor, James Mann, were welcomed particularly by slaves. Mann died after a short but successful ministry in 1830.[1]

The English Baptist minister William Knibb (1803–1845) arrived as a missionary in Jamaica on 5 November 1824 with his new wife, Mary Watkins. Originally sailing to replace his brother as a missionary and schoolmaster, Knibb worked at the Baptist mission school in Kingston before moving to Savanna-la-Mar in 1828. In March 1830, he arrived in Falmouth with his wife and two children to assume the responsibilities of minister at the Baptist church.

Best known as an advocate for abolition, Knibb often defended black slaves' rights. When he arrived in Jamaica in the 1820s, Knibb, other Baptists, and the Methodists opposed the House of Assembly's re-enactment of the Consolidated Slave Law which, by prohibiting the assembly of slave congregations and taxing Nonconformist churches, sought to prevent slaves from inciting rebellions.[2] Knibb also publically defended Sam Swiney, a falsely accused slave, first by publicizing his case in an island newspaper and eventually by advocating to the secretary of state for the colonies in London; the secretary ultimately dismissed the magistrates responsible for Swiney's wrongful conviction.[3] In addition to preaching, Knibb was known for teaching slaves how to build houses. Records show that Knibb bought more than one hundred acres at Granville Pen, a cattle farm in Trelawny, which was subdivided and sold as lots, possibly to former slaves in Falmouth who belonged to his church.[4]

FIGURE T5.2. William Knibb Memorial Baptist Church, 2009.

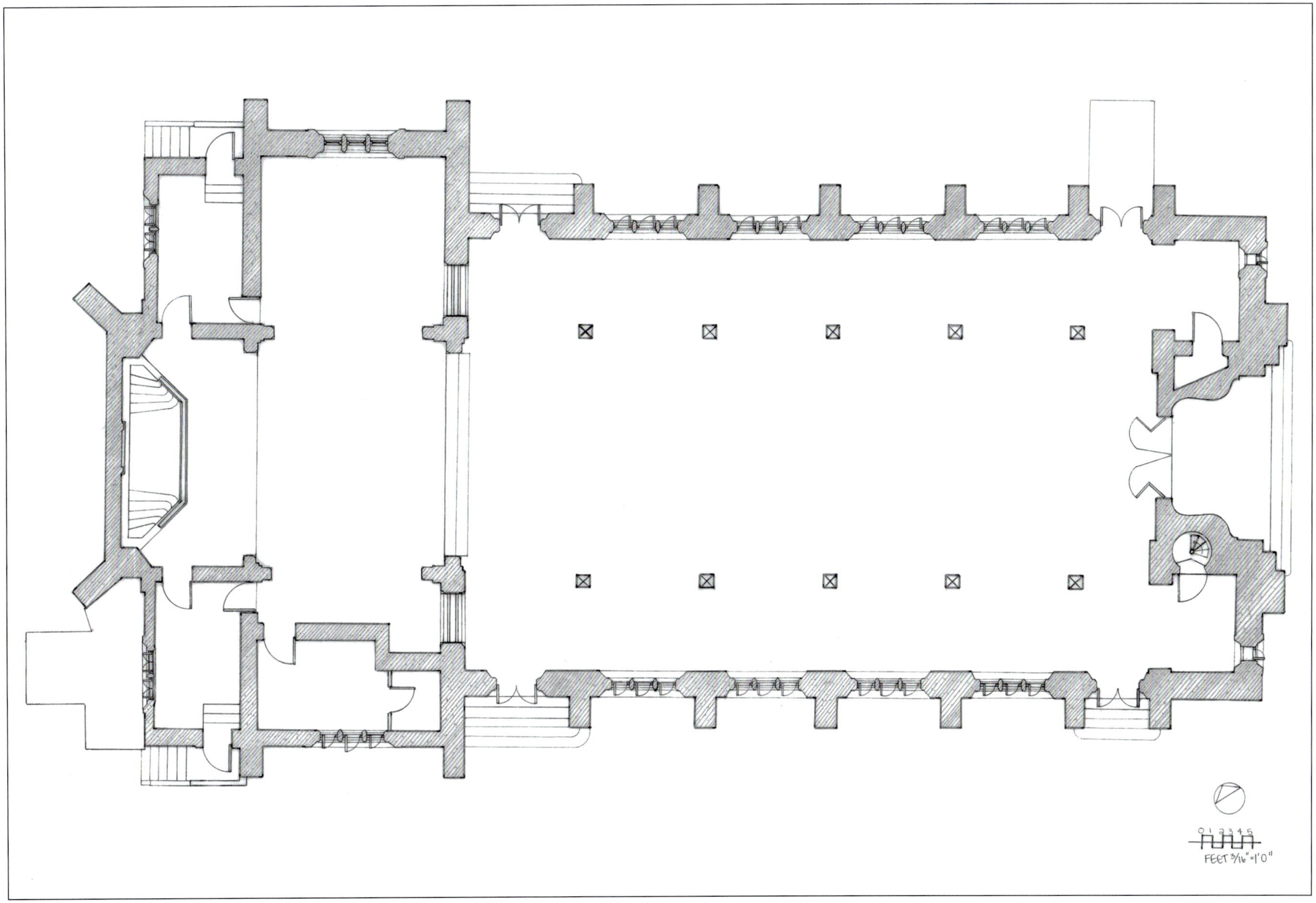

FIGURE T5.3. William Knibb Memorial Baptist Church, plan drawn by Susie Ranney, 2010.

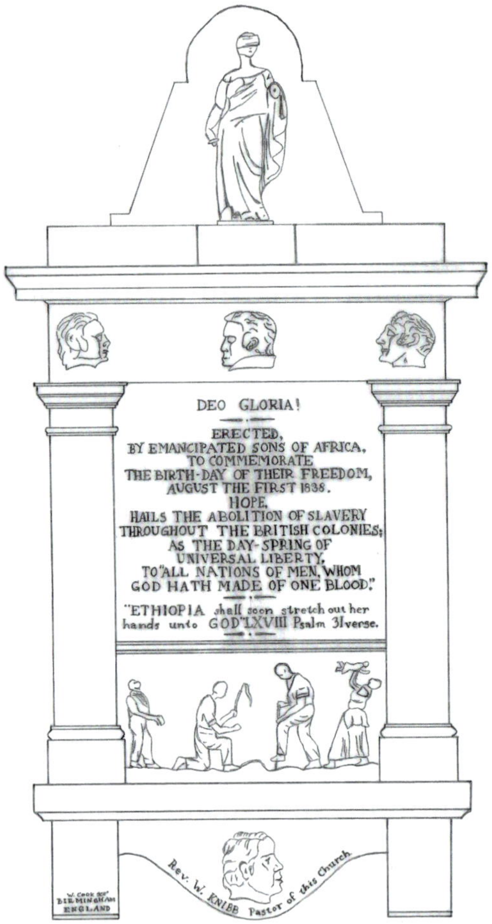

FIGURE T5.4. Emancipation memorial, William Knibb Memorial Baptist Church, drawn by Kelsey Reynolds, 2010.

FIGURE T5.5. William Knibb monument, William Knibb Memorial Baptist Church, drawn by Anna Danz, 2010.

In January 1832, Knibb used the Falmouth Baptist chapel as a barracks for the St Ann's regiment during the Great Jamaican Slave Revolt. The revolt, led by a slave named Samuel Sharpe, encouraged as many as sixty thousand of Jamaica's three hundred thousand enslaved persons to rebel. Magistrates and officers of the militia suppressed the events. As the militia prepared to leave Falmouth on 7 February, John W. Gaynor, a magistrate and ensign, Adjutant Samuel Tucker and the Colonial Church Union encouraged their men to demolish the chapel, making it one among many across the island destroyed after aiding the insurrecting slaves.[5]

Knibb was sent back to England by the Baptists of Jamaica in 1832 to plead their cause and fight for emancipation. Knibb travelled to public meetings in England and Scotland and discussed the work being done by the Baptist church for slaves in Jamaica. In May 1833 the Bill for the Abolition of Slavery in the Colonies was introduced in Parliament, and on 1 August 1834, slaves throughout the British empire were liberated. Knibb returned to Falmouth later that year.[6]

A system of apprenticeships took effect in Jamaica, and full emancipation was ultimately achieved in 1838. With full emancipation came the Jamaican Awakening, a religious revival lasting from 1838 to 1845 that involved the baptizing of twenty-two thousand former slaves as Baptists, including six thousand by Knibb. The Baptists in Jamaica also built forty-seven new chapels during this revival, and Knibb's church congregation grew from 650 to 1,280 members.[7]

In 1836, Reverend William Knibb erected a chapel 80 feet by 60 feet that seated three thousand people and five hundred Sunday school children, and cost nearly £16,000 to build. This church survived decades of storms and hurricanes until it was destroyed by the cyclone of 20 August 1944.[8]

Two monuments originally placed within this second structure survive today at William Knibb Memorial Church. The first recognizes emancipation, "erected, by the sons of Africa, to commemorate their freedom, August the first 1838". Imported from Birmingham, England, this neoclassical marble monument depicts both leaders of the efforts for abolition and daily activities of former African slaves. The second monument was erected in memory of William Knibb and, while undated, both its neoclassical style and devotion indicate a mid-nineteenth-century date. Knibb died of yellow fever in Jamaica on 15 November 1845 and eight thousand African Jamaicans attended his funeral at Falmouth's Baptist church. Commissioned by emancipated slaves, his funerary monument not only praises Knibb's work for abolition, but also his preaching and ministering.

NOTES

1. Daniel L. Ogilvie, "History of the Parish of Trelawny" (manuscript, 1954), ch. 8. Available at http://www.jamaicanfamilysearch.com/Samples/histre.htm.
2. Peter Masters, *Missionary Triumph over Slavery: William Knibb & Jamaican Emancipation* (London: Wakeman Trust, 2006), 15.
3. Ibid., 13–15.
4. Ogilvie, "History", ch. 8.
5. Masters, *Missionary Triumph*, 23.
6. Ibid., 39.
7. Ibid., 47–48.
8. Ogilvie, "History", ch. 8.

19 Duke Street

(*c.* 1875–1925)

EMILIE JOHNSON

Nineteen Duke Street was a single-storey house that sat mid-block between King and Queen Streets, directly across from the large townhouse at 20 Duke Street. Sadly, no deed information on the property has come to light, but treatment of the framing members, the presence of wire nails, the decorative treatment of the transoms and porch balustrade suggested a very late nineteenth-century or early twentieth-century construction date for the house. The house burned in 2008 soon after being recorded by the University of Virginia's Falmouth Field School, leaving only the brick piers and masonry steps as evidence of its presence.

The porch extended all around the house, except in the southwestern corner where there was a small room, only accessible from the porch, which may have been faced with reused clapboards from elsewhere in the house. A window opened from the back façade into the small patio room, suggesting the room was an addition. Wrap around porches are not common in Falmouth, but the sawn decorative balustrade was an example of Victorian era woodwork observed all over town, including the Thomas Davidson House at 1 King Street.

Both front and back façades had a central doorway, highlighted like the window frames and the plate, by a different paint colour. Paint was also used to suggest a sill at the lowest clapboard. The front double door had a transom, the back one did not. While the front façade had a symmetrical five-bay system the back had asymmetrical openings – single door, double door, narrow casement window, single door and blind window.

Raised 4 feet from the ground, the sills, joists and floorboards were attached to the brick piers; the studs, posts and down-braces seemed to float on top of the platform. The roof was fully exposed to show a common rafter roof system in one unit over the entire interior of the house. Two collar beams connected the rafters that sit directly on top of the non-corner posts on the front and back of the house, and a perpendicular collar beam ran out to the east and west sides of the roof. The ceiling rafters were joined to the plate by bird-mouth lap joints. Most studs, the plate, rafters, roofing elements and posts were all beaded. The building exhibited only wire nails.

The house had two rooms in front and three behind. The front door led into the largest room, which occupied about two-thirds of the front half of the house. This room had two finished walls, opposite the double front door and windows and the partition wall that created the other front room. The smaller front room had only one finished wall, opposite the front windows. Based upon wall finishes, the large front room was the fanciest in the house, with the small front room close behind. From the street, passersby would have seen finished walls in both spaces. The back three rooms had exposed framing members, suggesting uses as private spaces for the family.

FIGURE T5.6. 19 Duke Street, 2006.

FIGURE T5.7. 19 Duke Street elevation, drawn by Josi Ward, 2007.

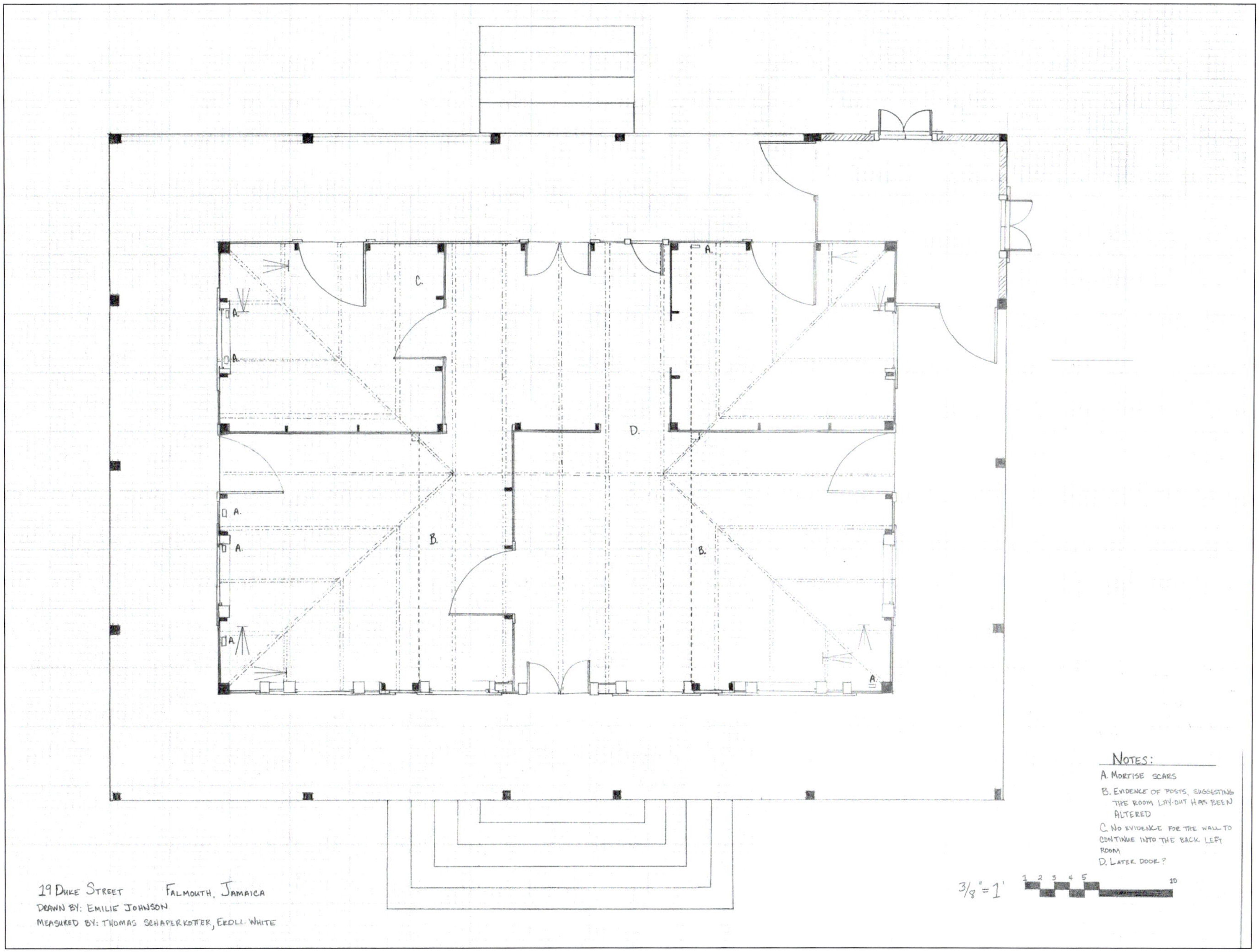

FIGURE T5.8. 19 Duke Street plan, drawn by Emilie Johnson, 2007.

20 Duke Street

(*c.*1797–1799)

SUSIE RANNEY

The house at 20 Duke Street is a residence unlike any other in Falmouth. It does not take the merchant storehouse form of a masonry ground floor with wood-framed upper storey found throughout the town. Rather, 20 Duke Street is a high-style Georgian townhouse, closer in architectural articulation and room usage to fashionable London and Dublin houses of 1800 than to its Falmouth neighbours.

James Hardyman, an esquire to the port, purchased the lot from Edward Barrett on 2 April 1797, and he likely built this house in the two short years between that purchase and the purchase of an insurance policy on the property on 15 May 1799. The policy details the buildings around the house; sadly, the description of the house – insured for an enormous £1,500 – has gone missing, but it describes "A range of Offices timber and shingled situate at the extremity of the same lot" and "Another range of Offices timber and shingled situate between the above House and Offices and at right angles with both", valued at £500.[1] The evidence for that range of offices can still be seen as partition scars in the perimeter property wall.

This entry depends on an extensive on-site field report and analysis of surviving historic fabric written by Edward A. Chappell in the summer of 2003.

James Hardyman died in Ireland in 1802. In his will, he designated John Burke to care for the house in Falmouth until it could be sold for a sufficient price. He also stated that if his kinsman Andrew Hardiman should go into the mercantile line of business, he should have rights to live in the Falmouth house for three years, rent-free, provided he did not sustain a loss.[2] Sadly, Hardyman's probate inventory does not list any of the furnishings in the house.[3]

On Duke Street, between King and Queen Streets, the house and property walls are constructed of yellow brick laid in Flemish bond. The property is a large lot with the main house on Duke Street and ten to fifteen ancillary rooms in two outbuilding rows on the north and west walls. Presumably the stables and carriage house, this area opens to King Street via an 11-foot-wide, round-arched carriage passage. Though not the largest in town, the house has a substantial footprint, 38 feet wide by 46 feet deep. The only original exterior door is located on the north façade, accessible through the courtyard; a mid-nineteenth-century addition of a door on the southern façade provided street access into what might have functioned as a business office.

Some of the richest architectural detailing in Falmouth is featured at 20 Duke Street. Double doors provide entry into the house, where a hallway opens into the large, formal reception room that occupies two-thirds

FIGURE T5.9. 20 Duke Street, 2009.

of the ground floor (see figures 2.29 and 2.30). A neoclassical mahogany stair complements the classical detailing in the architraves and cornices throughout the house and provides access to an elaborate entertaining area on the upper floor which occupies the same area as the first-floor reception room. The second floor features more sumptuous decoration than the ground floor, with painted faux panelling, contrasting paint colours, and a tray ceiling in the grand salon.

The builder indicated his plans for room usage through decoration and roof structure. The upper floor has two different roof systems masked on the exterior as identical, parallel, hipped roofs. However, the

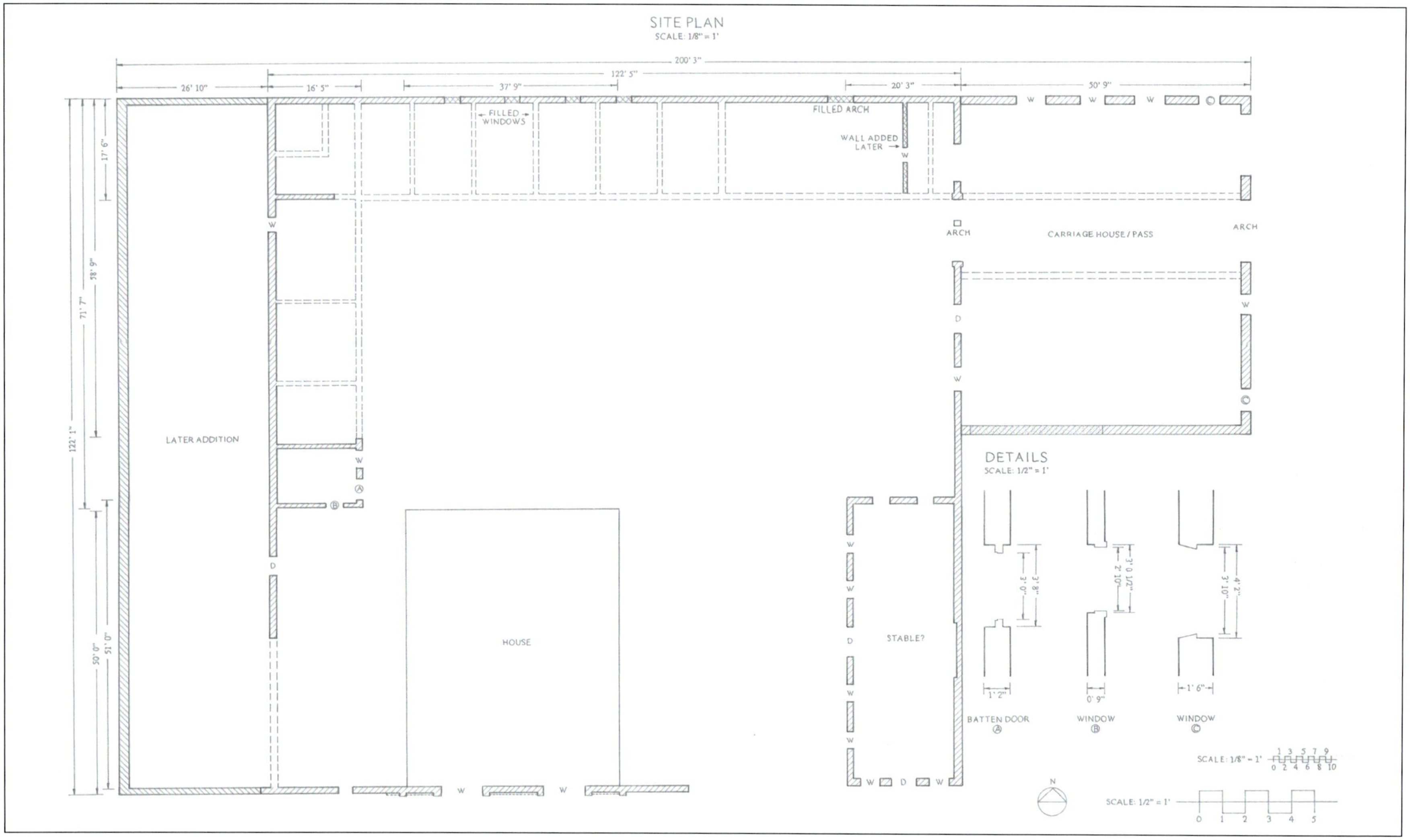

FIGURE T5.10. 20 Duke Street site plan, University of Virginia Field School, 2004.

roof over the southwest and middle rooms is comprised of minimal rafters covered by larger boards and painted masonry and plaster. A common rafter roof shelters the east rooms, but the rafters were coupled with joists to create a board ceiling in the southeast room. The upper reception room, the most refined room in the house, has a tray ceiling with beaded sheathing over its sumptuously embellished wall surfaces.

NOTES

1. Bristol Record Office (UK), reference no. 12151, Records of the Miles Family, 1800–1801.
2. James Hardyman Will, Wills, Island Record Office, volume 70, folio 107.
3. James Hardyman Inventory, Inventories, Jamaica Archives, volume 99, folio 19.

21 Duke Street

(*c.*1805–1825, 1890–1910)

WILLIAM CANUP AND EMILIE JOHNSON

In 1780, carpenter Thomas Hanlon purchased Barrett lot 87, on which this substantial home was later built. At the same time, Hanlon bought lot 73, located directly across Duke Street from this property, paying £100 Jamaican for the two parcels.[1] The sum of £50 Jamaican per lot in this part of Falmouth seems to have been the going price in the 1780s, as deeds record that people paid equal sums for surrounding lots during this period. It is uncertain how Thomas Hanlon used his Falmouth properties; we do not know if he built on the site, used it as a shop, or simply purchased these lots as a real estate investment. It seems unlikely that he built this house, which dates from the first quarter of the nineteenth century.

The exquisite masonry of this early nineteenth-century Georgian house is perhaps its most distinguishing feature. The three-bay façade contrasts yellow brick with the rose brick of the jack-arches. Unlike most brick houses in town, all four walls are laid in Flemish bond with generous use of closers and soldier brick where needed under the first floor windows. A two-course belt course – one course with all headers – separates the first and second floors. This Georgian house also features a base composed of squared limestone blocks and raised joints, resembling those at the Baptist Manse/Masonic Hall on Market Street.

It appears that the front double doors originally opened into what was the largest room, running the width of the house; a twentieth-century partition wall was later added to create a waiting room to satisfy the needs of a physician's office (see figures 2.21 and 2.22 for plans of 21 Duke Street). This large room is spanned by two planed and beaded traverse summer beams, which carry beaded longitudinal joists. These joists in turn form a base for tongue-and-groove floorboards, planed on both faces and beaded below. The first-floor bathroom walls are also a later addition and feature square louvres near the ceiling like those seen in about 1890 to 1910 Jamaican houses, suggesting that this portion of the plan was modified around 1900.

The interior moulding varies greatly from room to room and even from opening to opening, as a result of replacement and renovation over the years. The earliest and most prevalent type of moulding is a double architrave with an extra fillet or quirked ovolo and beaded backband which dates to 1805–25. A plain, open neoclassical mahogany stair rises in two runs at the southeast corner of the house, with moulded rails carried by square balusters and column-and-urn newels similar to those on the richer but now derelict stair at 20 Duke Street. The staircase cuts

---

This entry depends on an extensive on-site field report and analysis of surviving historic fabric written by Edward A. Chappell in the summer of 2004.

FIGURE T5.11. 21 Duke Street, 2009.

across a first-storey window because of the insistence on the preservation of the window-bay alignments and façade symmetry common in Georgian architecture.

At the top of the stairs, a pair of wide double doors with sunken-panel pilasters, turned bull's eye blocks at the intersections, and crown mark the entrance to a more stylized reception room overlooking the street. This Greek-flavoured detail is repeated inside the reception room with a costly dentil cornice which contrasts with familiar double architraves present in much of the rest of the house.

NOTE

1. Edward Barrett to Thomas Hanlon, 23 November 1780, Deeds, Island Record Office, volume 329, folio 176.

Neale Tavern

23 Duke Street (*c.* 1781)

BRIAN L. COFRANCESCO

This two-storey, masonry and timber-frame building was once the tavern of Thomas Neale and his wife, Eleanor, extremely wealthy tavern-keepers, plantation owners and free people of colour. The building's masonry ground level and timber-framed upper level echo the form of the merchant storehouse found throughout Falmouth. The ground floor likely included the tavern itself and probably housed tavern supplies and some spaces for lodging, with the Neale's living quarters and other available rooms upstairs. Its exterior street-front terrace – unique in this form in Falmouth – was likely a popular gathering place, allowing the activities in the tavern room to spill outside.

Neale purchased this lot from Edward Barrett on 10 September 1781 and built the tavern on the site. A 1796 probate inventory of Neale's possessions describes a lavish collection of tavern items, including 20 mahogany tables, 14 Windsor chairs, 10 bedsteads, 6 feather beds, 6 mattresses, 19 pillows, 6 lawn mosquito nets, 18 mahogany and walnut chairs, and 1 backgammon table.[1] Clearly, Neale ran a large and presumably successful tavern in the growing town of Falmouth.

The earliest reference to Thomas Neale is a plat, dated 12 February 1780, entitled "Rough Draught of the Cane Piece's at Jones' Castle Estate, the property of Mr. Thomas Neale". The plot of land shown was in the parish of Trelawny, and consisted of 49.1 acres divided into nine small sugar cane fields.[2] Until his death in early 1796, Thomas Neale continued to acquire land. By 1791, he owned 274 acres, much of which was his plantation in Trelawny. Neale's 15 March 1796 probate inventory listed him as the owner of "23 mules . . . 41 steers . . . 6 horses . . . 1 calf . . . 52 new hoes . . . 4 copper axes . . . 4 adzes . . . 13 hand saw files . . . 32 head of sheep", and as well as implements for processing sugar cane. This inventory also lists the names of ninety-six slaves that Neale owned, another testament to the incredible wealth of this free man of colour.[3]

After Thomas Neale's death, his property in Falmouth transferred to his wife, Eleanor, who held it until her death, although the lack of information in her probate inventory suggests that another person ran the tavern by 1806.[4] In her 5 June 1809 will, Eleanor was listed as owning land in Falmouth, no fewer than seven slaves and a sum of money to be divided among her children.[5]

The old, now-ruined tavern which stands on the southwest corner of Duke and Queen Streets is a rare artefact from the early development and prosperous period of Falmouth, just after its founding in 1769. More importantly, it tells the story of a successful entrepreneur and free couple of colour.

FIGURE T5.13. 23 Duke Street, 2007.

NOTES

1. Thomas Neale Inventory, Inventories, Jamaica Archives, volume 83, folio 262.
2. Estate Map T378, Special Collections, National Library of Jamaica.
3. Thomas Neale Inventory, Inventories, Jamaica Archives, volume 83, folio 262.
4. Eleanor Neale Inventory, Inventories, Jamaica Archives, volume 107, folio 59.
5. Her inventory listed ten slaves, who ranged in value from £100 to £200. The extent of her estate, as recorded in her inventory, was £1,300. By contrast, Thomas Neale's estate was valued at £20,131.6.8 . Eleanor Neale Will, Wills, Island Record Office, volume 76, folio 111.

FIGURE T5.12. 23 Duke Street, 2007.

28 Duke Street

(*c.*1800)

JENNIFER HUGMAN, LAUREN TRICE AND EMILIE JOHNSON

Located at the corner of Princess and Duke Streets, this single-storey, rectilinear building has a remarkable history. Its construction materials are a combination of original masonry and timber framing with poured concrete additions and a corrugated metal roof. The front bay of the house is made of traditional timber frame and local coquina stone, sedimentary rock composed primarily of shell fragments. Coquina is a material used in early Falmouth construction but abandoned by the mid-nineteenth century and is also found at the Neale Tavern and the Barrett House, both of which are buildings with secure late eighteenth-century dates. The 1844 Duperly lithograph of Falmouth from the Anglican church tower shows this building as a two-storey structure with a masonry ground floor and a wood-frame upper storey, now missing (see figure 2.2).

On 10 October 1793, Sarah McGhie, a free woman of colour, bought this lot from Edward Barrett for £90.[1] Wills or inventories for Sarah McGhie have not come to light, but she may have been related to James McGhie, a wealthy planter who owned three estates and 353 slaves in partnership with two others.[2] James McGhie was one of the executors for Thomas Neale, the wealthy free man of colour who owned the tavern at the corner of Duke and Queen Streets, one block from this house.[3] The exact relationship between Sarah and James McGhie is unknown, but the location of her house on racially and socio-economically integrated Duke Street and the presence of early building materials suggest that this house may have been built for Sarah McGhie.

Double doors centred on the front five-bay façade give access to a sizeable three-bay chamber in the southwest corner; a sense of openness is maintained from the open-air porch, through the wide double doors, into the large entrance chamber, and through the open doorway on the back wall that leads to the next room. The front chamber once led into a central hallway, presumably flanked by rear chambers like many other houses in town, as ghosting on the wall across from the front door shows an arched doorway that has since been walled over. The two front rooms have either masonry or finished board walls while the two back chambers have exposed frame walls, suggesting their subsidiary role to the front chambers.

This entry depends on an extensive on-site field report and analysis of surviving historic fabric written by Edward A. Chappell in the summer of 2008.

FIGURE T5.14. 28 Duke Street, 2005.

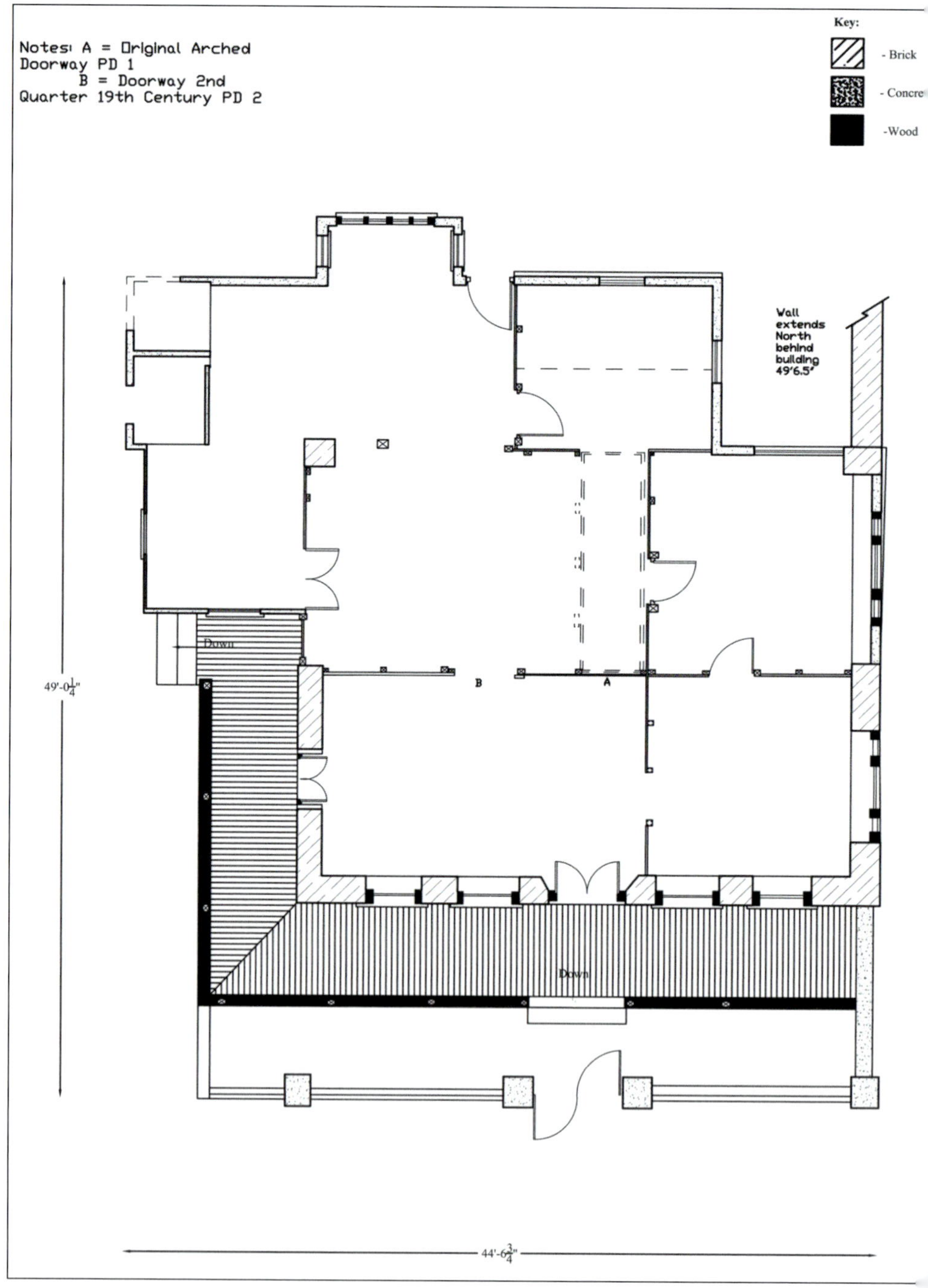

FIGURE T5.15. 28 Duke Street plan, drawn by Lauren Shepulski, 2006.

NOTES

1. Edward Barrett to Sarah McGhie, Deeds, 10 October 1793, Island Record Office volume 416, folio 68.
2. James McGhie Inventory, 18 April 1807, Inventories, Jamaica Archives volume 108, folio 131.
3. Thomas Neale Inventory, 15 March 1796, Inventories, Jamaica Archives volume 83, folio 262.

31 Duke Street

(*c.*1815–1835)

KATELYN CRAWFORD

Standing at the southwest corner of Duke and Princess Streets, 31 Duke Street is the smallest of the recognizably well-made and early houses in Falmouth and dates to approximately 1815–35 (see figure 2.4 for a photograph of 31 Duke Street). This two-room house measures 10 feet 1 inch by 17 feet 2 inches and is oriented towards its yard rather than the street.

The building is sheathed with wide weatherboards (10-inch to 11- inch exposure) which are straight, mill-sawn and planed only at the upper edge. The interior boards are set flush, with beads at their upper edges. There are other examples of this interior sheathing in town at 36A Cornwall and 7 Market Streets, however they lack beading. Wide 6-inch boards, beaded at the inner edge, are nailed over the weatherboards around the doors and windows to form outside frames. The joints below the board sills are covered with the flat boards common to Falmouth, and the original board that survived on the east wall has cyma mouldings. The external doors are also made of boards with cyma-edged stiles and rails nailed to the outer face to form six panels of conventional elevation, with wide lock rails and thin upper rails framing square upper panels. These doors, along with the simpler board-and-batten interior door, are hand planed.

The interior of the house is divided into a larger north and a smaller south room (see figure 2.5 for a plan of 31 Duke Street). Even before its restoration, the house showed careful and attentive craftsmanship, with virtually every wooden surface in the house planed and beaded. Two windows illuminate each of the rooms, with well-made six-over-six sash windows facing Duke and Princess Streets. Framing for some of the openings was renewed or rebuilt during the twentieth century, but in all cases, small mortises remain visible indicating the location of original studs that framed the openings.

The window sashes are well-made with boxed jambs that contain round weights hung on iron pulleys for the lower sash. The facing is beaded on the inner edges, but does not hide the studs (also beaded) to which it was attached. It is these windows, combined with the use of straight mill-sawn lumber, HL hinges and cut nails, that suggest the date of about 1815 to 1835.

Though there is little extraneous interior woodwork, the fully exposed frame was diligently planed and beaded, with the finish favouring the larger north room. The interior door between rooms is beaded on both sides, with bevelled battens and beaded studs exposed on the side of the

---

This entry depends on an extensive on-site field report and analysis of surviving historic fabric written by Edward A. Chappell in the summer of 2002.

smaller room. The partition between rooms has horizontal sheathing on the side of the larger room only, though it is planed and beaded on both sides. All of the studs and braces are exposed and beaded inside, more extensively than in some contemporary comparable or larger Falmouth houses. Some of the corner posts and studs were replaced in the twentieth century.

Clearly, in early nineteenth-century Falmouth, size did not define the level of finish and craftsmanship found in a residence. This small house shows an attention to construction detail not found in many larger dwellings. Deed research has shown that free black Jamaicans – or freed blacks after emancipation – were often the builders and residents of board houses like 31 Duke Street, indicating the socio-economic stability attained by some former slaves in the years after emancipation.

Falmouth Heritage Renewal restored the house in June 2004, retaining intact framing and finishes but replacing substantial portions of the wall and floor framing due to termite damage.

FIGURE T5.16. 31 Duke Street, 2007.

32 Duke Street

(*c.* 1800–1825, 1875–1925)

EDWARD BARNES

Falmouth contains a number of two-room timber-frame houses that date from the early nineteenth century. These buildings, thought to be the homes of Falmouth's sizeable free black artisan class, display quality workmanship and sophisticated finishes despite their small size. Though late nineteenth- and early twentieth-century additions have tripled this building's size, the hipped roof clearly marks the original two-room structure, a prime example of a Falmouth board house. The rectangular first-period core of the house measures 12 feet by 21 feet 6 inches. Typical of this housing type, the building has been situated on the lot with a narrow end facing the street to the south. Probably the location for entertaining, the formal function of the street-facing end is evident from the large tripartite, six-over-six sash window with flanking slender louvred openings that dominates the façade.

The east elevation, which overlooks the side work yard, contains the primary entrance with the door near the front end of the house. Immediately adjacent to the door is a six-over-six sash window smaller than the window on the south wall and lacking the tripartite configuration. Though now obscured by a late nineteenth-century shed addition, a large sash window originally overlooked the yard on the east elevation towards the rear of the house. By comparison to the south and east façades, the west elevation is relatively simple, featuring only two small evenly spaced sash windows. Before additional rooms were constructed at the rear of the house starting in the late nineteenth century, the north elevation contained the secondary entrance – a single, centrally located door that originally opened into the rear yard of the house. This basic fenestration plan of an impressive tripartite window facing the street, primary entrance on one side of the building facing a work yard, and secondary entrance at the rear is found in nearly all examples of this housing type in Falmouth.

On the interior, the first-period construction of 32 Duke Street is divided into two rooms. The primary entrance in the east wall opens into the front room, well lit by windows on the south, west and east walls. A partition wall of unornamented horizontal boards nailed to the south side of a row of studs separates the more formal front room from a smaller rear chamber. A door centrally located in the partition connects the two chambers.

As is common in Caribbean timber-frame construction, the substantial framing system of posts, studs, plates and braces are exposed on the interior; the high quality of workmanship is evident in this exposed timber frame. All of the framing members below the wall plates are planed,

---

This entry depends on an extensive on-site field report and analysis of surviving historic fabric written by Edward A. Chappell in the summer of 2008.

FIGURE T5.17. 32 Duke Street, 2007.

beaded and held together by mortise-and-tenon joints fastened with pegs. There is no ceiling and the beaded rafters, shingle lath, and the underside of the wood shingles are also visible. However, the visual effect of the exposed rafters is diminished due to the absence of paint above the wall plates. Often in the Caribbean, houses are constructed without ceilings to allow hot air to circulate throughout the building. The need for good air circulation influenced the construction of the partition wall between the front and rear rooms of the house; the board wall of the partition termi-

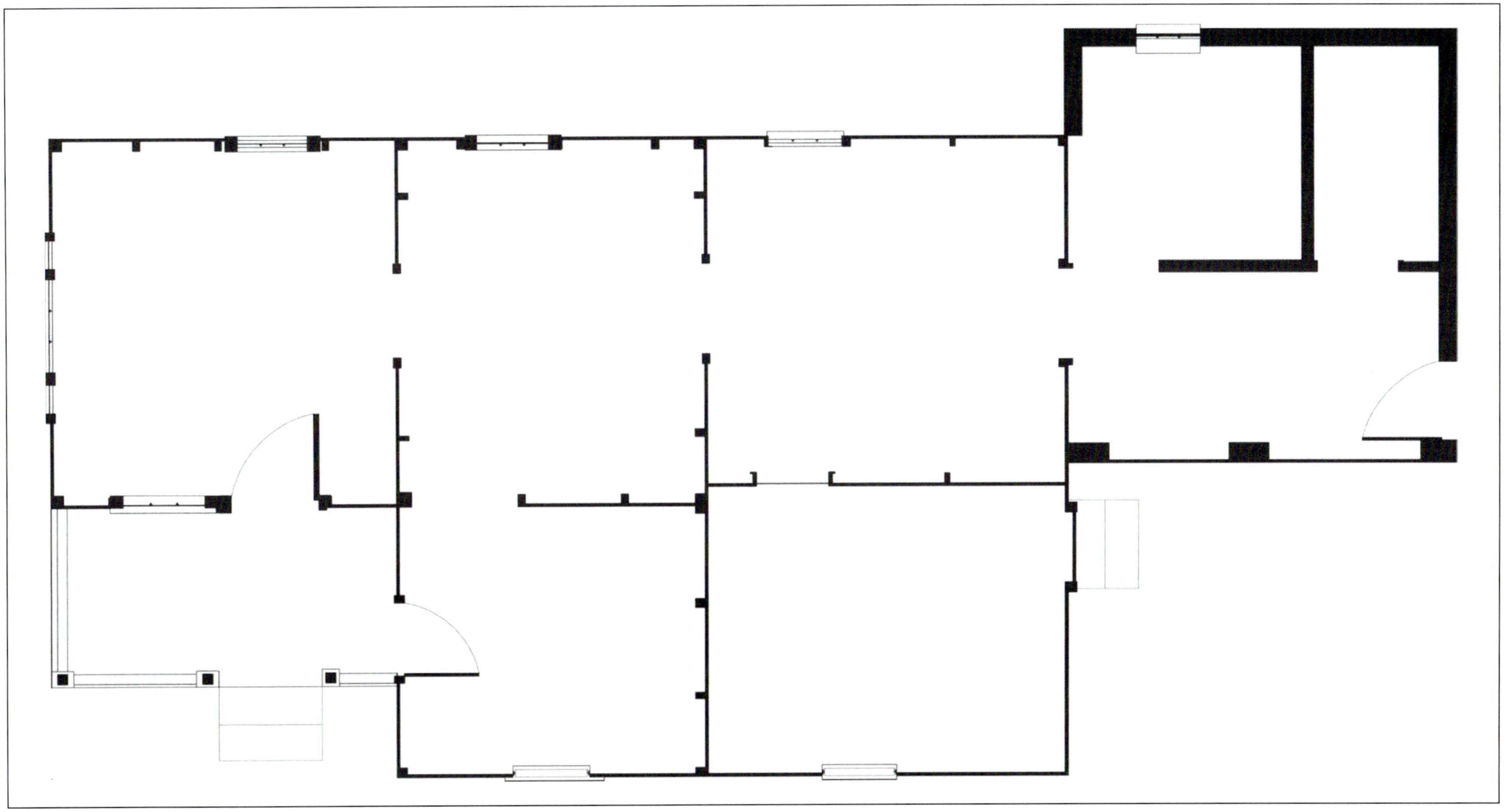

FIGURE T5.18. 32 Duke Street plan, drawn by Margaret Burke, 2008.

nates at the wall plate and studs carry spaced horizontal lath from the partition up to the rafters, providing ventilation between the two chambers.

A series of additions were made to 32 Duke Street starting in the late nineteenth century or early twentieth century. A small room with a shed roof attached to the east wall of the rear chamber was the first alteration. Not long after, a two-room portion was added to the north wall of the original rear chamber and shed roof addition. Finally, a cast-in-place concrete wing was added to the north wall of the third-period rooms in the middle of the twentieth century. The side porch with its chamfered posts and decorative sawn splats can also be dated to the turn of the twentieth century. Other twentieth-century alterations to the original structure include replacement siding and the corrugated zinc metal roof. However, the original hand-planed bevelled siding remains in place in the north wall of the north room. No original doors survive, but iron HL hinges fastened with rose head nails remain in place in the north (secondary) doorway of the north room.

27 Newton Street

(*c.*1800–1825, 1875–1900, 1900–1925)

BEN HAYS

The house at the northwest corner of Duke and Newton Streets features construction from three different periods: two front portions that date to the early and late nineteenth century and a twentieth-century addition at the rear. The two nineteenth-century bays are defined by hipped roofs of unequal width and wood exterior walls while the twentieth-century addition is marked by a cross-gabled roof and concrete walls.

The earliest portion of the house – the western bay topped by the largest hipped roof – predates 1844 as it appears in the Adolphe Duperly's lithograph of that year. This part of the house includes two nearly square rooms (roughly 12 feet by 11 feet) of approximately the same size. Both the wall and roof framing are fully exposed on the interior, revealing planed and beaded siding and roofing. The posts, studs and braces are tenoned, and most framing joints are also pegged. The interior is painted white up to 1 foot past the plate, before giving way to older red paint or stain on the underside of the roof.

Original fenestration visible today includes a large, south-facing tripartite window in its original stud spacing and one six-over-six, counterweighted, double-hung windows on the west façade. According to the Duperly lithograph, a door on the west wall provided access into the southern room; today, a window replaces the door. Visual evidence suggests windows or doors on the east façade may have matched up with the openings on the western face, though the first addition changed this wall significantly.

Late in the nineteenth century the narrow, full-length gallery-style room was added to the east of the original building. It measures approximately 7 feet 6 inches by 22 feet long. This room is also topped by a hipped roof, though the narrower width made the hip shorter in height. Unlike the early portion, the wall sheathing is unbeaded and the underside of the roofing is sheathed in matchboard, typical of the early twentieth century.

This entry depends on an extensive on-site field report and analysis of surviving historic fabric written by Edward A. Chappell in the summer of 2008.

FIGURE T5.19. 27 Newton Street, 2007.

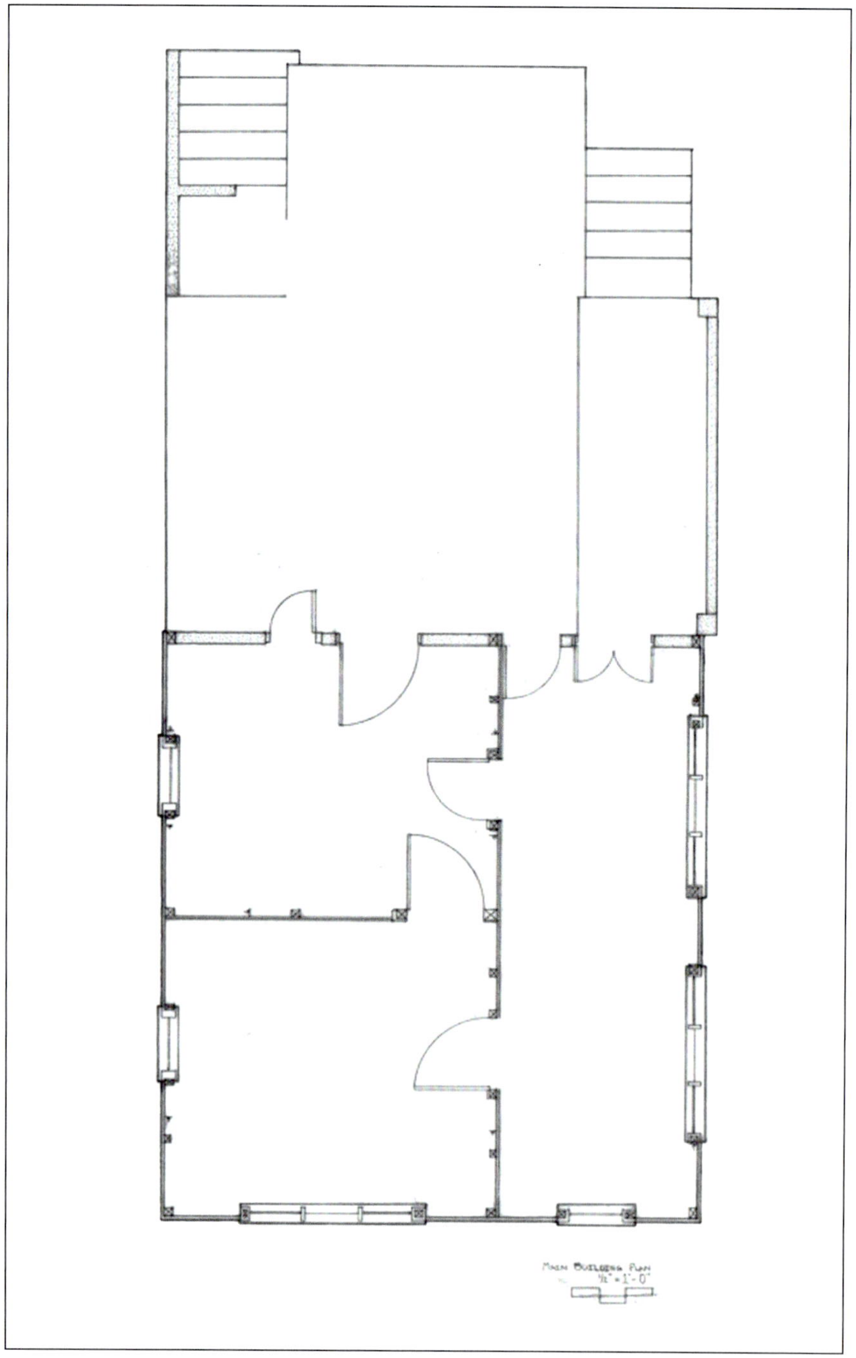

FIGURE T5.20. 27 Newton Street plan, drawn by Katherine Boles, 2010.

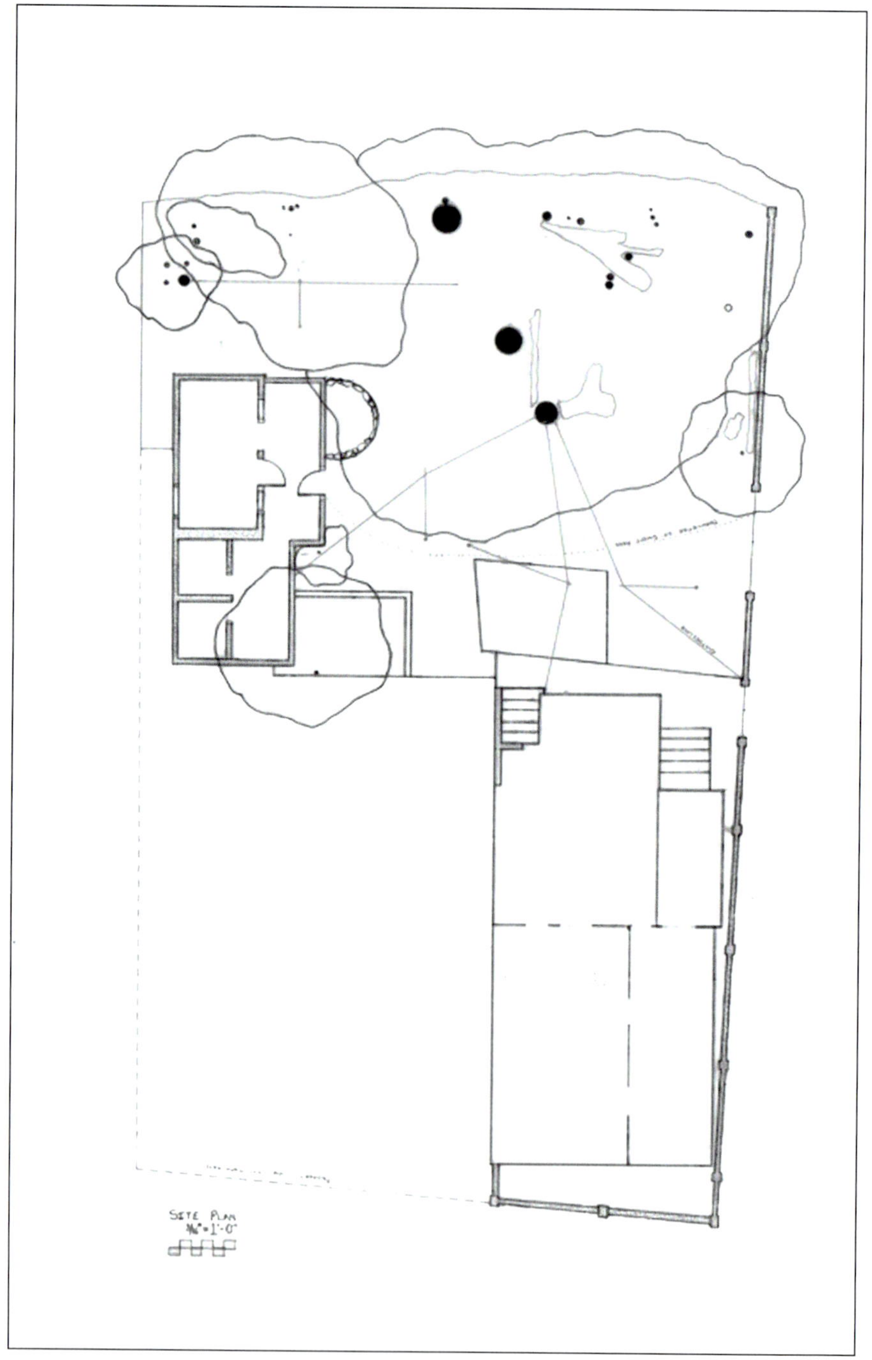

FIGURE T5.21. 27 Newton Street site plan, drawn by Katherine Boles, 2010.

43 Cornwall Street

(*c.* 1812, 1900)

JAMIE FRIELING AND BRIAN L. COFRANCESCO

The house at 43 Cornwall Street was built by Edward Hoole soon after his purchase of two lots in 1812. Hoole was a prominent citizen of Falmouth, active in local politics and serving as the clerk of the vestry in 1816.[1] In 1826, he was the deputy notary public, the deputy receiver-general and public treasurer, and the deputy naval officer, clerk of the navy, clerk of the peace, court and police, and the distributor of stamps at Falmouth.[2] That Hoole occupied all these offices at once suggests that the public offices were limited to a small community of powerful individuals. Listed as a "gentleman of Trelawny" in the deed, Hoole purchased two connecting lots from Samuel Barrett Moulton Barrett for £260 on 24 June 1812 and built his house on both lots. Hoole's property on Cornwall Street was a section of Falmouth just developing in 1812; the deed indicates that the lots were bound to the west on "streets not quite completed and called or intended to be called Pitt Street".[3] Set back from the street, the house is a three-bay structure with an open plan, large hipped roofs, and front and rear yards.

This entry depends on an extensive on-site field report and analysis of surviving historic fabric written by Edward A. Chappell in the summer of 2008.

Though one of the largest houses in Falmouth, 43 Cornwall ignored many of the architectural conventions established for other elite houses in town. It is not a two-storey merchant storehouse and while it has a masonry lower level, its upper storey is brick not frame. Living spaces for the family occupied both floors, not just the upper level. In a new section of town, off the primary commercial corridors of Falmouth, the materials and organization of 43 Cornwall Street suggest it was built by someone with significant personal wealth.

The ground floor is built of squared stone (ashlar) with raised mortar joints, whereas the upper floor is built of bricks laid using Flemish bond. On the interior, there is a clear system of hierarchy in which materials and finishes distinguish elaborate public spaces from private spaces, which feature exposed wood frame and unpainted surfaces and ceilings. In contrast, the doors leading to the two side rooms on the ground level face the best room and are made of rich materials and are more detailed than other doors throughout the house.

The central entrance opens directly into a large front room, one of four on the first floor. The front room is plastered, and each of the openings – except for the arched doorway – has double architraves. Directly ahead of the two front rooms is an arched opening creating an axial passage to

FIGURE T5.22. 43 Cornwall, 2007.

the two rooms at the rear of the house. These materials as well as the layout can be seen throughout other houses in Falmouth.

An enclosed stairway, which rises along the right wall of the house, leads to a front reception room with a circa 1900 tray ceiling. The room runs the length of the façade, lit by six-over-six sash windows. In the centre of the room is an original double door that opens onto the upper porch. The upper level utilizes a floor plan and architectural details similar to those on the ground floor, with an elaborate arched doorway with panelled piers, a double architrave arch, a scrolled keystone and dentil caps. The archway creates an axial passage and provides access to two rear corner rooms and an enclosed rear porch. The porch shows traces of having had a wide window at the rear, which may have been similarly coordinated on the left side. A six-panel neoclassical door on the right side of the porch, possibly salvaged, gives access to an exterior masonry stairway. The rear yard boasts an early kitchen with its masonry stack still intact.

NOTES

1. Second postscript to the *Cornwall Chronicle*, 20 January 1816.
2. *Jamaica Almanack 1826*.
3. Deed, Samuel Barrett Moulton Barrett to Edward Hoole, 24 June 1812, Island Record Office, volume 620, folio 30.

FIGURE T5.23. 43 Cornwall interior, 2007.

18 Pitt Street

(*c.* 1800–1825, 1900–1925)

EDWARD BARNES AND EMILIE JOHNSON

The house at 18 Pitt Street is one of the few examples of a three-room board house that survives in Falmouth from the early nineteenth century. Situated right at the street's edge and raised over 3 feet off the ground on a cut limestone foundation, the building presents an imposing façade that belies its rather modest scale. It seems likely that street presence was important to the builder, considering that the front façade is the only portion of the building supported by a solid foundation and is the only symmetrical face of the structure, with a double door flanked by six-over-six sash windows. At the northwest corner, original wide board sheathing – mitred to fit tightly together – is visible under a layer of twentieth-century wood shingles. Recently, a concrete and tile stair replaced the rotted twentieth-century wooden stair with the same orientation.

The front double doors open into a rectangular room, one bay deep (see figure 2.8 for a plan of 18 Pitt Street). Originally, this room stretched across the entire front (west side) of the house; however, a twentieth-century frame partition just south of the double door now divides the room in two. This originally long and narrow room was lit by the two aforementioned windows in the front wall and an additional window in the north wall which overlooks the north side yard. A door was cut in this wall directly adjacent to the window in the twentieth century. At the other end of the room, the south wall contains a door which opens into the south side yard where cooking and other work activities took place. The back (east) wall of the room is pierced by two doors that provide access to the two rear chambers of the house. Unlike the other three walls in the room, the framing system of this wall is not exposed. Instead, the wall is sheathed in boards, presenting a formal surface to guests when they enter the house. This front room performed a variety of functions, serving as both the main living area as well as the formal entertaining space. Direct access to the kitchen yard suggests that the room also served as the main dining space in the house.

The two rear rooms differ from each other in size and finish. The north room is the larger and more formal of the two. The presence of a three-part window – a six-over-six sash flanked by louvred openings – in the north wall suggests this room was used for entertaining; three-part windows were a common feature of the two-storey merchant storehouse buildings on Market Street, built and occupied by some of the wealthiest residents of Falmouth. The south room faces the work yard and probably was used as a sleeping chamber. The two rear rooms are separated by a first-period wall containing an original door. Flanking the partition on the back wall of the house is a pair of doors that provide exterior access to each of the two back rooms.

FIGURE T5.24. 18 Pitt Street, 2005.

The size of a residence in Falmouth is not an immediate indicator of its builder's wealth or social standing. Even the large, two-storey merchant storehouse limited living space to a single level. Another board house, though smaller, less imposing, and lacking architectural references to local and contemporary symbols of wealth and gentility, was built on a lot owned by John Harris, noted as a "gentleman of Trelawny".[1] The masonry foundation, symmetrical façade, large front room and three-part window in this building indisputably prove the unknown builder's familiarity with elite houses in town.

Eighteen Pitt Street is one of the few small, early nineteenth-century board houses in Falmouth with a surviving range of service buildings. This five-celled service complex was built in several different periods and is a mix of concrete, frame and nog construction. At the time of initial construction around 1820, these spaces would have housed cooking and washing facilities and possibly quarters for enslaved workers.

NOTE

1. Samuel Barrett Moulton Barrett to John Harris, Deeds, Island Record Office volume 638, folio 160.

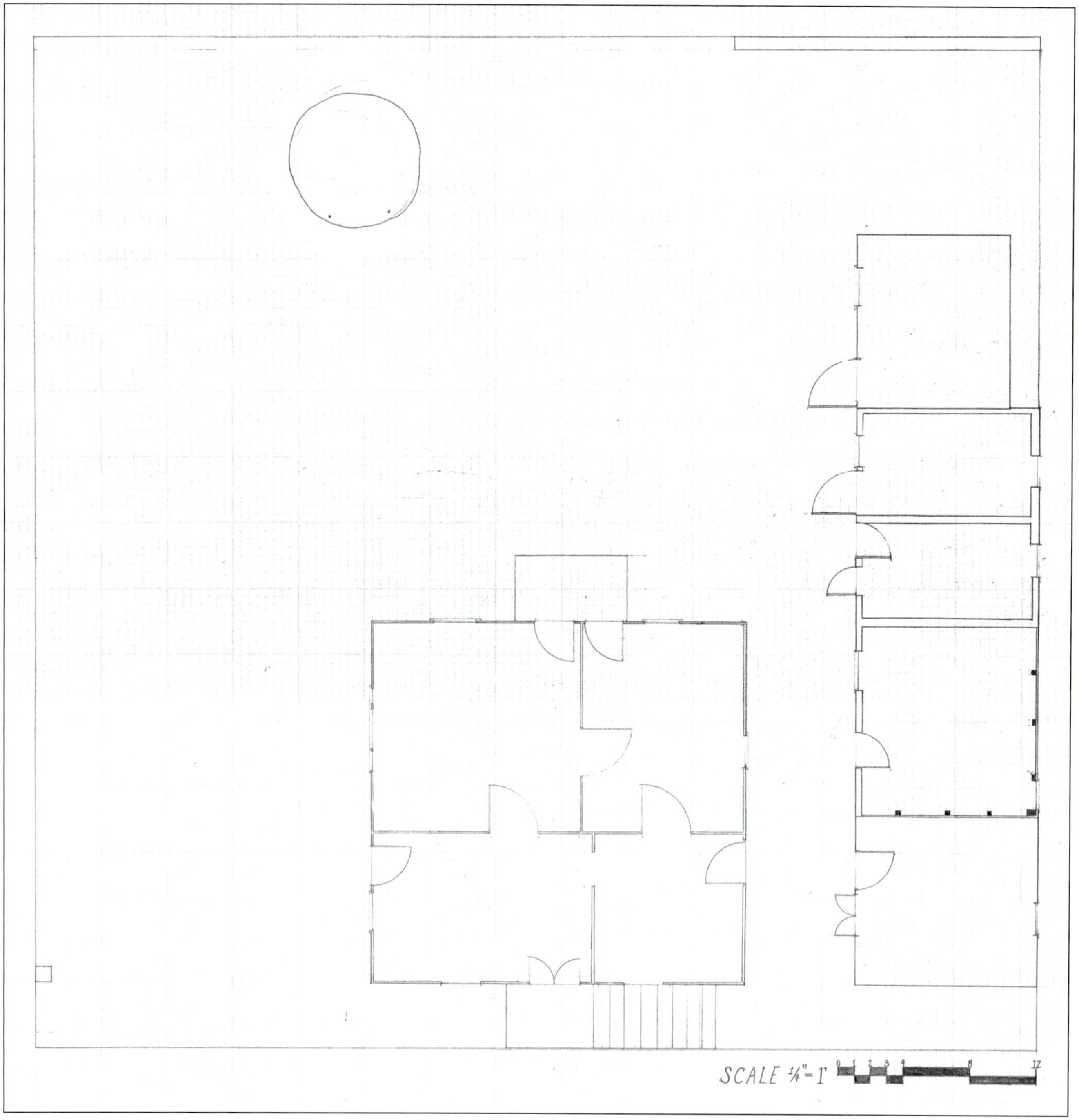

FIGURE T5.25. 18 Pitt Street site plan, drawn by Maggie Hansen, 2007.

St Peter's Anglican Church

Duke Street (*c.* 1796)

BRIAN L. COFRANCESCO

Although the British took control of Jamaica in 1655 and brought the religious traditions of the Church of England, Falmouth did not have an Anglican church until the 1790s. Construction of a church had been under consideration for decades, and wealthy landowner Edward Barrett designated half an acre in the centre of his property – known as Palmetto Point Pen – for a church as early as 1771. On 14 March 1791, the justices and vestry of Trelawny parish met at Martha Brae – the parish seat at the time – and decided that a "national church" should be built in Falmouth on the land allocated by Barrett. John Tharp, who owned Tharp's Wharf, a townhouse and Good Hope plantation, gave the rest of the parcel occupied by the Anglican church and churchyard in 1794.[1] The contract for the church and the sum of £9,000 were awarded to William Danny in 1791. Danny's requirements were a church with walls 3 feet thick and 20 feet high, with accommodations for three hundred people, and using the best white limestone available. Danny was to complete the church in eighteen months. The church was finally completed in 1796, with the exception of four interior column capitals, which were installed soon after September 1800.[2]

The original contract and church specifications did not include plans for a clock tower and on 29 June 1796, the church wardens were charged with seeking someone to "erect a sufficient Belfry for suspending the Town Bell and Clock and pay the expenses thereof". Within the year, a 60-foot tower was constructed and three bells along with an eight-day, three-dialled clock were installed. Two years later, in 1798, Messrs Burmingham and Robertson were paid £750 to build a dome or cupola atop the belfry to protect the clock tower and clock devices from the rain.[3]

Nearly forty years later, in 1837, a font was given to the church, a gift which marks the beginning of a period of renovations and construction. Calls for a new organ began in January 1839, increasing in 1840 when the organ committee deemed the instrument "unfit for any place of worship".[4] They recommended the purchase of a new organ, and the old one to be fixed and sent to Swanswick Church in Clark's Town. Apparently, with some attention, the organ would be fine at a smaller parish. The year 1841 brought discussions about expanding the church and a period of substantial building changes. The most significant change was a sizeable addition to the structure. James Gerard won the contract for construction, bid at £1,570 sterling, with an additional £1,300 sterling for his masonry. Work was nearly complete by April 1842, and by January of the following year, only decorations and steps needed to be finished. The addition stretched westwards, into the burying ground, built atop the graves of those already interred; in the 1950s, Daniel Ogilvie stated that these gravestones remained visible beneath the addition. In early 1845, Reverend Griffith Griffiths, Rector, requested the repositioning of the pulpit and reading desk inside the church, citing bad lighting and expo-

sure to excessive heat as his primary complaints, and the addition of the Creed, the Lord's Prayer and Decalogue on imported wooden panels above the altar. Soon after, the clock tower was heightened to allow the clock to run for eight days, and in 1848, the cupola was repaired and sheathed in sheet lead. In 1866, the church was disestablished and public funds could not be used for the maintenance of Anglican churches in Jamaica, perhaps the reason for no further changes to the church (with the exception of modifications to the cupola).[5]

Today, St Peter's parishioners enter on the longitudinal side of church, pass through an entrance vestibule, and arrive in the nave with the altar to the left. Four columns enclose a square space centred in the nave, two of which are the originals made of wood, stipulated in the contract with William Danny in September 1800, and two of which are replacement masonry. Much of the interior has remained untouched since the mid-nineteenth-century additions, and the ceiling cornice, font, pulpit, pews and "Bible table" are original. The clock in the tower is original with intact gears and parts but is no longer functional.

The exterior of the church is Georgian in appearance, an early example of the architectural tradition apparent across Falmouth. The façade is bilaterally symmetrical with a clear distinction of volumes and the use of classical quoins to distinguish building corners. String courses on the exterior denote the height of the interior space, and a parapet tops the roof of the nave, hiding the shallow gabled roof from view. A wooden balustrade surrounds the conical cupola on the clock tower. The main entrance and tower are centred on the structure and emphasized by a slight protrusion of the central bay.

St Peter's Church is a well-preserved artefact from early Falmouth. With much of the original fabric intact, it is an outstanding example of monumental construction in Trelawny parish and Anglican church-building practices in colonial Jamaica.

FIGURE T5.26. St Peter's Anglican Church, 2009.

FIGURE T5.27. St Peter's Anglican Church elevation, drawn by Grace Goldstein (n.d.).

NOTES

1. John Tharp to the Anglican Church, 1 August 1794, Deeds, Island Record Office volume 424, folio 170.
2. Daniel L. Ogilvie, "History of the Parish of Trelawny" (manuscript, 1954), ch. 6. Available at http://www.jamaicanfamilysearch.com/Samples/histre.htm.
3. Ibid.
4. Ibid.
5. Ibid.

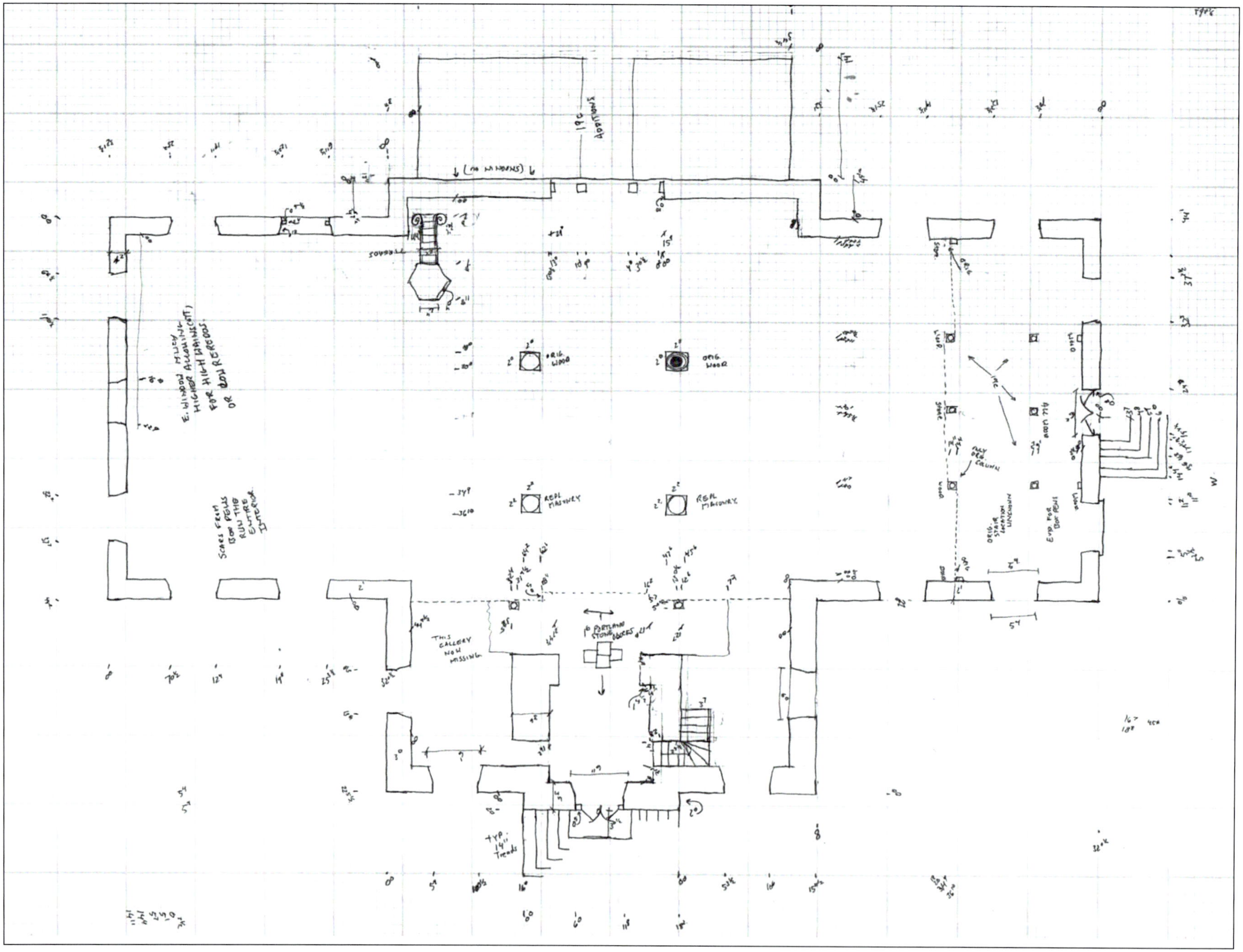

FIGURE T5.28. St Peter's Anglican Church plan, drawn by Louis Nelson (n.d.).

FIGURE T5.29. St Peter's Anglican Church, stair tower, 2009.

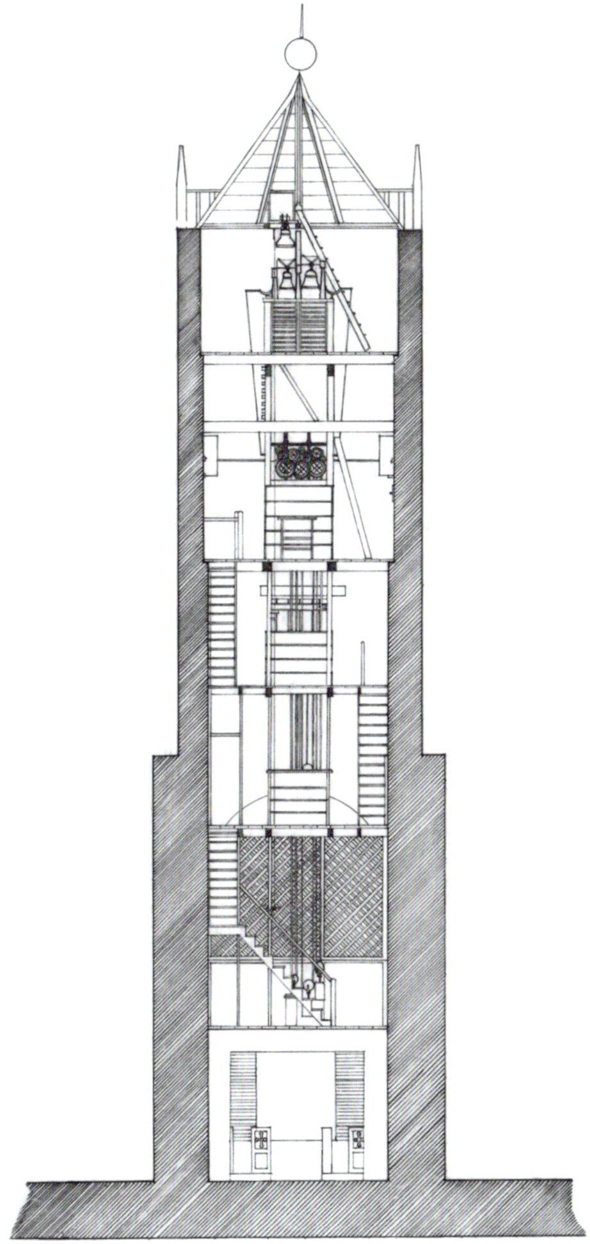

FIGURE T5.30. St Peter's Anglican Church, stair tower section, drawn by Charles C.W. Smith, n.d.

Church View

54 Duke Street (*c.* 1900–1925)

BEN HAYS

Towards the western end of Falmouth, across from the Anglican church, the house at 54 Duke Street is in a part of town developed in the 1820s and 1830s. Even though the church and churchyard had anchored this part of town since the 1790s, residential development was slower to move in. "Church View" on Duke Street is an example of the small, early twentieth-century, one-storey residence building type found throughout Falmouth. The central mass of the house is constructed of timber-frame walls and brick nogging covered with stucco, demonstrating the persistence of traditional building techniques into the twentieth century. The house, excluding the porch and addition, is raised on stone piers to elevate it above the ground and help ventilate the interior. Other details, such as the wood vent transom above the front door, are strategically used for ventilation. The front porch takes up nearly two-thirds of the front elevation and includes a decorative cement block railing. A concrete addition with a shed roof, which directs water away from the slab foundation, extends across the entire back of the house. A typical hipped roof sheathed in corrugated metal covers the earliest part of the house. A short roof crown tops the ridge of the roof, an architectural detail that links this building to older structures found throughout Falmouth.

The fenestration displays simple trim patterns that include mitred and butt-joined trim. The front windows are three-over-three double-hung sashes while the side elevations feature vertically oriented six-over-six sashes, matching the verticality of the three-over-three windows on the front. The height and narrowness of the windows emphasize height over width, an aesthetic decision to solve the problem of balancing openings in the wall expanse. Two casement windows in the shed addition are less finely detailed in terms of trim and window style.

FIGURE T5.31. 54 Duke Street, 2009.

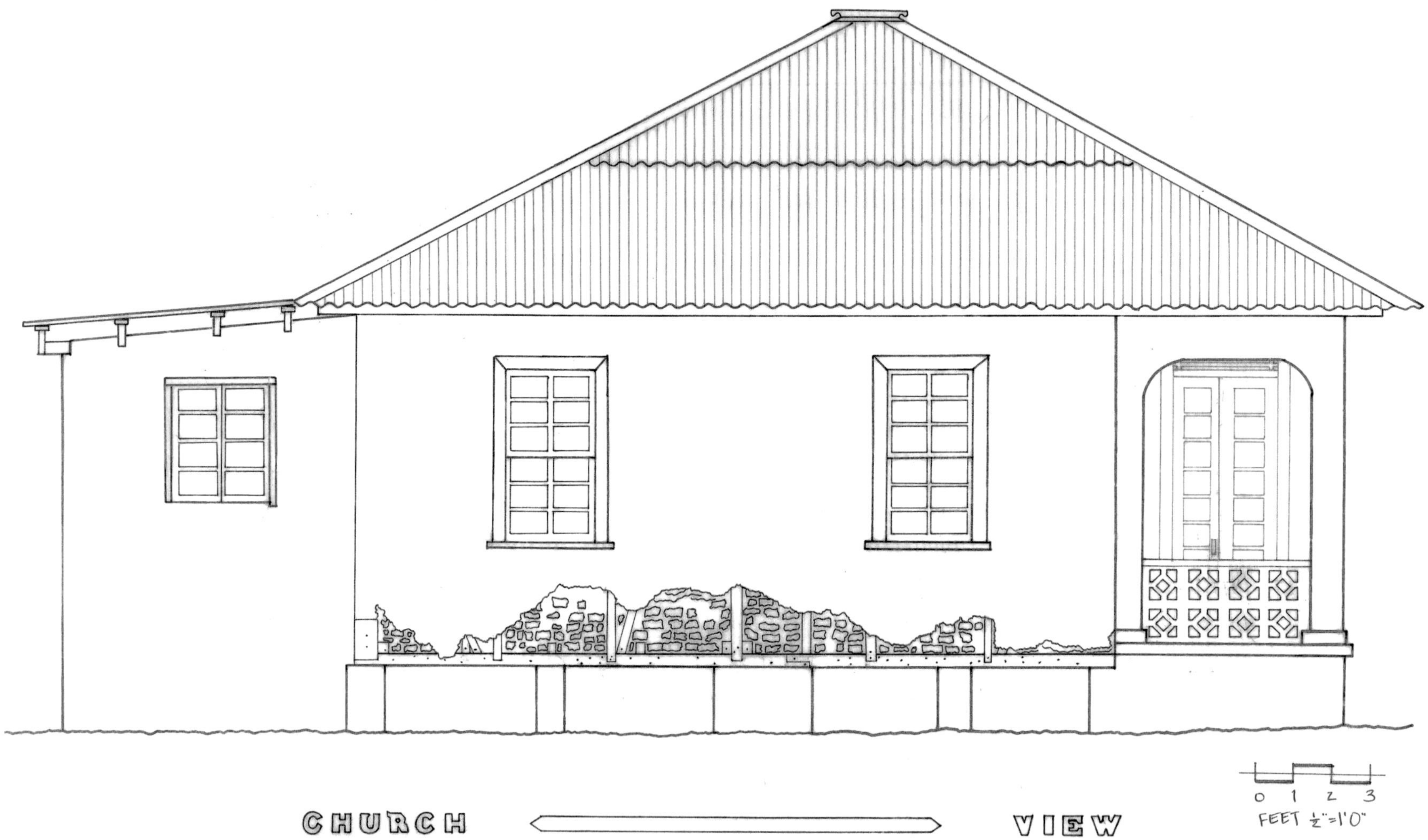

FIGURE T5.32. 54 Duke Street western elevation, drawn by Kathleen Smith, 2010.

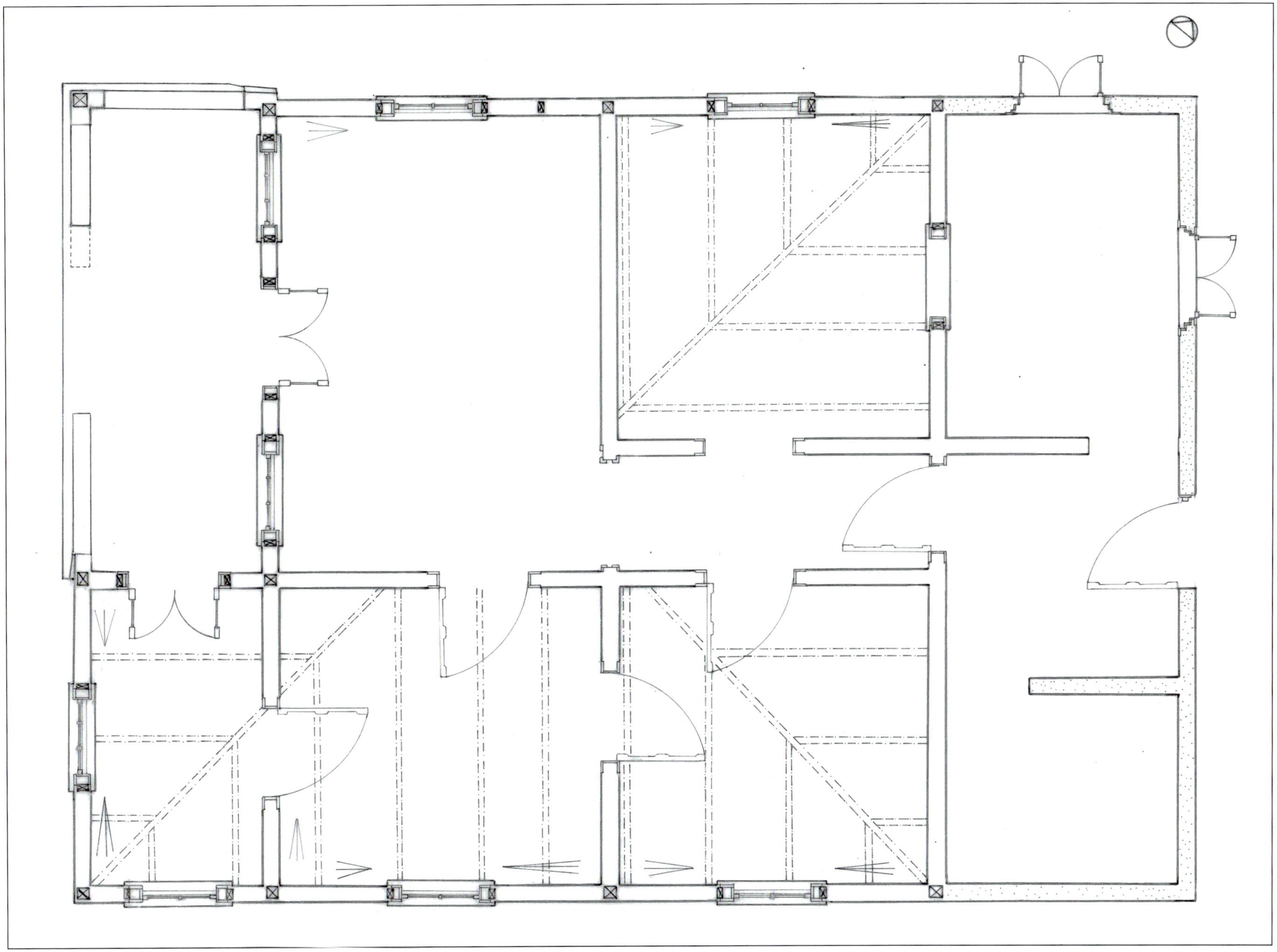

FIGURE T5.33. 54 Duke Street plan, drawn by Susie Ranney, 2010.

3

Poverty in Paradise

The Challenges of Preservation in the Developing Caribbean (2011 Report)

KATE BRADY AND CATHERINE H. REDFEARN

In the fall of 2007, the Port Authority of Jamaica announced the Historic Falmouth Jamaica port development project. The Port Authority, in partnership with Royal Caribbean, broke ground in October 2009, with the first ship on target to arrive in February. While the word "historic" is meant to be a marketing hook for cruise passengers, the development is historic in other ways as well. If one considers emancipation the first dramatic and traumatic shift in Falmouth's economic base, and the closing of the port in the 1950s as the second, then the coming of the global cruise industry, with all of its profound impacts on the town's economic, physical and social structures, rightly deserves attention as a third major moment in Falmouth's history.

In the spring of 2010, we led a research team to study how the wharf development might change Falmouth, and write an open report – available to all interested parties – about what if anything might be altered to better maximize the benefit to the residents while minimizing the detriment. Our project, funded by the Jefferson Public Citizens Program at the University of Virginia, consisted of undergraduates Brian Cofrancesco, Todd Mattocks, Molly McDonald and Christoph Wilhelm, we graduate students, and faculty member Louis Nelson. Our team incorporated the disciplines of architecture, architectural history, commerce and urban planning. All had participated in the University of Virginia's Falmouth Field School in Historic Preservation, where we had heard about the possible development of the wharf as a cruise ship destination. The community's opinion (and by community we include non-local stakeholders of the local preservation organization) seemed divided: some saw the wharf as the town's salvation, while others saw its demise. We felt that the future probably lay in the grey area between these two extremes. Because of our backgrounds, we chose to study the public history, built environment and community and economic development aspects of the project, to identify small changes that might tip the outcome closer to salvation. Our team conducted a semester of research including ten days of fieldwork to study the complexities of the wharf development. Stateside, we studied documents related to the history and design of this wharf development, and case studies of other cruise developments. In Jamaica, we conducted interviews with almost twenty stakeholders and conducted surveys of townspeople whose daily lives might be affected by the development. While we were expecting, indeed seeking out, nuance, we were nonetheless surprised by the complexities of a project of this scale in a developing country like Jamaica.

This is a story of money. Some players have it; others need it, desperately. It is also the story of an effort to preserve buildings and a community in a complex context. Falmouth's historic resources, although in desperate condition, are nonetheless a significant factor in the wharf developers' interest in the site. Area preservationists are ambivalent: the wharf's promise of resources for building restoration is compelling and yet this development will permanently change the town that they love.

Can the historic town of Falmouth survive the wharf development? Can it survive without it? How does preservation of the built environment contribute to the future of the vibrant community that exists there now? Economic development of the scale of the wharf development is necessary but not sufficient for the town's preservation. This chapter looks at the complex social, economic and political context of historic preservation in Falmouth and summarizes our recommendations to support the preservation of both the built and social environments of this unique town.

Falmouth is located on Jamaica's north coast, between two major tourist ports, Montego Bay (Mo Bay) to the west and Ocho Rios to the east. Its natural port is its main physical asset, but commercial shipping enterprises ceased in the 1950s, as global shipping operations outgrew the local facilities. Falmouth, the Trelawny parish seat, is the commercial centre of the region, offering commerce and services to the largely agricultural hinterland. Governmental agencies, banks and social services have locations in Falmouth. The weekly market – known to locals as the bend-down market – continues a two-hundred-year history in the town. The bend-down market is unique in the Caribbean, according to Trelawny mayor Colin Gager, and attracts both buyers and sellers from across the island.

Despite its close proximity to all-inclusive resorts, two major port developments and Montego Bay's international airport, tourism has largely overlooked Falmouth, until now. A few isolated destinations in the parish currently serve the tourists coming into Montego Bay or Ocho Rios, including Glistening Waters and rafting on the Martha Brae, but these pale in comparison to the developed destinations, such as the Great Houses and Dunn's River Falls, in neighbouring parishes. Only the hardiest tourists venture into Falmouth itself. The dearth of amenities catering to tourists – as of summer 2010, Falmouth's restaurants and stores cater to locals, and few if any overnight accommodations exist in town – is further proof that its economy is not dependent upon foreign tourism.

Even beyond the tourism sector, Falmouth struggles to find a dependable economic base. Employment is scarce and poverty is widespread. The lack of viable economic development projects in Falmouth is not for want of initiative. Several projects in the recent past, including the Trelawny Multi-Purpose Stadium, built for the ICC Cricket World Cup in 2007, and a possible extension campus of the University of Technology have dangled promises in front of local officials and residents. These were backed by the local government, with high hopes for resulting development, but insufficient resources have hampered follow-through. In the case of the stadium, the facility was built and hosted one of the cricket championship matches, and a few concerts and football games in the years since, but many feel the investment has not seen sufficient return.

The assumption was that if it was built, users would come, but it seems few resources were put towards long-term management of the venue. It is a very visible reminder of shortcomings in Jamaica's current political, economic and social situation, which make development efforts very difficult.

Jamaica's current situation can seem intractable. It is a developing country with a heavy debt load, profound poverty and high unemployment.[1] The national government is mired in entrenched partisanship, which in turn affects agency efforts and local governments as well.[2] Due to the economic and political situation, the national government is frequently unable to provide basic services for its citizens, opening the door to influence from organized crime syndicates.[3] Jamaicans use demonstrations and riots as an outlet for disaffection with their government and economy.[4]

Jamaica has one resource that other countries in similarly dire situations lack, however. Jamaica has something that North American and European markets want, which can neither be imported nor exported: the sun, sand and surf of the tropics, and for cruise liners in particular, a fresh water filling station. Jamaica's national government is heavily reliant upon revenue from tourism, primarily from foreigners, much of which comes in the form of all-inclusive resorts and cruise destinations. New tourism development is the country's prime approach to alleviating debt, unemployment and poverty.[5]

Just as Jamaica is blessed with something foreigners want, so too is Falmouth. Its rich collection of eighteenth- and nineteenth-century buildings has international significance, although the intervening years have not been kind to the town. The lack of significant economic development is evident in the architectural fabric of the community. While scant economic activity has meant that neglect and abuse continue to take their toll on the historic structures, few sweeping changes have occurred in the last 130 years, leaving the historic fabric crumbling, though largely intact. Preservationists' interest in Falmouth's historic resources began nearly twenty years ago and continues with the work of Falmouth Heritage Renewal, which is the main historic preservation nonprofit operating in Falmouth. Falmouth Heritage Renewal has done tremendous work in the town, restoring many homes with limited resources. But they are fighting an uphill battle against the elements, neglect and perceived irrelevance, and they are simply not big enough to keep up with Falmouth's tremendous collection of resources. While they work on structures one by one, they lack the means to maintain the houses for residents. In anticipation of the wharf development, Falmouth Heritage Renewal has shifted some of their focus of work from residences to monumental, civic buildings and spaces in town, including the courthouse, churches and a park.[6] Falmouth Heritage Renewal has certainly done a tremendous service to the community and its historic resources, but far more is needed for the community to retain its internationally recognized historic fabric.

Falmouth is considered by some to be the most intact Georgian seaport in the Western Hemisphere. Its historic district, as designated by Jamaica National Heritage Trust, includes 764 structures, including 392 of national, regional or local historic significance. Of the significant structures, 134 or 34 per cent were deemed in danger of being lost to deterioration or demolition, and therefore a priority for preservation.[7] That sort of work requires a great deal of money over a long period of time. Labour is inexpensive, but tools and materials are difficult to get, making restoration and maintenance work in Jamaica roughly the cost of restoration in the United States, but with less than one-fifth the per capita gross domestic product.[8] Funding for the restoration of buildings has and will continue to come in large part from outside the country. The restoration of some buildings (Barrett House, Tharp House, the foundry) may be paid for by Royal Caribbean, the restoration of others is being taken care of by Falmouth Heritage Renewal and private grants, but anecdotally most of the structures are privately owned and maintained (some of which are in imminent danger of owner demolition).[9] In order to achieve wide-scale preservation, money for the maintenance of buildings must come from within the community.

Falmouth Heritage Renewal cannot manage the preservation of the entire community alone, and they are working very much alone. For all practical purposes, Falmouth Heritage Renewal is the only preservation organization in town. Though the Jamaica National Heritage Trust declared the historic district in 1996, and wrote detailed district guidelines, the trust is not present in the community, and their guidelines are not well known by district residents, are difficult to find and are largely ignored.[10] According to a local historian, the Jamaica National Heritage Trust has the power by law, but no resources or support for enforcement of the district guidelines.[11] Falmouth Heritage Renewal's core concern with restoration takes most of the small organization's time and energy, leaving little for education, interpretation and outreach to make the case for preservation. Consequently, the relevance of historic preservation to the townspeople is largely related to potential future economic gain through tourism.[12] Prior to the wharf development that seemed like a slim possibility.

Given his experiences on the ground in Falmouth, Falmouth Heritage Renewal's executive director James Parrent is supportive of economic development in Falmouth to bolster the economic base of the residents and convince them of the need for preservation. Falmouth Heritage Renewal has served in an advisory capacity for the new wharf as community economic development. Economic reality requires some sort of development, and unfortunately, history suggests that the community cannot afford to be particular. The preservation of the community depends on a large-scale influx of capital, such as would come from the new wharf development, Historic Falmouth Jamaica, the most recent economic development project to hit Falmouth.

Based in part on the attention that Falmouth Heritage Renewal and other entities have brought to the resources in Falmouth, the Port Authority of Jamaica turned to Falmouth and the promise embedded in its historic fabric to increase the country's income from tourism. Seeking new revenue sources, the Port Authority first approached Royal Caribbean about the possibility of a wharf development several years ago and has since collaborated with the company on the project, with Port Authority owning the new land and Royal Caribbean owning all vertical development.

Royal Caribbean, based in Miami, Florida, is the second-largest cruise purveyor in the world. Including its subsidiaries, it controls approximately a quarter share of the world cruise market.[13] It operates thirty-eight ships with a passenger capacity of over eighty-four thousand at any given time (with that projected to increase to approximately one hundred thousand by the end of 2012). The company has over four hundred destinations worldwide and profits of US$1.6 billion in the second quarter of 2010.[14] Both Jamaica and Royal Caribbean are aware of the power dynamic, which puts Royal Caribbean in the negotiator's seat. This is not unusual, and in fact, Royal Caribbean shares the industry-wide poor reputation as exploiters of developing countries.

Take, for example, the criticism levelled at Royal Caribbean for continuing to route cruise passengers to their port at Labadee, Haiti, in January 2010, just sixty miles from extreme suffering at the epicentre of an earthquake, which decimated the capital Port-au-Prince.[15]

However, in partnership with IDEA, Inc., an Orlando-based marketing and branding firm specializing in creating experiences in tourist destinations, Royal Caribbean appears to be designing a new sort of cruise port in Falmouth, offering the potential for a different experience for passengers and locals alike. Although the industry standard is for restricted access between the development and the surrounding area, Royal Caribbean proposes planning this development as an extension of the community. They decided to develop on eleven acres of infill in the bay,

FIGURE 3.1. Historic Falmouth, Jamaica, map. Courtesy of IDEA, Inc., and the University of Virginia.

extending the streets from the existing grid in the commercial area of the historic district. The decision to add acres to the community will serve to protect the town from high water and limit incursion into the historic district. They will have full control over the look and feel of the end product, which mimics the town's Georgian period, ideally offering a smooth transition from the new to the old.[16] They intend to rent space within the development to any local business people who can afford the cost of rent, and are planning public space within the development to be open to townspeople even when the ships are not docked.[17]

FIGURE 3.2. Comparison of Falmouth in 2009 and 2010. *Top:* Falmouth, June 2009; *bottom*: Falmouth, March 2010

The developers appear to be trying hard, but still, our team had concerns. Initial descriptions of Royal Caribbean's development certainly offer the potential for townspeople to maintain their own houses, in the form of jobs and the motivation of tourist interest. But Royal Caribbean's development is imperfect as a means to preserve the built environment of the community. The infill, built over the historic waterfront, has irrevocably damaged the context of a port town. By rigidly adhering to the Georgian period of significance, the development undermines large swaths of interesting and important local and national history, including emancipation, post-emancipation (the era of the board houses, some of the most interesting vernacular architecture in town), independence and recent history. The development loses the opportunity to interpret not just the early history, but also the periods that connect the Georgian buildings to the current conditions. This is vital to the complete understanding of Falmouth's history.

Despite the new inclusive wharf design, the development could still be economically successful for Royal Caribbean, even if no tourists leave the compound and interact with the community.[18] Cruise ships are inherently all-inclusive, with all of the amenities a tourist could want on vacation. While IDEA sees Falmouth's sense of place and authentic architecture as supplying something valuable to the travellers, Royal

Caribbean is primarily concerned with attracting people off the ship and into the all-inclusive land-based experience of the new wharf. Further limiting the tourists' interaction with the community would be any sort of barrier between the wharf and town. As of March 2010, we received different answers to the question of whether there would be a barrier, either permanent (a wall) or temporary (a fence) between the wharf and the town. Presumably, the developers would want a barrier to protect their on-site investment should the country or the town destabilize, but practically a barrier would limit the tourists who come into town to only the most adventurous.[19]

As currently envisioned, the project will not live up to its potential for economic development in the community. There must be ways for the economic benefit from the development to get into the hands of Falmouth Heritage Renewal and the people who live in and maintain the historic properties, and that is not currently the case. Profit stays with the developers, and the people and businesses who are granted (or can pay for) locations within the compound. These businesses are often not local, as the cost of rental within the development prices out all but the most prosperous local businesses.[20] According to parish custos Paul Muschett, King Pepper, a large and successful manufacturer of condiments located in Hague, Trelawny, plan to have a kiosk in the port complex, but few others can afford the rental prices set by Royal Caribbean.[21] The residents of Falmouth, almost to a person, see the benefit of the wharf in jobs for locals within the compound.[22] As Falmouth has not really had a tourist economy up to this point, the skills required to serve tourists are not readily available in the unemployed and underemployed of the community, and our team had concerns about whether the local workforce development agency, HEART, is capable of readying people fast enough for the initial, significant rounds of hiring.[23]

FIGURE 3.3. Playground of the Falmouth All-Age School, 2009.

We were concerned that the development as conceived, both through its design and its economic base, would result in a segregated and selective town, a place belonging not to residents, but to outsiders who can afford to work or visit there.[24] While the initial infill phase – phase I of the construction process where earth was dredged from the ocean floor and packed between iron and concrete retaining walls – created new acreage for the bulk of the development, subsequent phases require the relocation of vital community resources, including the fishermen's village, the all-age primary school, the bend-down market and much of the local commerce on Water Square, away from the centre of town to free up more acreage for support facilities.[25] While the reasons are ultimately practical, this will serve to further

FIGURE 3.4. Falmouth fisherman, 2009.

separate the town into space belonging to the development and space belonging to residents. Further, the continued use of the historic district by residents will ensure a necessary, critical alternate voice to keep the history complex, layered and true, as well as a reminder to connect the history of the development with Jamaica's current situation.[26]

Our team shared the concerns voiced by some residents about what history, and whose history, is told through this development. The period of significance, as identified by Royal Caribbean and IDEA, Inc., is the Georgian era, representing less than fifty years of the community's 240-year history. Most of the remaining architecture in the community is more recent, including the board houses constructed by freed blacks after emancipation, of much interest to scholars of vernacular architecture. Selecting the Georgian period to the exclusion of all later history eliminates the social and educational pieces necessary to sell residents on the importance of preserving the board houses (which are small and more prone to termite damage than modern cinder-block construction), challenging the engagement of owners in private preservation efforts. Further, a programmatic focus on Georgian history ignores some major events, such as emancipation and national independence that both matter to the residents and are relevant to understanding contemporary Jamaica. Limiting the scope of what is considered "history" will do little to make preservation more relevant to residents and confounds anyone's efforts to interpret the town, the board houses and William Knibb into a cohesive story.[27] Focusing solely on Falmouth's Georgian past would also serve to exclude modern history, such as Jamaica's independence from Britain, or its success in international athletics, both sources of great price for community members.[28]

Royal Caribbean has made it clear that the responsibility for development in the community, to entice travellers out of the new development and into the historic district (the ultimate reason for the port of call in the first place) lies wholly with the community of Falmouth and the country of Jamaica. Their development is an enormous investment and undertaking, adding a great deal of physical capital to the town, and so some would argue that they have done enough. It was our research team's conclusion, however, that the wharf development alone will fail to preserve the community (or even the buildings). We feel that in fact, their new, inclusive design suggests that future success of the development will strongly depend on shared success in the community. Preservation is contingent upon development in the community continuing apace.

In our report, we sought to address the wharf development as more than a tourism enterprise, as community development in addition to a way to address national revenue shortfalls. We saw the port's potential as much more than simple profit. We want to see Royal Caribbean and the town of Falmouth push historic preservation further, to enhance the community. Drawing on our three study areas – public history, built environment, community and economic development – we defined success in Falmouth as shared history, shared space and shared wealth, and we

FIGURE 3.5. Water Square, Falmouth's main commercial area, 2010.

FIGURE 3.6. Town site plan by the Falmouth study team, 2010.

produced a report outlining some specific recommendations to further these goals.

With a community focus, our work centred on the Water Square area, seeing it as a hinge, spatially connecting the new development to the historic town. We felt Water Square was important because of its location and its history. The square has been the functional centre of the community for much its history: first as the location of the courthouse, the communal fresh-water cistern (hence the name) and the marketplace, and now because it houses the taxi stand, the courthouse and modern retail enterprises.

At the same time, because of the historic fabric around the square, there is discussion of making it a pedestrian space, surrounded by tourist-related retail that would be a comfortable and welcoming space for passengers in town. Because of its history and these competing interests, we felt that Water Square would be an ideal nexus for demonstrating our

ideas of shared history, shared space and shared wealth. To that end, we made the recommendations outlined below.

To create a shared history, we recommended that the Water Square space, controlled by the community, become a location for the interpretation of the diverse post-emancipation history of Falmouth. We suggested the interpretation of the town's political and legal history at the parish courthouse, in such a way to permit the continuing active use of the building as municipal space. The Albert George Market offers an opportunity for the interpretation of the role of the square in the town's commerce throughout history. We recommended that Water Square highlight the importance of access to and supply of water to the history of the town. Because Water Square borders the more residential areas of the community, an overview of the history of vernacular board houses could be located in the square, to entice visitors into the residential area. Finally, we suggested that a community group be formed to oversee cultural programming in Water Square, to continue its current role as the location for revivals, concerts and other community events.

Regarding architectural and design concerns, we sought ways to create a shared space where Water Square and surrounding areas remain open, accessible and welcoming environments for both residents and tourists. We recommended that the city improve pedestrian use in and access through the square while maintaining low volumes of traffic. A street cleanup and improvement programme, emphasizing the Water Square and historic district areas would go a long way with few resources to making the area inviting to all. We recommended clear connections, spatial, directional and programmatic, between the wharf area and Water Square. And finally, we suggested the addition of a public site on Water Square dedicated to musical heritage interpretation and contemporary performance. We also strongly recommended that the community and the Jamaica National Heritage Trust update and enforce the historic district guidelines, to ensure that new development and changes to existing, historic structures adhere to the historic character of the town.

Shared wealth is of vital importance. The economic development of the wharf needs to reach the residents of town, and access to opportuni-

FIGURE 3.7. Albert George Market, 2009.

ties and services currently located in Water Square must remain or be enhanced. To that end, we recommended the creation of a Water Square Business Association to offer the locally owned downtown business community cooperative access to wharf-related economic opportunities. The association could offer services to the business community that they do not currently have. We wanted to ensure that member businesses of all kinds – including storefronts, kiosks and pushcarts – have access to additional reasonably priced advertising outlets geared towards tourists. Leveraging cooperate force, the Water Square Business Association can act as a single point of contact within the business community for interactions with entities involved with the development, including national and local agencies, private interests and nongovernmental organizations.

FIGURE 3.8. Main commercial area as envisioned by IDEA, Inc.

An organization of businesses could be an ideal source of access to micro-credit for new and existing business owners seeking improvements to their businesses. We also felt it was important that the square continue to serve as a main social and shopping district for residents in the midst of tourist-related development pressures. We recommended that at least two social service organizations related to wharf-focused economic development obtain or maintain a physical office presence in the Water Square business district. We also suggested that the parish council, lessors of the Albert George Market, offer preferential rental rates to locally owned commercial ventures aimed at tourists, in order to preserve the local business presence on Water Square.

Royal Caribbean's new cruise ship port development in Falmouth, Jamaica, is without question an ambitious undertaking; impressive in not only size, scope and cost, but also in the paradigm shift it suggests for the role such developments can play in developing contexts. Unfortunately, as currently envisioned, such massive development as Royal Caribbean's falls short of its full promise to Falmouth – it is necessary but not sufficient for the preservation of the historic, physical and social fabric of the community. The fate of the town is now dependent upon the development, but to a large degree whether the wharf lives up to its potential ("giving visitors a taste of Jamaica that they wouldn't find anywhere else", according to one blogger) also depends upon the town.[29] It was our opinion that Royal Caribbean needed to do more, but the community was by no means excused from responsibility. We felt that community members and the nation needed to rise to the occasion and take advantage of the opportunity, to the extent possible, that has presented itself before it is too late. We also felt that if our report were to have any influence, it would be with townspeople, not a multinational corporation. So, while we did make recommendations for Royal Caribbean, we also pinpointed actions for a variety of local and national stakeholders, including: Falmouth Heritage Renewal, IDEA, Inc., HEART Trust (Jamaica's national workforce training agency), the Institute of Jamaica (a Smithsonian equivalent), Jamaica National Heritage Trust, the Social Development Commission, the Tourism Product Development Corporation (a quasi-governmental agency), the Trelawny Parish Council and the Urban Development Corporation. That was perhaps the real lesson of this project: in addition to shared history, shared space and shared wealth, we could add shared responsibility for the community's future.

Examples of tourism developments which fail to live up to their promises are plentiful worldwide. The town of Falmouth and Royal Caribbean have an opportunity to illustrate how development can be different. But they do not have a lot of time. Throughout our research we heard that

FIGURE 3.9. Oasis in port. Courtesy of IDEA, Inc.

there is a narrow window of time to establish a solid framework for investment and cooperation towards the preservation of Falmouth, and at the time of writing this article, we are another nine months down the road. While Royal Caribbean received our report well and agreed to make some changes, the answer to the question we opened with – Can the historic town of Falmouth survive the wharf development? – has not yet emerged and may not for many years. If all stakeholders (developers, townspeople, preservationists) rise to the challenge, this development has the potential to become a new model tourism development in Jamaica. Our study aimed to give all parties an objective view for how they might help create that new future. Now, we can only hope that this story of money, politics and preservation will have a happy ending.

FIGURE 3.10. Site plan for the shorelin
Courtesy of IDEA, Inc.

Existing Shoreline
RBO
N
S
E
W

Epilogue

This essay was written in early 2011, before Historic Falmouth Jamaica had opened. As the development was very much a work in progress at the time of writing, we were asked to update this essay in 2013. While phase one of the development is complete, the dynamic between Falmouth and Historic Falmouth Jamaica remains a work in progress. Positive responses are afoot within the community, but the pace of change in Jamaica falls far short of the speed of the cruise industry. Despite good intentions to the contrary, the wharf currently functions the way other cruise wharves do, largely independent of the local community.

As of the Vernacular Architecture Forum conference in Falmouth in June 2011, the land-based portion of the wharf development (including the retail plazas) was still under construction, although the wharves were open and received the staggering total of 214,906 passengers and 75,893 crew members between February and September 2011.[30] Although neither of us has returned since the conference, we maintained contacts with some of our original stakeholders and used the opportunity to undertake additional interviews. We also researched statistics and data on tourism and cruise industry websites. We hesitate to base in-depth analysis on internet sources and opinions of people close to the development, but we found clear examples of both positive, encouraging elements and disappointing developments.

We had expressed concern in the original report about preservation of the residential historic district areas and enforcement of the district guidelines. Jamaica National Heritage Trust has recently developed new partnerships with the Georgian Society and Falmouth Heritage Renewal to act as their local agents for monitoring adherence to the Historic District guidelines.[31] Falmouth Heritage Renewal intends to represent the Jamaica National Heritage Trust at the Trelawny Parish Council's planning committee, enabling it to respond to potential developments that might affect the historic districts as part of the planning process.[32]

Similarly, a group of governmental and nongovernmental organization stakeholders formed the Falmouth Project Committee in the summer of 2013 to implement short-term enhancement projects, focusing initially on ones that could be complete by the winter tourism season. Longer term, the Project Committee is particularly interested in rehabilitating sections of the old wharf complexes, transforming that area into a hub of cultural activity, including a museum and a centre to interpret the history of Jamaican music. Ke Vaughn Harding, Falmouth Heritage Renewal's coordinator of architectural resources, is particularly encouraged by their work with the history of Jamaican music and sees an opportunity for the interpretation of post-emancipation history through the stories of prominent individuals from Trelawny, including people familiar to foreigners (such as sprinter Usain Bolt) and people known primarily to Jamaicans (such as politician Hugh Lawson Shearer).[33] It seems encouraging that local agents are organizing to tell their own stories and enhance their own community, even if it is happening nearly two years after the wharf opened for business.

The Tourism Product Development Company has done quite a bit of façade and signage work within the streetscape of Water Square and its environs, although they have spent little time or energy on the desperately needed material preservation of the building fabric.[34] Falmouth Heritage Renewal, whose leadership has transitioned away from its founder Jim Parrent, has broadened its attention to include grander buildings in town while continuing to work on small houses.[35] High hopes that the wharf's success would spur private, individually funded residential rehab has yet to materialize.[36] A new housing

FIGURE 3.11. Cruise ship at the harbour. Courtesy of Hugh Darley.

FIGURE 3.12. Fence at the cruise pier. Courtesy of Hugh Darley.

development of nine hundred middle-income homes has opened;[37] even so, the perception is that rents have increased in town, fuelled by speculation.[38] Despite higher rents, there is still a strong presence of local families in the community;[39] feared displacement has not occurred. Some of the historic fabric is in danger of demolition and redevelopment for more modern, commercial use.[40]

As we feared, the town seems to be growing increasingly divided. Because of the infill design, and the phased development (which left parking and staging areas between the development and town) the new area feels isolated and far from Water Square.[41] As designed, the streets of the new development seamlessly integrate with the original town street grid. This continuity, though aesthetically pleasing, is functionally compromised by the permanent wall and fence that was constructed after June 2011.[42] While security issues may necessarily have trumped any promises made to the community, the fact remains that a design that had intended to be porous now functions as "a new sterile, controlled Falmouth meant to be occupied by tourists" in Ke Vaughn Harding's words.[43] Signage leaves little doubt about who is welcome inside the gates.[44] While some areas have been opened to residents for special occasions with permission or for lease,[45] this only serves to underscore that on a day-to-day basis, that part of town belongs to the tourists. We do not know the schedule for future phases, or what is planned to further enhance the connection between town and wharf.

Before the wharf development, Water Square was the centre of the community, with the courthouse, grocery stores, the taxi stand and various offices on or just off the square. Slowly but surely these functions are being moved elsewhere. First to go was the fishing village, as its original location was subsumed by the infill for the wharf.[46] The fishermen were moved several blocks west, to a location that has had ongoing problems with erosion and land access.[47] The tax office has been moved from its location beside the Jamaica National Building Society (directly between the new wharf and Water Square) to the Hampton Wharf Build-

FIGURE 3.13. Falmouth fruit vendor, 2009.

ing (near the wharf but just to the east) and the taxi service has been relocated out of the now-exclusively pedestrian Water Square to surrounding streets, complicating the traffic pattern for pedestrians and motorists alike.[48] Bend-down market, just to the east of Water Square, is a vibrant organic mess of a market, unique in Jamaica. It has yet to move, but the Trelawny Parish Council and the Port Authority have partnered to build a new facility in reclaimed wetlands south of town, well out of the historic core and away from the wharf. They have prepared the site and poured the foundation,[49] so the market's days of being downtown are numbered. As these sites of normal daily life slowly move out of the historic commercial area, the functional centre of the community steadily moves away from the wharf, effectively transferring ownership of the historic centre of the community from Jamaicans to the global corporation and the tourists.

FIGURE 3.14. Vendor space at the wharf. Courtesy of Hugh Darley.

The sense from our stakeholder contacts is that even some of the opportunities that Royal Caribbean promised have not panned out as hoped. Rental space within the wharf is technically available to qualifying local vendors, but the rent is set relative to the global economy, not the Jamaican economy.[50] Most of the shop spaces are too pricey for locals and are occupied by international chains, but there are some local vendors inside, primarily selling things like fruit and crafts from kiosk-type space.[51] Locals had hoped that cruise-sponsored excursions would serve to draw people off the ship, out of the gates and into town. While one local historian guides historic foot tours of the town,[52] most of the excursions seem to be supporting well-established destinations out of town, failing to market the historic core of Falmouth to the cruisers.[53]

Historic Falmouth Jamaica was ambitiously designed as a wholly new and novel sort of cruise destination, placed in close proximity to an established town and physically designed to reflect the historic built environment of that community. This development was conceived as a notable new direction for the cruise industry, deliberately tying a development's success to its location and the future economic and social success of its community. Preliminary findings suggest that, as feared, the wharf instead mirrors the usual pattern of cruise destinations: Historic Falmouth Jamaica currently operates fundamentally independently of modern Falmouth, Jamaica. The local community, with very limited resources, is largely left responsible for answering whether or to what extent the physical and social makeup of the town survives or changes. This is the sort of messy story of money and power that plays out in communities across the world where great economic inequality manifests itself. It is tempting to conclude, a mere two years after the development opened, that Goliath has won. We are unwilling to do that; two years is simply not long enough to draw any definitive conclusions about the fate of the town.

ACKNOWLEDGEMENTS

This article was written in the winter of 2010–2011 in advance of the Vernacular Architecture Forum Conference in Falmouth. The article as originally written, with minor edits for clarity, is presented below. An epilogue offers additional information about what has happened in the few years since.

NOTES

1. Jamaica continues to face a variety of development challenges, including a persistent fiscal deficit and heavy indebtedness. With a debt-to-GDP ratio approaching 126 per cent, giving Jamaica the unenviable rank of fifth in the world for public debt according to the CIA's *World Factbook*. To give some perspective, the debt-to-GDP ratio of the United States is 53 per cent, higher if the calculation included intra-governmental borrowings, for a public debt world ranking of forty-seventh. A summer 2010, Gallup poll showed debt tied as one of the two-largest threats to America's future well-being (http://www.gallup.com/poll/139385/federal-debt-terrorism-considered-top-threats.aspx). The Government of Jamaica is therefore severely constrained in public expenditure for critical investments in education, health and justice, considered the foundations of economic growth. Jamaica is heavily dependent on other countries to import a host of necessities. Although it was historically agricultural, a large portion of its food is imported, including most fresh vegetables. (In 2007, the UN Food and Agriculture Organization designated Jamaica as one of the world's thirty-seven most food-insecure countries.) All petroleum is imported, as are many manufactured goods (CIA, *World Factbook*). Approximately one-fifth of the gross domestic product comes from remittances from Jamaicans living overseas and sending cheques home to support family (CIA, *World Factbook*).
2. Jamaica's government is bipartisan, with the People's National Party and the Jamaica Labour Party being the two major parties. Our anecdotal evidence suggests that partisanship runs much deeper than it does in the United States, with ministries, towns, agencies, funding sources and even families having deeply rooted party affiliations. A complex system of influence means that the funding of even appropriate and necessary economic development projects may be held up by party differences between a community and the funders or agencies.
3. Because of its economic and political situation, the national government is frequently unable to provide basic services for its citizens. A USAID report from 2008 details that the Jamaican government's debt service and personnel costs leave less than 15 per cent of the budget available for government operating costs and capital expenditures in health, education and infrastructure. As in other countries in similar situations, extra-governmental individuals and entities, including suspected organized crime rings, step up to meet the needs. They are in-turn supported by the Jamaican citizens, and in effect "own" or "govern" neighbourhoods. These individuals are then in a position to deliver votes in blocs to favoured politicians, often intertwining the interests of government and organized crime. A visible example of this was the social unrest in late spring 2010, when the United States demanded extradition of Christopher "Dudus" Coke, an alleged drug lord, on US federal drug and weapons charges. Dudus had ensured support and votes from Kingston neighbourhoods for then-prime minister Bruce Golding's Jamaica Labour Party administration, but the United States supported the Golding administration in other ways, so the extradition put Golding in a tight spot. When Golding finally bowed to American pressure and announced the search for the suspect, Dudus's supporters armed themselves and revolted in the streets of Kingston, shutting down the city for almost a week.
4. This is only the latest example of Jamaicans using demonstrations and riots as an outlet for disaffection with their government and economy. A significant, economically motivated example was the gas riots of April 1999, which were also centred in Kingston but stretched into the countryside, in which poor citizens rioted to draw attention to the hardships posed by proposed hikes in the cost of gasoline. The gas price hikes, designed to raise revenue for the country, were the result of a highly partisan review committee. The committee reviewed other options, including raising property taxes and selling government assets. The riots that ensued are blamed for the loss of nearly US$100 million in cruise ship tourism dollars, as ships were unable to dock due to riots (*Gleaner*, 24 April 1999)
5. Tourism comprises more than 20 per cent of Jamaica's total national revenue. Manufacturing (alumina and bauxite) and agriculture are the other large revenue generators (CIA *World Factbook*). The recent closure of many bauxite/alumina mines, a direct result of the declining international demand for the product, leaves tourism as the major revenue generator for the country. In direct opposition to the shrinking of the alumina/bauxite

industry, tourism continues to grow on average 3 per cent a year, internationally (www.unwto.org). By investing in tourism, Jamaica is following models set by international organizations. The World Tourism Organization supports tourism as a sound investment for developing nations as it is able to finance growth in other sectors while simultaneously increasing foreign exchange, increasing income and increasing employment.

6. Based on interview with Jim Parrent, president, Falmouth Heritage Renewal, March 2010.
7. In 2008, the University of Virginia's Falmouth Field School did an extensive building-by-building survey of the historic district. These statistics came from that survey.
8. The extreme disparities between labour and material cost and the informal nature of much construction work in Jamaica make direct cost comparisons difficult to track and estimate. The estimate cited here is based on correspondence with Matthew Webster, Falmouth Heritage Renewal board member and director of architectural conservation at the Colonial Williamsburg Foundation. CIA, *World Factbook.*
9. Interview with Hugh Darley, president of IDEA, Inc., Royal Caribbean's design firm; the 2008 historic district survey included questions about tenure and owner demolition, but that data has not yet been analysed to give solid figures.
10. The Jamaica National Heritage Trust's guidelines are not available online, and a historic district survey of residents completed by our research team in March 2010 revealed that few district residents are aware of or abide by the regulations. Furthermore, anecdotal evidence from Falmouth residents suggests that many building projects take place at night or incrementally in order to avoid official scrutiny. The second-floor addition to Club Nazz, located in a historic storefront on Market Street, is one notable example.
11. Interview with Marina Delfos, Georgian Society of Jamaica, March 2010.
12. Results of historic district survey and stakeholder interviews. An overwhelming number of interviews with stakeholders and responses from two surveys conducted by our research team – one of vendors and shoppers at the bend-down market and the other of residents of the historic district – revealed this sentiment.
13. http://en.wikipedia.org/wiki/Royal_Caribbean_International.
14. http://www.juneauempire.com/stories/072610/loc_683634459.shtml.
15. http://www.guardian.co.uk/world/2010/jan/17/cruise-ships-haiti-earthquake, http://news.yahoo.com/s/ynews/20100119/ts_ynews/ynews_ts1063.
16. A 2007 concept plan created by IDEA, Inc., lays out the components of the wharf development, including replicated structures, stylized new Georgian architecture and restored and enhanced existing buildings. In a March 2010 interview, IDEA president Hugh Darley asserted that the use of stylized Georgian architecture within the wharf complex would make it "practically indistinguishable from the town".
17. Interviews with Peter Brand, Royal Caribbean, and Hugh Darley, president, IDEA, Inc.
18. Based on information received from IDEA president Hugh Darley, Royal Caribbean estimates about 45 per cent of their passengers will disembark when cruise liners are in port. Darley made a rough guess that another 10 to 15 per cent might leave the wharf complex. A ship the size of the *Oasis of the Seas*, carrying nearly fifty-four hundred passengers, might only see 250 tourists leave the wharf to explore the town.
19. Interviews with Peter Brand, Royal Caribbean, and Hugh Darley, president, IDEA Inc. It is important to note that those interviews took place in March, 2010, before the riots in Kingston.
20. According to a price sheet of retail lease information produced by Royal Caribbean, dated 22 February 2010, rentals for market kiosk within the wharf development range from US$1,250 to US$1,500 per year with a US$6,500 non-refundable deposit. Compare these prices to the average Jamaican annual income, which is only US$7,400/year (CIA, *World Factbook*).
21. Interview, Custos Muschett, 9 March 2010.
22. Based on results from the March 2010 survey of bend-down market vendors and shoppers.
23. In a March 2010 interview, HEART director Althea Samuels relayed that because of budget constraints HEART has been unable to meet current demands for tourism industry training and certification. Furthermore, most HEART training sessions last twelve months. With the first ships slated to arrive in November 2010 and very few local training opportunities available for Falmouth residents, the outlook for preparing a local wharf workforce seemed slim.
24. This sort of conclusion is strongly suggested by wharf developments elsewhere throughout the developing world, including Labadee, Haiti and developments along Mexico's Caribbean coast.

25. Bend-down market, considered by many residents and developers to be a dangerous and unsightly facility, but nonetheless a keystone of Falmouth's economy, is slated for demolition and relocation to a site outside of town limits along Market Street. The new market will be part of a transportation hub – for use mainly by residents. The all-age school, currently located west of the wharf complex along the waterfront has been marked for relocation to make room for wharf expansion. While these relocations seemed like certainties – based on information provided by IDEA – there was much confusion in the town as to when and how these relocations were happening.
26. One Caribbean, the official tourism lobby for the Caribbean, promotes cultural and heritage tourism as a means promote and share the authentic stories of the people of the Caribbean. The question remains: How authentic a story can you tell without the people. This is a basic tenet of sustainable tourism – to retain the economic and social advantages of tourism development while reducing or mitigating any undesirable impacts on the natural, historic, cultural or social environment. This is achieved by balancing the needs of tourists with those of the destination (www.unwto.org).
27. The missionary and emancipator William Knibb established a Baptist parish in Falmouth and is buried there. The regard with which the community holds him is reflected in the variety of schools, churches and other institutions that bear his name even today.
28. Usain Bolt, the three-time Olympic gold medalist was born in the parish of Trelawny and attended William Knibb Memorial High School. During interviews, many residents spoke with pride when talking about Bolt, and more than a few recalled the stretch of road on Market Street where Bolt sprinted a 100-metre exhibition.
29. http://mindyjoyce.com/2010/05/31/uncovering-jamaican-history-through-it%E2%80%99s-most-recent-and-significant-tourism-development-historic-falmouth/.
30. http://jamaica-gleaner.com/gleaner/20110916/lead/lead5.html.
31. Ke Vaughn Harding, private email communication, 26 August 2013, and Marina Delfos, private email communication, 30 August 2013.
32. Ke Vaughn Harding, private email communication, 26 August 2013.
33. Ibid.
34. Ibid.; Marina Delfos, private email communication, 30 August 2013.
35. Ke Vaughn Harding, private communication, 26 August 2013. Authors' personal observations.
36. Marina Delfos, private communication, 30 August 2013.
37. Hugh Darley, private communication, 26 August 2013.
38. Ke Vaughn Harding, private communication, 26 August 2013. Marina Delfos, private communication, 30 August 2013.
39. Marina Delfos, private communication, 30 August 2013.
40. Ibid.
41. Ke Vaughn Harding, private communication, 26 August 2013.
42. Ibid.; Marina Delfos, private communication, 30 August 2013; Hugh Darley, private communication, 26 August 2013.
43. Ke Vaughn Harding, private communication, 26 August 2013.
44. Ibid.
45. Ibid.; Marina Delfos, private communication, 30 August 2013.
46. Authors' observation, summer 2011.
47. Ke Vaughn Harding, private communication, 26 August 2013. Authors' observation.
48. Marina Delfos, private communication, 30 August 2013.
49. Ke Vaughn Harding, private communication, 26 August 2013.
50. Marina Delfos, private communication, 30 August 2013; Ke Vaughn Harding, private communication, 26 August 2013.
51. Ke Vaughn Harding, private communication, 26 August 2013.
52. Marina Delfos, private communication, 30 August 2013.
53. http://portoffalmouth.com/index.html, accessed 13 August 2013.

Acknowledgements

The authors thank the following students from the University of Virginia's Falmouth Field School for Historic Preservation for their essays in this book: Edward Barnes; William Canup; Ivor C. Conolley; Katelyn Crawford; Leeann Dickerson; Jamie Frieling; Laurin Goad; Grey Graham;Justin Greving; Ben Hays; Jennifer Hugman; Sophie Johnson; Stephanie Langton; Kathryn Lasdow; Marilyn W. Moedinger; Ann Pfunter; Susie Ranney; Kevin Riddle; Kristin Rourke; D.P. Sefton; Katherine H. Spicer; Lauren Trice and Callie Williams. The authors thank Ivor C. Connolley, Ke Vaughn Harding, Chris Ohrstrom, James Parrent and Matthew Webster for their aid with documentary research, fieldwork and editing. We would also like to acknowledge the numerous contributions of former students who participated in the Falmouth Field School: Jasper Adams; Jesse Adams-Doolittle; Sara Anderson; Stephanie Arbieto; Hunter Armstrong; Sela Bailey; Hayden Bassett; Hannah Beckman; Katherine Boles; Eryn Brennan; Sarah Brummett; Kristin Buchanan; Stephanie Burcham; Margaret Burke; Sam Carr; David Casteel; Alisha Clark; Jonathan Coble; Robert Cox; Katherine Cullinan; Colin Curley; Anna Danz; Erika deBroekert; Eduardo Diaz-Etchevehere; James Dunnigan; Sarah Eissler; Elizabeth Engel; Adam Erby; Robert Erickson; Tahinee Felix-Marin; Stephanie Fernandez; Jason Fox; Marina Freckmann; Laura Frye; Molly Garfinkel; Mike Goddard; Grace Goldstein; Jennie Graves; Margaret Hansen; Jennifer Harris; Ethan Heil; Kristen Hennings; Rachel Himes; Rachel Jessup; April Johnson; Matthew Jungclaus; Katie Klepper; Kosova Kreka; John Kupstas; Erin Kuykendall; Anna Kvan; Alexandra Lauzon; Lawrence Lazarides; Tran Le; Yun-Fong Lin; Jennifer Lindblom; Whitney Martinko; Jordan Matthews; Todd Mattocks; Lindsay McCook; Molly McDonald; Meagan McFadden; Maureen McGee; Elizabeth McGinley; Meghan McLoone; Francis McMillen; Elizabeth Milnarik; Amy Moses; Noel Mukubwa; Effie Nicholaou; John O'Hara; Jennifer Pack; Camila Quinteros-Casaverde; Philip Redpath; Kelsey Reynolds; Elizabeth Rice; Julie Robert; Rachel Robinson; Jerold Rosema; Alison Ross; Blythe Rowe; Kedryn Samson; Maria Sanchez-Carlo; Tommy Schaperkotter; Lauren Shepulski; Richard Sidebottom; Charles Smith; Deborah Smith; Kathleen Smith; Kristen Sparenborg; Mark Stephongzi; Todd Stovall; Jackie Taylor; Jessica Terdeman; Anh Thai; Katherine Thaxter; Sarah Thomas; Kimberly Toney; Alyssa Turner; Jessica Underhill; Jessica Vanecek; Josi Ward; William Watkins; Leah Werner; Christoph Wilhelm; Michael Wsol; Steven Yena; and Chris Young.

Contributors

LOUIS P. NELSON is Associate Dean for Research and International Programs, School of Architecture, University of Virginia.

EDWARD A. CHAPPELL is the Shirley and Richard Roberts Director of Architectural and Archaeological Research, Colonial Williamsburg Foundation, Virginia.

BRIAN L. COFRANCESCO is Head of Education, Connecticut's Old State House, Hartford, Connecticut.

EMILIE JOHNSON is Assistant Curator, Monticello, Thomas Jefferson Foundation, Virginia.

KATE BRADY is Principal, Partners for Place, Charlottesville, Virginia.

CATHERINE H. REDFEARN is Principal, Partners for Place, Charlottesville, Virginia.